National
Standards
in American
Education

Diane Ravitch

National Standards in American Education

A CITIZEN'S GUIDE

The Brookings Institution
Washington, D.C.

Copyright 1995
THE BROOKINGS INSTITUTION
1775 Massachusetts Avenue, N.W., Washington, D.C. 20036

Library of Congress Cataloging in Publication data:
Ravitch, Diane
    National standards in American education : a citizen's guide
  / Diane Ravitch.
        p. cm.
    Includes bibliographical references and index.
    ISBN 0-8157-7352-8 (alk. paper) :
    1. Education—Standards—United States. 2. Education—United
States—Evaluation. 3. Educational tests and measurements—United
States—Evaluation. 4. Education and state—United States.
I. Title.
LB3060.83.R38   1995   94-39663
379.1'58'0973—dc20   CIP

9 8 7 6 5 4 3 2 1

The paper used in this publication meets the minimum
requirements of the American National Standard for
Information Sciences—Permanence of Paper for Printed
Library Materials, ANSI Z39.48-1984.

Set in Sabon and Avant Garde

Composition by Harlowe Typography, Inc.
Cottage City, Maryland

Printed by R. R. Donnelly and Sons, Co.
Harrisonburg, Virginia

*This book is dedicated,
with thanks and love,
to my dear friend Mary*

Foreword

WHAT SHOULD AMERICAN students know and how does society know they have learned it? Those are the two questions at the heart of the debate on creating national education standards and assessments for the nation's public school students. It is a debate fraught with controversy and anxiety. Opponents fear that the federal government will mandate what their children should be taught. Proponents believe that national standards can improve academic achievement and equip the nation's youngsters to deal with the challenges of the twenty-first century.

In this study Diane Ravitch seeks to put the debate in perspective. She reviews the role that standards of all sorts play in everyday life, traces the development of standards and expectations about academic achievement in American education, and examines the events that led to passage of recent federal legislation creating a process for establishing national education standards and assessments. Along the way the author raises questions and issues that each participant in the debate must address as the standard-setting process moves forward, and she recommends several steps that she believes will lead to credible standards and higher academic achievement for all students.

One of the country's leading education historians, Diane Ravitch is a senior research scholar and adjunct professor of education at New York University and nonresident senior fellow at the Brookings Institution. She is the author of dozens of articles and several books, among them *The Troubled Crusade: American Education, 1945–1980* (1983) and *The Great School Wars: New York City, 1805–1973* (1974).

This study was conducted under the auspices of the Brown Center for Education Policy. Funding was provided by the Andrew M. Mellon Foundation and the Pew Charitable Trusts. The Brookings Institution is most grateful for their support.

The views expressed here are those of the author and should not be attributed to the persons or organizations whose assistance is acknowledged, or to the trustees, officers, or other staff members of the Brookings Institution.

Bruce K. MacLaury
President
The Brookings Institution

November 1994
Washington, D.C.

Contents

Preface

 IN MID-1992 BRUCE MACLAURY, president of the Brookings Institution, invited me to write a book at Brookings after I concluded my government service. At the time, I was Assistant Secretary for the Office of Educational Research and Improvement (OERI) in the U.S. Department of Education, and my assignment from Secretary Lamar Alexander was to promote public understanding of the national education goals and of the value of high standards for all students. After the 1992 elections and change of administrations, I accepted Mr. MacLaury's invitation. His offer afforded me the opportunity to step back, reflect upon, and assess an activity in which I had been deeply involved.

There was never any doubt in my mind that I would write a book at Brookings about standards in education. During my eighteen-month stint in the Department of Education, no issue consumed more of my time and energy than the role of standards in improving education. Government agencies tend to move slowly, but in a matter of months, OERI made awards to major organizations of teachers and scholars to develop national standards in science, history, geography, civics, the arts, English, and foreign languages. (These awards were made in collaboration with other federal agencies, including the National Endowment for the Arts and the National Endowment for the Humanities.) In addition, we awarded grants to states to prepare new curricula that embodied high standards for all students. Through conferences, publications, and collaborative activities with the National Science Foundation, we supported the recently developed standards of the National Council of Teachers of Mathematics. The message that OERI delivered consistently to teachers, supervisors, teacher educators, researchers, city and state officials, textbook publishers, journalists, and others was that education without standards would fail to achieve either equity or excellence.

Having known of Brookings' sterling reputation as a think tank, I was somewhat apprehensive about whether I would fit into this august institution. I imagined a stuffy place peopled by experts who were both world renowned and unapproachable. To my delight I found that my preconceptions were totally wrong. The scholars, researchers, and other staff members at Brookings were unfailingly open-minded, helpful, and collegial. I must say that Brookings is the most pleasant and productive environment in which I have ever worked. Casual conversations—over the lunch table, at the water cooler, or in the frequent luncheon seminars—were invariably stimulating. The facilities, including the library and the computer services, are state of the art, and the institutional tone is one of personal and professional considerateness.

I especially appreciated Brookings' air of intellectual and political freedom, free from any whiff of what is now called "political correctness." There are no strictures, formal or informal, on what may be said, written, or argued. There are no political views that are excluded. The only claims that may draw polite reproof are those that are not supported by sound reasoning or solid evidence.

My own work was helped immeasurably by the many opportunities to discuss it with colleagues from different fields, not only in informal discussions, but in occasional research seminars.

As I worked on this book, I discovered a problem that I had not anticipated. I began the book as an advocate of a particular approach to the issues; as time went by, events changed my perceptions and my point of view. I continued to support strongly the idea of standards but had become deeply concerned about the problems of their implementation and the possibility of their politicization. My experience, I suppose, reflected my transition from policymaker to policy analyst, from advocate to critical supporter.

Readers looking for simple answers will not, I think, find any here. They will find, I hope, a reasonably accurate description of how and why the movement for national standards became a federal priority. And I hope they will also find useful discussion of some of the problems that have not yet been addressed and that may—if left unaddressed—prevent this initiative from achieving its laudatory aims.

In the course of writing this book, I was helped by many people to whom I owe deep gratitude. I am certainly grateful to Bruce MacLaury for extending the invitation to spend an intellectually exhilarating fourteen months at Brookings. And I appreciate the encouragement that I received from Thomas Mann, head of Governmental Studies. I am grateful too to the many scholars and research associates at Brookings who listened, pointed out errors, and encouraged me. I especially thank Susan Stewart, Inge Lockwood, and Cindy Terrels of the Brookings staff for their steady help. My summer helper, Margo Weisz, was invaluable. Mary Ann Noyer did a fine job as research verifier for this book. Max Franke prepared the index.

Several people read all or part of the manuscript and made valuable editorial suggestions, including Cliff Adelman, Paul Barton, John Burkett, Chester Finn, Jr., Claudia Golden, Jeanne Griffith, Jeffrey Mirel, and Maris Vinovskis. I thank them for doing so. Because I did not accept all of anyone's suggested changes, none of them should be held responsible for the final manuscript. Of course, any errors of fact or interpretation are solely my own.

Among others to whom I owe special thanks are Lamar Alexander and David Kearns, who persuaded me to join them at the U.S. Department of Education and to take on the standards portfolio. I also thank Francie Alexander, Jan Anderson, Eve Bither, Joseph Conaty, Emerson Elliott, Terri Ferinde, Ray Fry, Paul Gagnon, Sandra Garcia, Cheryl Garnette, Milton Goldberg, Eunice Henderson, Patty Hobbs, Dave Mack, James Mitchell, Janice Morris, Jeanette Randolph, Ted Rebarber, and Lydia Spencer, with whom I collaborated on standards-related issues at the Department of Education. Although I left the federal government with mixed feelings about the way Washington works, I hold unreasonable affection for my associates at OERI.

I also want to thank Nancy Burton, Nancy Irving, and Len Ramist of the Educational Testing Service; Janice Gams of the College Board; and Ina Mullis of the National Assessment of Educational Progress, all of whom helped locate and interpret elusive data.

The arduous process of editing this book was managed by Marty Gottron, who displayed patience, care, and intelligence. For meeting high standards of performance, I award her an "A."

I am also grateful to the Brown Center for Education Policy and to the Andrew M. Mellon Foundation and the Pew Charitable Trusts for their generous support.

DIANE RAVITCH

Introduction

 IN THE LAST TWO DECADES of the twentieth century, dissatisfaction with the performance of U.S. schools grew strong enough to permit serious consideration of major structural changes in American education. Perhaps the most striking initiative, because it departed so dramatically from tradition, was the bipartisan effort to create a national system of standards and assessments. Support from a diverse coalition of governors, educators, business leaders, and two successive presidents gave momentum to the movement. The push toward national standards also attracted intense opposition, largely because of widespread concern about the possibility of a national curriculum and increased federal control of education.

Other nations, whose education systems are controlled by centralized national ministries of education, follow paths that to American eyes seem logical and orderly. In the United States, with its 15,000 local school districts, fifty state boards of education (plus the District of Columbia), and the federal Department of Education, educational change is a messy affair. Add to that already crowded list of actors a slew of interest groups, elected officials, the state and federal judiciaries, schools of education, researchers, universities, unions, publishers of tests and textbooks, and journalists, and the sheer complexity of educational decisionmaking becomes clear. Because there are so many different centers of power, changes in education policy are brought about through public argument, campaigns, crusades, and movements. To succeed, education reformers must persuade many people, including parents and taxpayers. This system of change may or may not be the right way, but it is the American way, a way determined by the decentralized politics of American education and by this society's use of public schools not only as educational agencies, but also as instruments of social policy.

The movement for national standards and assessments began after an agreement in 1989 between President George Bush and the nation's governors to set national education goals. Two of the six goals were pledges to increase academic achievement. The third goal declared that by the year 2000 "American students will leave grades four, eight, and twelve having demonstrated competency in challenging subject matter, including English, mathematics, science, history, and geography; and every school in America will ensure that all students learn to use their minds well, so they may be prepared for responsible citizenship, further learning, and productive employment in our modern economy." The fourth goal stated that by the year 2000 "U.S. students will be first in the world in science and mathematics achievement." The other goals focused on helping preschool children (with a promise that "all children in America will start school ready to learn"), raising the high school graduation rate to 90 percent, increasing adult literacy, and pledging that all schools would offer a disciplined environment, free of drugs and violence.[1]

This list of ambitious goals was intended to focus the nation's attention on the need to improve education for all students. It was a stimulus for public and private sector collaboration. It encouraged many different kinds of programs and activities in government and in local communities. The Bush administration's AMERICA 2000 plan spurred the creation of thousands of community-based organizations across the nation to work toward the goals. The Clinton administration's Goals 2000 program was enacted into law in 1994. Both administrations recognized that goals three and four implied the need for national standards, to describe what children are supposed to learn, and comparable assessments, to determine if they have learned it. Both administrations pledged that any national standards would be voluntary.

Policymakers and the public were ready to consider these unusual initiatives for several reasons.

First, in the late 1970s measured declines in student performance on tests led to a host of critical reports by national and state commissions about the quality of education. The well-publicized declines heightened public concern about the inadequate preparation of students entering college and the work force. Many governors, legislators, and business leaders began to recognize that student achievement had to improve.

Second, the public was repeatedly dismayed during the 1980s by the poor performance of American students on international assessments of mathematics and science. The results were particularly unsettling because Americans had long been accustomed to thinking that their schools were the best in the world.

Third, in the 1980s many public officials and education leaders embraced the idea that schools should be judged not only by their "inputs" (resources, facilities, number of advanced degrees among teachers, and so forth), but also by their "outputs," or results (that is, student performance). Dissatisfied by the returns on increased education spending in the 1980s, many policymakers demanded accountability for results; in a major conceptual change, the focus of reform shifted to student performance as the best measure of the success of a particular school or school system.

Fourth, the persistence of large gaps in educational achievement among students of different racial and ethnic groups hindered the quest for social equality. It became clear that education could not serve as a significant route to upward social and economic mobility unless the educational performance of minority youngsters was strengthened.

Fifth, many of those concerned about educational equity concluded that low expectations were contributing to the poor performance of students in the bottom half of the age cohort. Educators usually explained wide variations in achievement by noting that the United States educates almost everyone while other nations educate only their elites. Several other nations, however, now educate an even larger proportion of their population than does the United States.[2] The comparison with other nations raised questions about the customary practice of "tracking" weak students as early as age eleven or twelve into undemanding programs, instead of introducing them to the kind of instruction that would challenge them to learn more.

Sixth, changes in the economy increased inequality between those who were well educated and those who were not. During the 1980s international competition eliminated many semiskilled jobs; as demand for less-educated workers fell, the earnings gap between high school graduates and college graduates grew. Economists predicted that international competition, new technology, and the restructuring of the workplace would continue to favor educated workers with portable skills. In the future not everyone would need a college degree, but every successful worker would need to be literate and numerate and have the ability to solve problems, work with others, and keep learning new skills.[3]

Seventh, Americans worried that badly educated youngsters might impair the nation's productivity and international competitiveness. Although the schools should not be blamed for the loss of major industries to other nations or for fluctuations in international trade, nonetheless the knowledge and skills of the labor force can affect the overall productivity of the nation. Just as investment in education is good both for the individual and for society, inadequate education or low educational performance is not good for society or for those individuals who are not well prepared for citizenship and productive work.

Eighth, in trying to assess the health of American education, many of the concerned parties—educators, public officials, parents, and business leaders—came to realize that there is no clear agreement about what elementary and secondary students are supposed to learn and that there are no reliable measures of individual student performance. Thus, debates flourished in the late 1980s and early 1990s about whether the schools were doing a good enough job and whether they were better or worse than they used to be. Without generally accepted standards or any reliable measures of individual student achievement, no school or school district could say with any assurance whether its students' performance was higher or lower than it was at some time in the past.[4]

Ninth, the American public school—responding to the demands of courts, legislatures, governmental agencies, and interest groups— had become a catch-all institution, lacking in priorities or focus. In trying to be all things to all people, the school had lost its sense of mission. Much of the movement for standards aimed to reestablish priorities by clarifying that the schools were responsible, first and foremost, for developing the intelligence of their students. This was not meant to eliminate or disparage the numerous other social functions that had been assigned to the schools, but to emphasize that instruction in skills and knowledge was the sine qua non of the schools' responsibilities.[5]

For all of these reasons and more, a wide variety of individuals and organizations concurred that American education needed sharp improvement. By the early 1990s much of the public recognized that higher levels of education than were necessary in the past would be needed in the twenty-first century and that American schools must expect more effort and higher levels of performance from all students. And many of the actors in American education at the state and national levels had come to believe that national standards and assessments would help to provide accurate information and to raise the quality of schooling for all students.

No one suggested that standards and assessments might be a panacea, capable of curing all the ills of education. Standards and assessments are not a solution for the myriad other problems of schools or society. They are unlikely to make much difference in schools where adults have not established an orderly climate conducive to learning. No one is so naive as to believe that efforts to improve academic achievement would counteract deleterious social trends, such as the weakening of the family, the spread of drugs and violence, and the persistence of poverty. Nor would they be a substitute for preschool programs, decent recreational facilities, or sound nutrition. No, the purpose of establishing standards and assessments is to raise the academic achievement of all or nearly all children, to signal students and teachers about the kind of achievement that is possible with hard work, to emphasize the value of education for future success in college and careers, to encourage improvement of instruction and collaboration among teachers, and to motivate students to have higher aspirations in their school work.

The promise of standards prompted an unusual political convergence. People who worried most about excellence looked to standards to raise achievement; people who worried most about equality looked to standards to provide students with equal access to challenging curricula and learning experiences. Together they forged an unusual and effective alliance.

The purpose of this study is to explain the evolution of this significant movement in American education. Chapter 1 examines the idea of standards, why they are important in most walks of life, and what they mean in education. It also considers the cases for and against national education standards. Chapter 2 provides an overview of the history of standards and assessments in American education. Chapter 3 analyzes various indicators of educational achievement, including student performance on the Scholastic Aptitude Test, the National Assessment of Educational Progress, international assessments, and course-taking patterns.

Chapter 4 explores the major ideas of scholars and policymakers that shaped the national discussion of standards and assessments. Chapter 5 examines the politics of standard setting at the national and state levels. It reviews passage of the Goals 2000 legislation in Washington, as well as controversies over standards in the states. Chapter 6 offers recommendations.

This book is subtitled "A Citizen's Guide" because its purpose is to inform the concerned citizen who wants to understand the movement to create national standards in education. As the book was written, the federal legislation to establish a process to develop national standards was debated and passed. Whether this process will produce high education standards remains to be seen; whether it can be insulated from partisan politics remains to be seen; whether it will help to stimulate concerted and effective efforts to improve student achievement remains to be seen. What is not in doubt, however, is that universal education of a high caliber is more important today than ever before. Nor should there be any doubt about the imperative to improve the educational performance of all American youngsters.

1

The Idea of Standards

 WHAT ARE STANDARDS? The dictionary definition of "standard" suggests its dual meaning. Derived from similar words in Middle English, Old English, Old French, and the Germanic, the word refers first to "a conspicuous object (as a banner) formerly carried at the top of a pole and used to mark a rallying point esp. in battle or to serve as an emblem." In that sense, a standard is "something established by authority, custom, or general consent as a model or example"; it is a criterion by which judgments or decisions may be made. At the same time, a standard is *also* "something set up and established by authority as a rule for the measure of quantity, weight, extent, value, or quality." That is, a standard may also be defined as a "criterion, gauge, yardstick, touchstone. . . ."[1] Thus, the word "standard" refers simultaneously to both the "model or example" and the gauge or yardstick for determining how well one's performance approximates the model or example. A standard is both a *goal* (what should be done) and a *measure* of progress toward that goal (how well it was done).

7

According to Albert Batik, in a study of engineering standards, "the first function of any standard is to transmit information from those who have the knowledge to those who need and can use that knowledge." The earliest written reference to standards occurs in the Book of Genesis in the Bible, when the Lord commands Noah, "Make thee an ark from resinous wood sealing it with pitch." This, Batik comments, would today be considered "a standard specification for an ark"; he notes that the Bible also includes "an entire building code" for Solomon's Temple in Jerusalem. The history of standards is a history of people agreeing on ways to improve materials, processes, and products and communicating that information to people who need to know it. Much of that development has occurred in response to changing technology or as a result of wars or disasters. Thousands of industrial accidents occurred in the years immediately after steam power was introduced; eventually, the development of standards for boilers and other steam vessels virtually eliminated safety hazards. Similarly, the infamous Triangle Shirtwaist Factory fire in Manhattan in 1911, in which nearly 150 working women died, not only spurred workers to organize formally, but also led to the establishment of strict standards for fire safety.[2]

Americans clamor for standards in nearly every part of their lives. They expect strict standards to govern construction of buildings, bridges, highways, and tunnels; shoddy work would put lives at risk. They expect explicit standards in the field of telecommunications; imagine how difficult life would be if every city, state, and nation had incompatible telephone systems. They expect stringent standards to protect their drinking water, the food they eat, and the air they breathe. They rely on high standards for health and safety in restaurants, offices, factories, hotels, and schools. When they visit a lawyer, doctor, accountant, or any other professional, they count on his or her adherence to standards of professional conduct and assume that he or she has met the licensing standards for the field. When they open a can of beans, they assume that the producer met well-defined standards for canning and preserving set by the food industry and that the ingredients are truly what the label indicates. When they buy a crib for their infant, they assume that the manufacturer abided by product safety standards. When they fly, they count on the enforcement of security standards, rely on the airlines to observe strict maintenance standards, and expect the pilots to have passed the appropriate tests. When they buy a new car, they know that the automobile manufacturer was required to comply with standards for quality, safety, fuel efficiency, and auto emissions. In the workplace, they know that fair labor standards regulate wages and hours, child labor, and working conditions. If they buy a prescription drug or over-the-counter drug, they expect that it is safe because of the standards of the federal Food and Drug Administration. When they use a computer keyboard, they gladly accept the QWERTY standard setting out the order of the keys. On the roads, they automatically expect other drivers to stop when they see red lights, go when they see green lights, and drive on the correct side of the road.

Even the most ordinary transactions of daily life reflect the omnipresence of standards. U.S. coins and bills have a standard value, allowing them to be spent anywhere in the country. (The Constitution gave Congress the power "to coin Money, regulate the Value thereof . . . and fix the Standard of Weights and Measures.")[3] In debating whether to adhere to the traditional imperial system of weights and measures or to switch to the metric system, Americans must choose between two standards, each of which makes possible a common language of measurement. Furthermore, the language that each person speaks or signs reflects a standard of usage.

Standards are created and perfected because they improve the quality of life. Without them, life would be chaotic, unpredictable, and dangerous. Although it may be satisfying to complain about the "stultifying" effect of standards of dress and decorum, in truth everyone who lives in civilized society enjoys the protection and predictability that standards provide.

Even a cursory review of the pervasiveness of standards suggests the complexity of the subject. There are many different kinds of standards, and they are measured and enforced in a wide variety of ways. Every meaningful standard offers a realistic prospect of evaluation; if there were no way to know whether anyone was actually meeting the standard, it would have no value or meaning. So, every real standard is subject to observation, evaluation, and measurement. Standards may be mandatory (required by law), voluntary (established by private and professional organizations and available for use by anyone else), or de facto (generally accepted by custom or convention, such as standards of dress, manners, or behavior).

The global trend is to extend the reach of standards to facilitate communication and trade among different societies, as well as to improve the quality of life (or *standard* of living) for more and more people. There are already international standards for financial and monetary transactions, enabling people in different societies to buy and sell from one another; for telecommunications, enabling people to communicate with each other by telephone or fax across national borders; for data collection, enabling organizations such as the United Nations and the Organization for Economic Cooperation and Development to develop common statistical measures; and for human rights, bringing the pressure of world opinion on states that violate generally accepted standards of behavior. International standards are emerging in such areas as environmental protection, as nations recognize that environmental degradation is a common threat; product design and safety, as nations seek to sell their products in each other's markets; and food safety, as nations recognize that adulterated wine or beef will cause them to be excluded from international trade.

Standards in Education

In education, standards are also becoming international. This is happening in mathematics and science, in particular, not only because international assessments in these subjects have been administered to students in many nations since the mid-1960s, but also because these subjects are truly international in scope. The mathematics and science taught in one modern country are not—and should not be—markedly different from the mathematics and science taught in other modern countries. Number systems operate in exactly the same way regardless of the race, gender, ethnicity, or religion of the person performing the mathematical operation. Nor are the principles of science culturally determined. Although science is vulnerable to religious battles, especially regarding the origins of the world, the operations of science are everywhere the same: airplanes fly over all parts of the world in exactly the same way, without regard to the culture or color of the people in the plane or on the ground below. The laws of gravity and motion do not differ in different lands. Cultural groups may differ in their access to modern science and in the uses to which they put its findings, but the validity of the life sciences, earth sciences, and physical sciences does not depend on the identity of those who engage in their study or use. For these reasons, international assessments of mathematics and science pose precisely the same questions to students of the same age all over the world, with the expectation that they will have (or should have) studied the same material.

The internationalization of standards in mathematics and science has helped to promote the development of content standards in the United States. When testing experts gather to decide which topics to include on international assessments, they must agree both about what *is* taught and what *should be* taught in their subject. This being the case, American educators are forced to grapple with the same issues: if there are international standards in these fields, what should American students be taught? Should world standards be used to shape instruction only for students preparing for elite colleges, for all college-bound students, or for *all* students? Should international standards shape the teaching of these subjects in the early grades, long before students know whether they are college bound? These questions have pushed along the movement to identify external standards.

Discussions of standards tend to turn at once into debates about testing, such as whether tests are fair (however that word may be defined), whether tests discriminate against disadvantaged or minority students, whether test items are culturally biased by their vocabulary, whether multiple-choice tests discourage creativity, whether tests can measure what is really important, whether tests have too much influence on instruction, and whether tests should influence decisions about college admission or employment. Focusing only on testing makes it easy to forget that a standard is also a description of what is to be achieved, a model or example to be aimed for. Many educators also associate standards negatively with "standardization," and most especially with standardized tests, the multiple-choice tests that are scored by machine. But standardized tests are not the only means of measuring progress toward external standards; it can also be measured by essays, mathematical calculations, scientific experiments, projects, performances, or similar demonstrations of what was learned.

The term "standard" in education means different things to different people. Sometimes the word is bandied about with no concrete meaning at all, other than as a synonym for doing better in some nonspecific way ("we should improve our standards," for example, or "the standards are too low"). But a standard is not useful or meaningful unless there is some way to measure whether it is reached. Some state boards of education think that they have standards when all they really have are hortatory or obscure statements about aspirations that are inherently unmeasurable (for example, "all students can learn," or "all students should understand the basic processes of science"). Many states use terms such as "standards," "objectives," "outcomes," and "goals" interchangeably, without defining any particular meaning.

For purposes of this discussion, the meaning of the word "standard" as it pertains to education should be made clear. The term has three common uses, each with distinct meaning and purpose. These are:

Content standards. Content standards (or curriculum standards) describe what teachers are supposed to teach and students are expected to learn. They provide clear, specific descriptions of the skills and knowledge that should be taught to students. As a report to the National Education Goals Panel defined them, "those 'skills' include the ways of thinking, working, communicating, reasoning, and investigating that characterize each discipline. That 'knowledge' includes the most important and enduring ideas, concepts, issues, dilemmas, and information of the discipline."[4] A syllabus containing the content standards of each school district or state should be easily available to students and parents, so that the school's expectations are well understood. A content standard should be measurable, so that students can demonstrate their mastery of the skills or knowledge; if mastery of the standard is neither measurable nor demonstrable, then it is probably so vague that it has little meaning or value for teachers and students.

Content standards should be specific enough to be readily understood by teachers, parents, students, and others. They should be clear enough so that teachers know what students are supposed to learn and can design lessons to help them learn what is expected. In the absence of clear content standards, each teacher and each school must figure out what students are supposed to learn. Under such circumstances, students with educated parents and schools in affluent neighborhoods get a richer curriculum than students from poor families in poor neighborhoods; more gets taught in well-to-do schools, and the gap between students grows larger because they are not offered equal educational opportunities.

Performance standards. Performance standards define degrees of mastery or levels of attainment. They answer the question: "How good is good enough?" Performance standards describe what kind of performance represents inadequate, acceptable, or outstanding accomplishment. The report cited above held that performance standards "indicate both the nature of the evidence (such as an essay, mathematical proof, scientific experiment, project, exam, or combination of these) required to demonstrate that content standards have been met *and* the quality of student performance that will be deemed acceptable (what merits a passing grade or an 'A' grade)."[5] The National Assessment of Educational Progress has established clear performance standards to judge student writing, for example, on a scale of 0 ("not rated") to 6 ("extensively elaborated"). The meaning of each score is explained and illustrated with specific examples, so that different scorers share common criteria for what constitutes poor writing and what constitutes excellent writing.[6]

Opportunity-to-learn, or school delivery, standards. Opportunity-to-learn standards define the availability of programs, staff, and other resources that schools, districts, and states provide so that students are able to meet challenging content and performance standards. Initially described as "school delivery standards" in congressional debates during the Bush administration, the term was renamed "opportunity-to-learn standards" as part of the Clinton administration's Goals 2000 legislation. Because such standards have always been the responsibility of state and local governments, proposals to develop federal school delivery standards were very controversial during legislative debates in both administrations.[7] Proponents believed that students should not be expected to meet high standards unless their schools had adequate resources; critics feared that such standards would become a source of interference and unfunded mandates by the federal government.

These three types of standards are interrelated. Content standards without performance standards are meaningless. Content standards define what is to be taught and learned; performance standards describe how well it has been learned. Similarly, opportunity-to-learn standards cannot stand on their own, without content and performance standards. Some proponents want to use opportunity-to-learn standards as a lever to force new spending and equalization of spending among schools. But spending is not an end in itself. The end must be to provide children with the opportunity to learn what is taught (content standards) and to learn it well (performance standards). Without content and performance standards, there is no way to determine objectively whether resources are deployed effectively. Resources are, of course, important. Even critics of opportunity-to-learn standards agree that schools must meet fundamental standards of safety, healthfulness, and physical comfort and that students cannot be expected to learn or excel unless they have well-educated teachers, a sound curriculum, appropriate instructional materials, and a well-maintained environment for learning.

What is most controversial about these three types of standards is how they will be enforced and by whom. Will such standards be mandatory, voluntary, or de facto? Some standards, such as those governing pupils' health and safety, are already mandatory and regulated by state and local governments. Many educators fear that the federal and state governments will require uniform policies (under the mantle of opportunity-to-learn standards) on issues such as class size, disciplinary policies, teaching methods, teacher training, and other matters that should be left to professional discretion. Educators and elected officials generally agree that content and performance standards should be voluntary, not mandatory; that they should be created by professional associations of teachers and scholars, free of political interference; that they should serve as guidance, rather than as directives; and that there should be enough leeway in their implementation to permit continual revision and improvement.

An International Perspective

Many countries have external examination systems, external standards that provide both guidelines for instruction (what is to be taught, described in a published syllabus) and a means of gauging how well the subject has been learned (an examination based on the syllabus). The United States does not.

Some countries—such as Japan, France, and Great Britain—have a national curriculum that describes content standards. Other countries—such as the United States, Germany, and Canada—rely on states or provinces to define content standards. In the United States some school districts and states have curriculum guidelines (or curriculum frameworks) that contain clear content standards; most, however, do not. Many states have curriculum documents that list broad, diffuse objectives or behavioral outcomes or lofty goals, but these are rhetorical statements rather than content standards because no one is quite sure what they mean or how to measure them. Many educators regard the absence of guidance from the state as a good thing; they fear the imposition of a state or national curriculum. Theoretically, this allows freedom for experimentation, but in practice most districts, schools, and teachers follow the direction provided by commercial textbooks and mass-produced, standardized tests.

Nations that establish national standards do so to ensure equality of education as well as higher achievement. They make explicit what they expect children to learn to ensure that all children have access to the same educational opportunities. Japan has a well-developed national curriculum, prepared by its Ministry of Education, Science, and Culture. The national course of study is contained in three slender volumes, one for elementary schools, one for lower secondary schools, and one for upper secondary schools. The course of study contains content standards for every subject in every grade; it provides guidance to teachers about what students are supposed to learn in each grade, but it does not dictate what is to be done every day nor how teachers should teach. For example, elementary school science in Japan is organized around three topics: "living things and their environment," "matter and energy," and "the earth and the universe." Fifth graders are expected (among other things) to "understand the function of air in combustion, while examining the change of air when a substance burns and the properties of air by producing oxygen and carbon dioxide." In doing this, they are supposed to learn that "(1) air is essential for combustion, (2) substances burn more strongly in oxygen than in the air, (3) air contains oxygen, (4) oxygen is used and carbon dioxide is produced when plant substances are burned, and (5) carbon dioxide is heavier than the air and turns limewater cloudy and white."[8]

This description is typical of the Japanese approach in every subject area throughout the national curriculum. Clear and free of jargon, it identifies the main ideas that children should learn; in each grade, new concepts and skills are added to what has previously been learned. Japanese textbooks reflect the central ideas contained in the national curriculum.

In the United States, by contrast, schools have a haphazard approach to teaching science in the elementary grades; there is no agreement about what content is appropriate, and the teaching of science often depends on the interest or experience of the teacher. Because the schools have no particular expectations about what is to be taught, science may not be taught at all in some grades. In addition, textbooks often fail to explain the big ideas of the field in ways that children can readily understand; instead, the texts commit the cardinal sin of "mentioning," to be sure that every fact, idea, and definition is included and that everything is surrounded by flashy—although not necessarily relevant—illustrations and graphics.

Japanese children begin to learn about geometrical figures in the first grade, when they observe and construct objects with different shapes. In each following grade, their knowledge of geometric concepts is deepened. By sixth grade, teachers are expected

1) to help pupils understand plane figures more thoroughly,
   a. To know the meaning of axial and point symmetry and to study the fundamental figures from the viewpoint of symmetry.
   b. To summarize the understanding of the shape and size of the figure, and to read and draw simple reduced or enlarged figures.
   c. To investigate the mutual relations between the fundamental figures.
2) To help pupils know the fundamental prisms, circular cylinders, pyramids, and circular cones, and to enable them to represent and construct those solids.[9]

By contrast, most American students study no geometry until they enter high school; it is usually postponed until tenth or eleventh grade, after they have completed the study of algebra. In many schools geometry is considered appropriate only for college-bound students, and about one-third of high school students never study it at all.

The Japanese national standards are notably comprehensible and brief. The entire national course of study for all subjects in all grades is smaller in size than the documents prepared by subject matter groups in the United States for the teaching of a single subject. For example, the U.S. standards for mathematics, prepared by the National Council of Teachers of Mathematics (NCTM), are contained in a densely packed volume of more than 250 pages. The NCTM standards have had a tonic effect on the teaching of mathematics across the nation because they shifted attention from memorization to problem solving. But they are not presented in a clear and concise format; teachers must plow through a mountain of prose to figure out what is expected of them and their students.

In other nations large numbers of students prepare for national examinations at the end of high school, which concentrates their attention on learning. Many students in England and Wales spend their last two years of secondary school preparing for their A-level examinations; 31 percent of the age cohort took A-level examinations in at least one subject in 1992, and 25 percent of the age cohort earned passing grades. French students in their last year of secondary school prepare for national examinations that lead to a baccalaureate diploma. Regardless of the type of baccalaureate diploma—academic, technical, or professional—all students are expected to study a core curriculum that includes French, history and geography, mathematics, chemistry, and physics. In 1992, 71 percent of the age group prepared for a "Bac" examination, and 51 percent of the age cohort passed.[10] In Germany students in their last year of secondary education take a demanding examination called the *Abitur;* in 1991, 37 percent of the age cohort took the examination, and more than 95 percent of them received a passing score.[11] In each of these countries students must pass these subject-based examinations to qualify for admission to university.

By contrast, most students in the United States are not expected to take any subject-based examinations to enter college or university. About one-third of the nation's colleges accept all applicants, regardless of their performance in—or even completion of—high school; many other colleges require nothing more than a high school diploma for entry. A minority of colleges and universities is selective, requiring applicants to submit scores earned on a college-entry test, either the SAT or ACT, neither of which is directly based on what students have studied in high school.[12] An even smaller minority of colleges and universities is very selective and requires students to take achievement tests in subjects that they studied in high school, such as science, history, or foreign languages (about 10 percent of high school graduates take achievement tests for college entry). None of the college-entry tests that American students take is considered comparable in rigor to the English A-levels, the French baccalaureate examination, or the German *Abitur.*

The College Board's Advanced Placement (AP) examinations are closest in format and academic rigor to the exit examinations of other nations. Nearly half of all American high schools offer at least one AP course. Participating schools receive a course outline, and their teachers may attend special workshops. High school students who pass AP examinations can earn college credit in more than a dozen academic subjects. Students are told in advance the topics that might be on the examination, and they are given sample questions, so that they know the level of difficulty for which to prepare. In 1993 only 7 percent of American high school seniors took one or more AP examinations, and only 4 percent passed them.

The International Baccalaureate (IB) is another example of an authoritative, syllabus-based examination, modeled on the French baccalaureate. It is offered to students in seventy-two nations; in the United States, about 7,000-8,000 students in 150 high schools prepare for the IB examination. The syllabus guides, distributed to students and teachers, contain topics, sample questions, a prescribed book list, and themes that are likely to appear on the examination. Those who pass the rigorous IB examination receive college credit in universities around the world, in recognition of its consistently high standards.

Whether one considers the AP, the IB, or the French baccalaureate, the point that emerges clearly is that the test does not stand alone; rather, it embodies carefully delineated standards that have previously been communicated to teachers and students. The test is the measure of whether the standards have been met. It is not a mysterious process that students must puzzle out at the end of the year, or one that asks for a quick response to an unanticipated question. The examination is based on a syllabus that identifies what is most important and what students need to learn. Each examination is not just a test, but also an integrated, well-conceptualized set of standards and assessments.

The Case against National Standards and Assessments

Many people, for many different reasons, object to national education standards and national testing. Some object on principle to any effort to establish national standards, even voluntary ones, rejecting the presumption that there is value in uniformity. Others fear that any standards controlled by a federal agency cannot long remain voluntary, because of the federal government's power to coerce compliance by withholding funds. The critics range from conservatives, who have always opposed expansion of the federal role in education, to liberals, who fear that meaningful standards will cause poor children to fail or drop out of school.

There are genuine risks in any activities setting education standards; these risks are even larger when a federal agency controls the standards. These dangers cannot be dismissed out of hand; they must be confronted directly, and steps must be taken to minimize them.

As the possibility of creating national standards and assessments came closer to reality in the early 1990s, opponents voiced the following criticisms:

National standards will be minimal, reduced to the lowest common denominator, especially if they are controlled by a federal agency. This is a realistic fear, especially when the standards are to be certified by a politically appointed board that by law has a large representation of historically low-achieving populations. The best safeguard against inadequate standards is the public nature of the process; if national standards are not comparable to the best standards in the states and other nations, they will be ignored or ridiculed.

The government might impose controversial values and opinions. Critics warned that if the federal government gained control over curriculum and testing, it could impose political and ideological conformity. This has been a concern of many conservatives for years, but recently liberal academics have also expressed this view. Stephen Arons of the University of Massachusetts worried about allowing the government to define "official knowledge" and foresaw "zero-sum conflicts over conscience and belief in schooling."[13] Theodore R. Sizer of Brown University noted that, although forging agreement on standards for reading, writing, and mathematics was altogether possible, reasonable people might well disagree about what should be taught and read in history and literature classes. "The issue for me is not, thus, merely a scientific one about testing techniques," Sizer wrote. "It is, rather, a matter of philosophy, of intellectual freedom. *How much control should the state have over my child's mind?* Is there a limit to state authority here?"[14]

Critics are right to worry about the dangers inherent in setting standards in subjects such as history and English, where people hold divergent views. Americans are not likely to want any government agency, federal or state, settling historical debates and giving official sanction to certain ideas, values, and policies, when others have equal claims to truth. Any national (or state) board that oversees education standards must be scrupulously nonpartisan not only about the political parties, but also about disputes over fundamental values. Will the standards avoid controversy? Will they cause controversy by avoiding controversy? If government assumes the right and power to mold opinion on controverted topics, there will be controversy; but if government fails to establish the validity of basic values—for example, slavery and the Holocaust were crimes against humanity, a multiparty democracy is preferable to a dictatorship—there will also be controversy. The challenge is to pose issues and controversies without resolving them; to recognize that historical and scientific debates are always subject to investigation and evidence; and to acknowledge those instances where investigation and evidence have established conclusive facts. Diversity of opinion is a basic value in and of itself in a democratic society. If government-endorsed standards trample on freedom of thought or attempt to impose uniformity of opinion, they deserve to be short-lived.

National standards based on traditional subject matter disciplines such as mathematics, science, and history will narrow the curriculum. Critics charge that subject-based national standards will freeze the curriculum and stifle teachers who want to focus on real-life problems in an interdisciplinary or nondisciplinary manner. Some educators complain that national standards will be an obstacle to those who prefer to organize the school day around themes and problems rather than subject-matter courses.

What appears to be "narrowing" to some critics may also be seen as setting priorities and making sure that students have equal educational opportunity. Every student, regardless of background or interests, should study mathematics, science, history, English, the arts, civics and—one hopes—a foreign language. Identifying the essential skills and knowledge that students should master in each of these subjects in no way limits the creativity of teachers and may even make their lives easier. Teachers cannot engage in interdisciplinary instruction unless they have first mastered at least two disciplines. Even "nondisciplinary" instruction—if it is to be worthwhile—must ultimately incorporate key concepts, knowledge, and skills drawn from the disciplines, or it runs the risk of being unfocused and without educational value as well as nondisciplinary. Teachers must be free to adapt the standards in each field into interdisciplinary lessons, hands-on experiences, problem-solving activities, or anything else that they think appropriate.

National testing will harm children and will distort priorities in the classroom. Critics fear that imposing standardized national tests will trivialize instruction, enforce uniformity in classrooms across the country, and reduce learning to preparing for tests. They charge that, if test results are used for student promotion or graduation, teachers will spend too much time coaching students to perform well on the tests, and children will be labeled and discriminated against on the basis of their test scores. In other words, teachers will teach to the test, which will corrupt both the test and the test results.[15]

Critics of testing usually make two assumptions: first, that tests of the future will be the same kinds of multiple-choice tests that are in wide use today (and that are already used to label children); and second, that teaching what is tested or testing what is taught is bad. But should not tests incorporate the best aspects of performance assessment: essays, projects, portfolios of student work, open-ended answers, as well as a limited core of well-crafted multiple-choice questions? In the future many students will be tested by sophisticated computer programs that quickly eliminate questions that are too easy or too hard for a particular student, leaving ample time for students to answer open-ended questions or engage in challenging performance assignments.

"Teaching to the test" is bad in current practice because so many tests ask narrow questions about disconnected fragments of information, thus leading teachers to drill their students on right answers rather than to teach a deep understanding of the concepts involved. Suppose instead that the test is based on what is taught (similar to advanced placement examinations, for example). Suppose students know that they will be asked to write an essay or to solve an unfamiliar problem, using what they have learned in class. If the tests are thoughtful and thought-provoking, then teaching to the test makes sense, because the teacher is helping students prepare for the test. The test should be an opportunity for students to demonstrate what they know and can do, not just a guessing game for the fast and the lucky. Teaching to the test is appropriate if the test gives students a chance to show that they understand and can use what they have learned. If the test does not test what was taught by the teacher, what does it test?

National standards and national tests will do nothing to help poor inner-city schools. Critics argue that the most urgent need in inner-city schools is money, not standards and assessments. Michael W.

Apple of the University of Wisconsin denounced standards and assessments as "reform on the cheap" that would "ratify and exacerbate gender, race and class differences in the absence of sufficient resources. . . ."[16]

Standards and assessments are no substitute for resources. Schools that cannot afford to pay good salaries, make timely repairs, or buy adequate supplies may need additional resources, or they may be part of a school system that is spending a disproportionate amount on administration and bureaucracy instead of the classroom. But standards and assessments are nonetheless a crucial part of a strategy to increase equal educational opportunity. Absent standards, poor and minority children do not have equal access to challenging courses; absent assessments, no one can know the size of the gap between schools or groups of students or whether that gap is growing larger or smaller.

If there are national (or state) standards that identify what students need to learn in each major academic field, there should also be clear measures of whether school districts are providing equal educational opportunities in programs and courses offered, regardless of the race or social origin of the students. Similarly, consensus on the primary goals of the schools would support targeted investment in teacher education, staff development, instructional materials, technology, and testing. A national test, based on national standards, would give parents the accurate information about their children's performance that most do not now receive. Accurate reports about student performance might cause many parents to take a more active role in improving their children's schools.

National standards and assessments will not expand equality of opportunity. Critics complain that national standards and assessments will not improve the achievement of minority students nor reduce the achievement gap between minority and nonminority students. Setting high standards will discourage them, not help them, say these critics; nor will minority students be helped by a national test that merely confirms what is already well known about their lackluster performance.

If the act of setting standards is seen as the first step in educational reform, rather than the end of the process, then standards can become a means of ensuring equality of opportunity. In other countries national content standards ensure that all students have access to the same curriculum, no matter where they live, and that their teachers are prepared to teach it, because they know what is expected of them. In this country studies have shown that low-income black and Hispanic students tend to be enrolled in schools where they have "less-extensive and less-demanding science and mathematics programs available to them. They also have fewer opportunities to take the critical gatekeeping courses that prepare them for science and mathematics study after high school—algebra and geometry in junior high school and calculus in senior high school."[17]

Perhaps the most ambitious effort to demonstrate the connection between standards and educational equity is the College Board's EQUITY 2000 program. This program enlisted six school districts (Providence; Nashville; Milwaukee; Prince George's County, Virginia; Fort Worth; and San Jose), each with a large number of poor and minority students, in pursuit of a single goal: academic excellence for every student. The districts increased the percentage of children who study algebra (now up to 80 percent of all ninth graders) and agreed to place every middle grade and high school student in a college preparatory curriculum, eliminate all "watered-down" courses, retrain teachers, provide counseling for students to raise their aspirations, and work closely with local colleges. The program will eventually be judged by whether it substantially increases the enrollment of minority and disadvantaged youngsters in college.[18]

National standards and assessments will not improve achievement because most teachers will ignore them and do what they have always done. Larry Cuban of Stanford University argues that comparatively few teachers in California follow new state-developed guidelines but that most "adapt, modify, and even ignore what the state requires." Because teachers are likely to ignore national standards, he continues, such standards are not likely to produce "a higher degree of uniformity in what students learn. . . ."[19]

Whether standards are state or national, teachers *should* adapt and modify them to fit their own pedagogical skills as well as to take advantage of current events and student interests. The point is not to create uniformity of practice, but a challenging curriculum that is equally available to all students. If, however, teachers ignore the new standards, they are not likely to have any of the negative effects that critics fear.

The question, then, is under what circumstances will standards influence what happens in the classroom. Standards alone are not likely to change anyone's behavior and expectations. Whether developed at the national or state level, standards must precede and be linked to student tests; for the standards to matter to teachers and students, the tests must be based on the standards. If the two are linked, both teachers and students will know what the test is likely to cover, and both will know that what is taught counts. When a state (or nation) announces standards but continues to use old tests, then of course the new standards will be ignored. If the standards form the basis for the state's testing program, they will not be ignored.

The failure of national standards and testing will undermine faith in public education and pave the way for privatization of education. Critics charge that the information produced by a system of national standards and tests would be used so that "educational 'consumers' could discover which 'product' is better," allowing "free market forces to operate" by providing "product" information.[20] Providing information about performance and allowing parents to choose their schools would encourage demands for choice and, ultimately, privatization of education, they contend.

Parents and the general public should have the right to full information about educational performance, not only of their own children, but of all publicly funded schools. In the past the release of information about test scores and school segregation spurred important reforms that would not have occurred in the absence of public information. With standards and assessments (whether local, state, or national), parents know what students are supposed to learn and whether they have learned it. More and more public school systems have decided to issue report cards for individual schools and school districts. More and more public school systems have decided that parents and students should be free to choose their public school. If some schools are consistently low-performing (which can be determined only on the basis of valid standards and assessments), pressure to restructure or close them will undoubtedly build. Some communities have even been pressured to turn management of the public schools over to contractors, who would be subject to strict accountability for student performance. Without valid standards and assessments, there is no way to identify low-performing schools or to determine whether all students are receiving equal educational opportunity. It is hard to come up with a good reason for limiting the public's right to know about school performance.

National standards and assessments will accomplish little by themselves. Unless they are accompanied by better teaching, a better school environment, better instructional materials (including new technology), and more highly motivated students, student achievement will not improve. This is true.

Every one of the criticisms directed against national standards and assessments or national standards controlled by a federal agency contains a valid and important caution. Some of the eventualities that critics fear are clear and present dangers to educational quality. There is real reason to worry that education standards developed through a political process of give-and-take may be minimal and undemanding; there is also good reason to worry that any standards approved by a politically appointed board might reflect partisan views. Such developments must be rigorously guarded against to protect the integrity of the entire process. If, over time, the political process proves incapable of creating demanding education standards worthy of respect and emulation, then the standards will be discredited and rightfully disregarded by states and schools.

The Case for National Standards and Assessments

"Education" means to lead forth, but it is impossible to lead anyone anywhere without knowing where you want to go. If you do not know what you are trying to accomplish, you will not accomplish much. Content standards—what children are expected to learn—are necessary for educational improvement because they are the starting point for education. When educators fail to agree on what children should learn, it means that they have failed to identify their most fundamental goals. In the absence of such agreement by educators, decisions about what should be learned are left to the marketplace—textbook publishers, testmakers, and interest groups.

In 1994 Congress passed a law intended to begin the process of creating national content and performance standards (but not national assessments; states will continue to be responsible for assessment). Supporters of national standards in education make the following claims.

Standards can improve achievement by clearly defining what is to be taught and what kind of performance is expected. They define what teachers and schools should be trying to accomplish. They can raise the quality of education by establishing clear expectations about what students must learn if they are to succeed. If the goals of teaching and learning are spelled out, students understand that their teachers are trying to help them meet externally defined standards, and parents know what is expected of their children in school.

Standards (national, state, and local) are necessary for equality of opportunity. Standards establish the principle that all students should encounter the same educational opportunities and the same performance expectations, regardless of who their parents are or what neighborhood they live in. One essential purpose of standards is to ensure that students in all schools have access to equally challenging programs and courses of study, that expectations for learning are equally high for almost all children; and that all teachers are well prepared to teach.

National standards provide a valuable coordinating function. In the absence of explicit standards, the pieces of the educational system operate without coherence and often at odds with each other. Teacher education proceeds without sure knowledge of what is to be taught, giving rise to the frequent complaint that schools of education stress pedagogy and ignore content. In-service courses for current teachers focus on process and group dynamics, rather than building teachers' understanding of what they are to teach. The content of textbooks determines what is taught, and their content is based on the checklists of textbook adoption committees in big states such as California and Texas. Tests drive the curriculum, based on what testmakers think is being taught; teachers teach what they think is likely to be on the standardized tests that their students take. With teachers teaching to the test and using the textbook as their course guide, the textbook and test publishers—*faute de mieux*—define the curriculum and set the actual standards low enough so that every state can claim to be "above the national norm."[21]

Content standards make it possible to coordinate the various parts of the educational system to promote student learning. Teachers can use content standards to prepare their lessons. Textbook writers can use them to write materials for the schools. Colleges and universities can use them to prepare teachers so that they will know what they are expected to teach. Software designers can use them to create new technology that will teach what children are supposed to learn. Testing experts can use them as the basis for tests that children will take to determine whether or how well they have met the standards. Seen this way, explicit content standards clearly can become an or-ganizing force for education, in which all the different pieces of the system are focused on the same goal: helping children learn at high levels of achievement.

There is no reason to have different standards in different states, especially in mathematics and science, when well-developed international standards have already been developed for these fields. International assessments of mathematics and science have identified clear parameters for what is expected of students at various ages. Why should state and local standards depart radically from international standards? In addition, because so many Americans move from state to state and from region to region, there is no justification for extreme variation among state educational standards.

Standards and assessments provide consumer protection by supplying accurate information to students and parents. Who would willingly send their child to a school where a full curriculum was not available, where few students enrolled in advanced classes, where teachers did not know their subject area, where expectations for achievement were low, and where student performance was consistently poor? Students and their parents have the right to know whether their school offers a full curriculum, appropriate facilities (such as a library and science laboratories), and a well-educated staff; how student achievement compares to other schools in the district and the state; and how their individual performance measures up to the school's expectations.

Standards and assessments serve as an important signaling device to students, parents, teachers, employers, and colleges. Standards tell everyone in the educational system what is expected of them; assessments provide information about how well expectations have been met. Standards tell students what they need to do to succeed in school; assessments tell them whether they are making progress. Assessments also tell employers and colleges whether high school graduates truly possess the necessary knowledge and skills for work or further study.

The Complex Process of Setting Standards

The United States has educational standards, but they are not explicit, nor are they established by design. They are the incidental result of disparate decisions made in a variety of states and localities about tests, textbooks, and teacher preparation. Instead of being consciously selected and framed, these educational standards have emerged serendipitously from a patchwork of activities at the local, state, and national levels. Moreover, the same school may have different standards for different students, depending on whether students are in the college "track" or not. Instead of specifically setting standards for what students should know and be able to do, the national practice is to discover them in existing institutional arrangements. Depending on the circumstances and the students, standards are sometimes set by colleges, private testing organizations, state-mandated commercial tests, commercial textbooks, individual teachers, state or local graduation requirements, or a combination of the above. The problem is that there are many standards and that they are in the main low, unchallenging, and inconsistent. These standards establish minimal expectations for student learning and signal that what is learned in school is not very important, either in higher education or in the workplace.

The movement to establish national standards and assessments, it has been noted, began with the decision by President Bush and the governors to set national education goals. From the outset, it was not clear where responsibility would lie for implementing the goals, nor was there any agreement on who would establish national standards or devise national examinations. Would the federal government take the lead? The Bush administration and many governors, both Republicans and Democrats, did not want federally imposed standards and tests to usurp the traditional authority of local and state governments. The only consensus on issues of implementation was that any national standards and assessments should be voluntary, not mandatory, and national, not federal. But no one knew with any certainty how to launch a process for creating voluntary national standards that would remain free of federal control.

The Bush administration did not offer legislation to establish national standards and assessments precisely because it feared that congressional authorization would inevitably place the federal government in control of what the administration believed should be a voluntary process. The administration used the voluntary national standards of the National Council of Teachers of Mathematics as a free-market model for educational reform. The NCTM standards were created by a private organization of teachers and scholars, disseminated by voluntary efforts to classrooms across the nation, and adopted by teachers, local school districts, state education agencies, and schools of education because they embodied the best thinking about how to teach mathematics. Following that example, in 1991 and 1992, the U.S. Department of Education made grants to leading groups of teachers and scholars to create voluntary national standards in science, history, geography, foreign languages, the arts, English, and civics.[22] The department's intention was to have no federal oversight agency, but to encourage professional fields to shape a consensus about what students should know and be able to do. Eventually, the standards would make their own way into the schools (or not) by virtue of their quality, as the NCTM standards have, and not because of the coercive power of government to impose them. The results of a voluntary national test, when known to parents and teachers, would encourage schools, districts, and states to adopt high standards, or so the reasoning went.

The Clinton administration pursued a different path, enacting legislation with assurances of the voluntary nature of national standards. Its Goals 2000 legislation created a federal agency, the National Education Standards and Improvement Council (NESIC), responsible for certifying the national standards created by subject-matter organizations. The legislation rejected a national test, relying instead on the states to prepare their own standards and assessments, which could be submitted (if the states chose) to NESIC for certification.

In the United States, with its strong tradition of local control and decentralization, devising a credible public process for setting content standards will be difficult. NESIC will review the voluntary national standards proposed by the consortia of scholars, teachers, and others that received federal funding. It will also review proposals by other groups that have not received federal funding. It may be that the work of an unfunded group will be superior to that of a funded group. It is uncertain, however, whether certifying multiple national standards is sensible and whether multiple standards will make all competing standards ineffectual.

Over time, content standards might look like a three-tiered cake, composed of national, state, and local layers. The national standards might identify in broad strokes the essential skills, concepts, and knowledge of each field; state standards might build on the national standards, making them more concrete and adding content pertinent to the state; localities could tailor the national and state standards, making them more specific and adding content prized in that locality.

This may seem unduly complicated, but complexity is necessary in a federal system, where states and localities bear primary responsibility for education.

National standards, in other words, are a starting point, which states and localities can use to define their own curriculum frameworks. The content standards promulgated at the national level must be authoritative (in the sense that they must be based on the best scholarship, the best research, and the best classroom practice). They must define what children should know and be able to do to be prepared for citizenship, work, and a fulfilling life. They should be clear, precise, and brief, rather than encyclopedic compromises intended to satisfy every splinter group in the field.

The Challenge of Goals 2000

No matter which way the federal government moves, dangers loom: the danger of federal control, the danger of a federal curriculum—but also the danger of making a lot of noise yet accomplishing nothing. It is impossible to know whether the Bush strategy would have worked. And only time will tell whether the Clinton strategy will. The complexity of the challenge guarantees that doing it right will be hard; doing it wrong will be easy.

As the effort to establish national standards proceeds, questions must be raised again and again: Are they high enough? How will we know? Who will make sure that they contain no political or ideological bias? How will they be revised? What will be the relationship between national standards and state standards? How much power will federal agencies have in deciding what all children should learn? Can national standards be set without establishing a national curriculum? Should there be a limited national curriculum for fields such as mathematics and science? Will Congress try to regulate the curriculum, the textbooks, and the tests used in American schools? How will national standards affect the education of poor and minority children? Will they be a help or hindrance in the pursuit of equal educational opportunity? If the standards are voluntary, will anyone pay attention to them? Will anyone pay attention to the national standards if they are not used as the basis for a national test? When the new national standards are synthesized by state departments of education, will they end up looking very much like the status quo?

How much tolerance will there be for national standards if they are so high that some students are not likely to meet them? Will the standards be as high as those in other nations? How can we be sure?

The Clinton legislation does not provide for a national test nor for national performance standards; instead, it encourages states to create state standards and state tests. As matters now stand, the nation will have national content standards but not national testing. Questions must be asked about this arrangement. How will state tests connect to common national standards? Should there be a federal role in comparing state tests to national standards? What if some states have more difficult tests than other states? What should test scores be used for? Should they be used in decisions about college admission and employment?

All of these issues will be addressed sooner or later in Washington, in state capitals, and in local communities. The question is not whether the nation should have standards and tests; it already has plenty of both. The question is whether the existing ones are good enough, whether they can be improved, and whether the steps now under way will make them better or worse.

The most important new element in this discussion is the expanded role of the federal government. Education in the United States has always been a state and local responsibility. The federal government has been involved in education since the nineteenth century, when its primary responsibility was collecting statistics. But its role has always been limited, not least because of the Tenth Amendment to the Constitution. Since 1965, when Congress passed the Elementary and Secondary Education Act, which authorized federal support for the education of disadvantaged children, the federal role has supported specific activities, including research, aid for disadvantaged and handicapped students, and subsidies for students in higher education. By law the federal government has not been allowed to supervise, control, or direct curriculum. This restriction stems from fears that Uncle Sam might attempt to exert control over what children learn. Americans, for many different reasons, have long shared a consensus that federal control of education was not desirable; at bottom, people of various persuasions worried that political or religious partisans might gain power and distort what was taught in the classroom. The agreement to keep the federal government out of curriculum decisions was based on lack of trust; the political leadership of the United States at every level agreed not to create a centralized ministry of education, because of mutual fear that it would inevitably impose someone else's unwanted ideas into local schools.

To be successful, NESIC, the new federal panel created to certify national standards, will have to be strictly nonpolitical and nonpartisan, in the same way that government statistical agencies are. If NESIC approves standards that are not high or if it acts politically, its credibility as well as the credibility of the national standards it certifies will quickly be lost. Clear national standards can help to support excellence in education only if they are benchmarked to the best practices here and abroad and exemplify the learning that can be achieved under the best circumstances.

The purpose of setting standards is to raise expectations for all students. The object is not to make school more difficult, but to make instruction more challenging and engaging and to establish goals that the entire educational system will strive to reach. "World-class" performance will be reached not by producing a generation of smart robots, but by encouraging students to think about what they are learning and to become actively involved in their own education. The movement for standards is grounded in the faith that every human being is born with the capacity to learn, that the job of education is to improve the ability of people to use their minds well, and that expectations and incentives affect effort. Proponents believe that standards can be a lever for both excellence and equity. They argue that too little is expected of almost all American students and that the challenge to American education is to educate every youngster for full participation in the modern technological society.

The United States has begun the process of creating national standards. Although much remains to be resolved, one thing is clear. The development of national standards with the support of the federal government represents dramatic change in a nation whose educational system has always been extremely decentralized. How did it happen? Why did it happen? Will it improve education? These are some of the questions to be considered in the following pages.

2

A Historical Perspective

 TO MANY THE MOVEMENT for national standards and assessments seems a startling turn of events, a development unprecedented in American history. The fact is that American education has a long history of standard-setting activity, sometimes overt and purposeful, at other times implicit and haphazard. The current movement is grounded in a long tradition of efforts to establish agreement on what American students should know and be able to do and to measure whether and how well they have learned what was expected of them. Yet, despite this history of standard setting sponsored by various public and private agencies, never before has the federal government attempted to establish explicit national standards for what American children should learn in school.

Standards in Nineteenth Century Schools

The development of public education in the United States—the common school movement—coincided with the onset of waves of immigration from Ireland, Germany, and elsewhere in the 1840s and 1850s. As the nation's diversity grew, the schools promoted social cohesion by teaching a common language and shared civic values. The heralds of the common school, especially Horace Mann, described it as the great equalizer of opportunity. As secretary of the Massachusetts Board of Education, Mann championed the public's responsibility to provide equal opportunity, which in turn meant that the state had to play a large role, monitoring access and quality. Needless to say, equality of educational opportunity—a critical aspect of Mann's vision—implied that schools would not be wildly dissimilar in kind or quality.

Making sure that all children have access to schools that offer education of similar, high quality has been a primary reason to establish standards. Over the years standards—some purposeful, some serendipitous—have evolved to foster some degree of similarity in the quality of schooling, such as:

- The use of identical or similar textbooks

- The specification of requirements for high school graduation or college entrance

- The use of standardized or comparable achievement tests for promotion or college admission

- The prescription of curriculum patterns (for example, so many years of English, history, and so forth, as well as certain sequences of courses, such as biology, chemistry, and physics)

- The professionalization of teacher training, with shared norms and expectations (that is, standards)

Although critics periodically rebel against the constraints and stifling effects of conformity, uniformity, and standardization, educators and legislators have spent a great deal of time and attention trying to establish shared norms, expectations, and standards to achieve efficiency, equality, or both. This tension between the search for order and the rejection of conformity is healthy; Americans value individualism and imagination far too much to embrace mechanistic prescriptions. Nonetheless, the effort to ensure equal access to a good education for all students inevitably requires some form of standards.

After the American Revolution, Webster's "Blue-backed" speller provided something akin to a national standard for many years. Webster's speller was used not only in school but by adults for self-education; the speller set a national standard for spelling and pronunciation, as Webster had hoped. In the early nineteenth century, however, the Webster speller lost its near-monopoly as other book publishers turned out competing books in every subject. As early as the 1830s, school reformers complained about the burgeoning number of textbooks in every field. Despite the multiplicity of titles, however, the content of the books was more like than unlike. In some fields, one or two series, such as the McGuffey's reading books, dominated the market. The reading series that competed with McGuffey's looked much like McGuffey's, even including some of the same stories and poems. The similarity of the nineteenth century readers, history books, geography texts, and others vying for market share in the same subject area is striking. The uniformity found in the reading materials extended to classroom methods, with few exceptions.

American schools for most of the nineteenth century by and large had content standards, as defined by relatively uniform classroom materials, and they even had an implicit consensus about performance standards, with a broadly shared scale that ranged from A to F or from 100 to 60. It was not exact, but educators had a common vocabulary with which to gauge student performance.

Because no state or national testing systems had yet been developed, college admission requirements provided the only reliable external standard for student performance in early America. Each college had its own entrance requirements, and the president of the college and members of the faculty examined prospective students. The first admission requirement to Harvard in 1642 read: "When any Scholar is able to read Tully or such like classical Latin Author ex tempore, and make and speak true Latin in verse and prose, *suo (ut aiunt) Marte,* and decline perfectly the paradigms of nounes and verbes in ye Greeke tongue, then may hee bee admitted into ye College, nor shall any claime admission before such qualifications."[1] (*Suo, vestro,* or *nostro Marte* was a Latin proverb meaning by one's own exertions, without any help whatever.) The only significant addition to the college curriculum in colonial times was arithmetic, which appeared for the first time in the entrance requirements for Yale in

1745: "That none may expect to be admited into this College unless upon Examination of the President and Tutors, They shall be found able Extempore to Read, Construe and Parce Tully, Virgil and the Greek Testament; and to write True Latin in Prose and to understand the rules of Prosodia, and common Arithmetic, and Shall bring Sufficient Testimony of his Blameless and Inoffensive Life."[2]

As time went by, college entrance requirements became both broader and more specific. That is, they expanded to include more subjects, such as algebra, geometry, English grammar, science, modern foreign languages, history, and geography, but they also became more specific about the literary works that students had to master before their examination. Thus, Columbia College declared in 1785: "No candidate shall be admitted into the College . . . unless he shall be able to render into English Caesar's Commentaries of the Gallic War; the four Orations of Cicero against Catiline; the four first books of Virgil's AEneid; and the Gospels from the Greek; and to explain the government and connections of the words, and to turn English into grammatical Latin, and shall understand the four first rules of Arithmetic, with the rule of three."[3] Although the works required varied somewhat, the three constants in Latin were Cicero, Virgil, and Caesar. Students prepared themselves in accordance with these "content standards" and presented themselves for examination at the college of their choice.

In retrospect the requirements appear fairly uniform, yet the entrance requirements of different colleges varied enough to frustrate headmasters of academies and secondary schools. Headmasters complained of "unreasonable diversity," and students had to learn the specific text or oration that was demanded by the college of their choice.[4] Consequently, in the late nineteenth century, several associations were created to promote closer relations among schools and colleges and, especially, uniformity of college admission requirements. The collaboration was good for the schools, because it relieved them of the burden of preparing students for a wide variety of entrance examinations; it also benefited the colleges, because it enabled them to influence the curriculum of the secondary schools.

The Committee of Ten

As the last decade of the nineteenth century opened, many educators believed that the addition of new subjects had turned the high school curriculum into an anarchic mess. In 1892, in an effort to promote uniformity of curricular offerings in the high schools, the National Educational Association established a panel called the Committee of Ten to make recommendations to improve the curricula of the nation's high schools.[5] The chairman was Charles W. Eliot, president of Harvard University, and one of the most esteemed educators of his era. The committee included William T. Harris, the U.S. Commissioner of Education (and former superintendent in St. Louis); four other college presidents; and three high school principals (the tenth member was a college professor). The committee surveyed forty high schools and discovered that they offered thirty-six different subjects, including five foreign languages, six mathematics courses, four science courses, and a few miscellaneous courses such as stenography, penmanship, and music. This seeming disorder in 1890 stands in sharp contrast to the more than 2,100 course titles reported to the U.S. Office of Education in the mid-1970s.[6]

The Committee of Ten was the first national "blue ribbon panel" to study the curriculum of the high school. Since then, many forests have been felled to print the reports of numberless committees, commissions, panels, task forces, and study groups on the needs or future of American education. But in 1892, there was no precedent for a national body to issue recommendations to the many thousands of school districts, nor was there any mechanism to promote or require compliance. The committee had no way of knowing whether anyone would heed its proposals. Nonetheless, because of the stature of its members and sponsors, as well as the novelty of the undertaking, the committee's report received widespread attention and achieved some measure of influence upon the curricula of many schools.

The Committee of Ten had to wrestle with four difficult issues. The first was how to resolve the antagonism between the classical curriculum and the modern academic subjects such as science, history, and modern foreign languages. The second was how to promote uniformity in preparing students for college. The third was how to respond to demands by some educators to include practical courses such as manual training. The fourth was whether the high schools should offer different curricula for those who were college bound and those who were not.

The report of the Committee of Ten sought both to establish new curricular standards for high schools and to alter the admission standards for colleges and universities. Although other influences were simultaneously at work in schools and society, both complementing and subverting the proposals of the Ten, the report was fairly effective in changing standards at both levels of education in the years immediately after it was issued. The committee engaged nine subject-matter conferences to examine each major subject and to recommend how it should be taught, how teachers should be prepared, when the subject should be introduced, for how many hours each week and for how many years, and so on. Each subject-matter conference considered carefully what the course of study should consist of and how the subject should be assessed for college admission. The subjects were Latin; Greek; English; other modern languages; mathematics; physical science (physics, astronomy, and chemistry); "natural history" (biology, including botany, zoology, and physiology); history, civil government, and political economy; and geography (physical geography, geology, and meteorology).

The Ten recommended that the modern academic subjects should be equal in status to the classical curriculum for purposes of college entry. The report endorsed four model curricula, which differed mainly in the amount of time given to foreign languages: classical (containing three languages, including Greek and Latin); Latin-scientific (containing two foreign languages, one of them modern); modern languages (containing two modern foreign languages); and English (containing only one foreign language, either ancient or modern). This recommendation implied certain things that seemed radical to some educators: first, that neither Latin nor Greek was absolutely necessary for college preparation; and second, that students should be permitted to choose their course of study, so long as it included English, mathematics, history, science, and foreign language.

The Committee of Ten lined up unequivocally on the side of educational equality. The educational press was already printing demands that the children of workers be given an education different from that given to the children of privilege, but the Ten rejected this counsel. Instead, it took a firm stand against differentiation between those who planned to go to college and those who did not. All nine of the subject-matter conferences and the Committee of Ten itself agreed "that every subject which is taught at all in a secondary school should be taught in the same way and to the same extent to every pupil so long as he pursues it, no matter what the probable destination of the pupil may be, or at what point his education is to cease." The report concluded that "the secondary schools of the United States, taken as a whole, do not exist for the purpose of preparing boys and girls for colleges," but for "the duties of life," for which the best preparation is what today would be called a liberal education.[7]

Subsequent commentators complained that the Ten ignored those who were non-college-bound (the overwhelming majority of children at that time), instead of recognizing that the Ten meant that all children—*especially those who were not headed for college*—should have the benefit of a liberal education. This idea was as radical then as it is now, for the committee posited that all children had the intellectual capacity to benefit from an education that included foreign languages, history, mathematics, science, and English. The Ten saw this not as a college-preparatory curriculum, but as a curriculum that would prepare all children for a rich and full life, no matter what their ultimate vocation.

One immediate result of the report was the creation of the Committee on College-Entrance Requirements, established by the National Educational Association to promote the recommendations of the Committee of Ten. This committee, far less celebrated than the historic Ten, worked to formulate a common framework for college preparation, consonant with the recommendations of the Ten. It proposed that high schools adopt the use of "constants" or "units" to provide a uniform measure for all courses. The committee recommended a total of ten units (or years): four units of foreign languages, two of mathematics, two of English, one of science, and one of history. In a four-year program of sixteen units, the student would be free to elect six additional units. The consequence of this suggestion was that the curricular discussion—previously focused by the Ten on parallel, equivalent *courses of study*—shifted to the concept of interchangeable, equivalent *units*. This change not only advanced the notion of a standard unit of study, but eventually served to promote the principle of electives and of equivalency among all kinds of subject-matter. These units were eventually retitled "Carnegie units," after the Carnegie Foundation for the Advancement of Teaching defined a unit as a course of five periods each week for one academic year.

The College Entrance Examination Board

Another product of the movement in the 1890s to establish uniform standards for high school graduation and college entry was the

College Entrance Examination Board. Sponsored by President Eliot of Harvard, the College Board fulfilled his personal vision of "uniformity of standards and flexibility of programs."[8] The purpose of the College Board was to organize a common examination system for college admission. This arrangement assured colleges that they could continue to admit whomever they chose, regardless of test scores, without relinquishing authority to any outside body.[9] It was an ingenious solution to a vexing problem. The private sector took responsibility for creating a standard-setting process, which freed high schools from the burden of preparing students for many different examinations and left colleges free to admit whomever they wished.

The College Entrance Examination Board of the Middle States and Maryland held its first examination in June 1901 in nine subjects: chemistry, English, French, German, Greek, history, Latin, mathematics, and physics. The first examinations were based on standards set by recognized national committees—for example, the American Philological Association, the Modern Language Association, and the American Historical Association. In the second year botany, drawing, geography, and Spanish were added.

The College Board had to grapple with the issue of reviewing standards in the different subject areas. Initially, it assumed that it could rely on the continuing involvement of the various scholarly bodies, such as the Modern Language Association, but these proved to be uninterested in secondary school teaching. So the board created its own "committee of review," with responsibility to establish requirements for the examinations in each subject. This committee regularly assembled special commissions of school and college teachers to review and revise subject standards.

Even the act of reading and grading the examinations helped to support the implementation of what might be called voluntary national standards in the different subject areas. Each year large numbers of teachers from schools and colleges across the country would meet in New York to read the examinations. There they would talk, discuss papers, laugh about "boners," and work informally at defining performance standards for their field. In 1990s' terms, they "networked" as a community of scholars and teachers. At the same time they shaped standards and enforced them. The grading of the examinations was a professional development seminar of the highest order.

Many secondary schools prepared their students for the college entrance examinations. By reading through old examinations and by perusing the College Board's syllabus of English classics, teachers could be sure that their students were ready for the examinations. But these practices led to complaints about cramming and to criticism that the examination tested memory power rather than the students' ability to use what they had learned. Nonetheless, the secondary schools knew what their students had to learn to prepare for college and for the entrance examinations.

Commission on the Reorganization of Secondary Education

The College Board provided a standard for college preparation, at least for those students who wanted to apply to the selective colleges that were members of the board. But many educators continued to object to college domination, and the National Educational Association sponsored a Commission on the Reorganization of Secondary Education (CRSE), whose 1918 report established a pattern of standards that sharply diverged from the academic emphasis of the Committee of Ten and the College Board.

Unlike the Committee of Ten, which was chaired by the president of Harvard and included college presidents and secondary school principals, the CRSE was dominated by educationists. Its chair was Clarence D. Kingsley, the state high school supervisor for Massachusetts, and its members were drawn mainly from the world of professional education and colleges of education. Unlike the conferences of the Committee of Ten, which focused on academic subjects, the CRSE established committees not only for academic subjects but for industrial arts, household arts, vocational guidance, agriculture, and other nonacademic concerns. The report of this commission identified "the main objectives of education." These seven cardinal principles were "Health," "Command of fundamental processes," "Worthy home-membership," "Vocation," "Citizenship," "Worthy use of leisure," and "Ethical character."[10] Every academic subject was required to demonstrate its value in achieving these objectives; the emphasis was on utility (what was immediately useful for the student) and social efficiency (that is, how the schools could serve the perceived needs of society). Several academic subjects, especially the classical languages and history, were difficult to justify or rationalize in terms of the seven cardinal principles. Neither history nor geography survived as a subject; both were submerged into the new field of "social studies." The new "standard" for high schools was based neither on the intellectual development of all youngsters nor on a commitment to the ideal of liberal learning, but on preparing youngsters for present and future social and occupational roles. The goal—the standard—was social efficiency. The report endorsed differentiated curriculums, including agricultural, business, clerical, industrial, fine-arts, and household arts. At the time, this differentiation seemed an appropriate approach for schools that were suddenly overwhelmed with large numbers of immigrant children, many of whom spoke little or no English. The report legitimized the practice of diverting children into vocational programs, thus keeping them out of college-preparatory programs that appeared (from the viewpoint of the commission and many other leading educators of the day) to be a waste of time for these children.

The report gave strong support to the development of comprehensive high schools. Unfortunately, it also supported the practice of curricular tracking, whereby school officials could use their predictions about students' future vocation to "guide" students into a particular curriculum. Inevitably, these guesses tended to encourage differentiation based on social class, race, and ethnicity. Thus the academic track increasingly became a preserve for the minority who were college bound—the bright, the ambitious, the children of the educated—while the majority of students were directed into general or vocational programs.

The report of the CRSE reflected widely shared views in the education profession and in society. The term "academic" was increasingly used in a derisory fashion to refer to studies that had no practical value. Many educators, for many different reasons, converged on certain themes that appeared in the report: that an academic or liberal education was not appropriate for everyone; that the purposes of education should be derived from the activities of life, rather than from book-learning; that book-learning was sterile, "academic"; that children had different needs and should therefore have an education that was fitted to those needs; that the role of the school should change to fit the "needs" of society (and the needs of society were usually in the eye of the beholder). The overriding philosophy was social efficiency, which supported curricular tracking and a devaluation of liberal education.

The reports of the Committee of Ten and the CRSE, separated by twenty-five years, each claimed to be based on the principles of a democratic society. The Ten believed that all children should have the experience of a common academic curriculum, that all should be educated in the same way regardless of who their parents were or what their intended destination in life. The CRSE believed that the curriculum should be tailored and differentiated to meet the needs of society and of children. Beginning with similar premises, the two ended up in very different places. The compromise that was struck over time between the conflicting ideals was that the principles of the Committee of Ten applied to the academic track and the principles of the CRSE governed the vocational and general track.

Put another way, the CRSE won. The commission's ideas won not because they were argued more persuasively, but because they provided a good fit for the difficulties confronting the schools: the problems of mass education and of educating large numbers of children from poor and non-English-speaking backgrounds. Parents of these children did not demand that they be excused from the academic curriculum; what evidence exists suggests that immigrant parents did not want their children to have a curriculum different from what was studied in the best schools. Educating poor and immigrant children in the way prescribed by the Ten was possible, but it would have required enormous intellectual energy to reformulate the subject matter so that it was comprehensible to children with widely different backgrounds. Teaching academic subjects only to academically able children was easier than rethinking and redesigning the academic curriculum so that all children could learn and understand the material in the "college track." To do so would have been very difficult and very "inefficient" in an age when efficiency was highly valued. The path of least resistance was chosen, and in time most educators and parents came to believe that certain studies—such as foreign language and advanced courses in mathematics, science, and history—were only for the college-bound students, a distinct minority.

Aptitude and Achievement Testing

At the same time that the CRSE provided the rationale for differentiating curricula, the availability of the new techniques of standardized testing facilitated differentiation. After the debut of intelligence tests in World War I, the testing industry mushroomed, producing a broad array of tests of ability, intelligence, and educational achievement.

Standards, as applied to the academic curriculum, were defined during most of the twentieth century by college admission requirements. These consisted of the colleges' entrance requirements—a specification of so many years or units of certain academic subjects—and the college entrance examinations. Until the development of the American College Testing program in 1959, the only national examination for the college bound was that of the College Entrance Examination Board. While vigilant in protecting the quality of its examinations, the College Board also was sensitive to constant criticism that the examinations exerted too much influence on the high school curriculum. In the years immediately after World War I, the board took interest in the new movement for intelligence testing. Unlike the traditional college entrance examinations, which tested what students knew, the intelligence tests claimed to test students' innate intelligence, or what they were capable of doing. In 1922 the College Board expressed "favorable interest" in the use of "general intelligence examinations" and its readiness to administer such examinations when it became practicable.[11] Because none of the members of the board was an expert on psychological testing, the board appointed an advisory commission of experts, including Carl C. Brigham of Princeton, Henry T. Moore of Dartmouth, and Robert M. Yerkes of Yale. Brigham and Yerkes were pioneers in the development of intelligence testing. Brigham soon emerged as the driving force in a successful effort to reorient the college entrance examinations and to turn them into tests of intelligence or aptitude.

The Scholastic Aptitude Test

Brigham and his team of psychological experts built upon the board's interest in determining a student's readiness for college-level work to propose a new test altogether: the Scholastic Aptitude Test (SAT). There were skeptics on the College Board and among the secondary school representatives, but the experts had a mantle of authority—the authority of science—that swept along the doubters.

The first SAT was given in 1926 to 8,040 candidates, most of whom were applying to Ivy League colleges. Brigham became a salaried member of the College Board staff in 1930, where he continued to refine the test that he had devised. Although the SAT did not take the place of the traditional written entrance examination until the Second World War, the College Board recognized its value immediately. Throughout the 1930s the appeal of the SAT grew apace with faith in social science. The standardized, multiple-choice test saved the College Board from the wrath of those who complained that the college entrance examinations had too much influence over the curriculum of the secondary schools. It was the perfect answer to the angry headmaster who supposedly muttered in 1902, "I'll be damned if any Board down in New York City, with a college professor at its head, is going to tell me and my faculty what or how to teach!"[12] The SAT tested linguistic and mathematical power and had no connection to any particular curriculum, which left secondary schools free to require whatever they chose. The literature curriculum, which had been anchored by the college entrance examinations for many years, was completely abandoned by the SAT, allowing secondary schools to teach whatever books they wished and even to drop the traditional classics altogether.

Although some members of the College Board must have been uneasy about the shift from the old-style achievement tests to the new-style intelligence-aptitude testing, Brigham became "the policy maker" of the Board, "and whatever route was taken for the next few years was charted by him."[13] Colleges began to recognize the SAT's practical value for predicting students' ability to do college-level work, and each year the number who took the test increased. Then, on Pearl Harbor Day, December 7, 1941, representatives of Harvard, Yale, and Princeton, decided to cancel the June essay examinations because of the war. Normally an outcry would have issued from "conservative" educators, who continued to believe that an essay exam was preferable to a multiple-choice test of "aptitude." But the war emergency hastened what at the time seemed inevitable. With this decision, the SAT became *the* college entrance examination for the nation's most prestigious colleges and universities. The acceptance of the machine-scored exam meant, first, that the standard-setting force of the traditional (that is, written) college entrance examination was negated, and second, that the standard-implementing activities of those teachers and scholars who met annually to read the examinations were terminated.

During the 1940s and 1950s, the College Board claimed that the SAT was intended not to influence standards, but to help colleges identify students who were ready for college studies. Other examinations offered by the College Board, such as advanced placement examinations and achievement tests, defined and supported educational standards, however. Over time, it became clear that the advanced placement and achievement tests bolstered high school academic standards at the same time that the SAT undermined them. Except for its section on mathematics, the SAT was virtually curriculum free. Vocabulary and reasoning skills were of primary importance. The "old" College Boards required not only the ability to write and express oneself fluently, but also knowledge of science, history, geography, and literature; on the nation's premier college entrance examination, the SAT, such knowledge counted for nothing. Students could improve their performance on the SAT by attending special coaching sessions or by learning test-taking skills. Until the 1960s high school graduation and college entrance requirements buttressed the SAT. When those requirements were lowered in the late 1960s and early 1970s (in response to student demands), the SAT was left standing almost alone as the guardian of standards, a role for which it was not designed and to which it was not equal.[14]

Standardizing Tests and Textbooks

College entrance examinations were one source of educational standards; another was mandated testing, which was undertaken on a broad scale in the early twentieth century. In the 1890s educational reformer Joseph Mayer Rice introduced what may have been the first test to be administered to a large national sample (in spelling). Edward Thorndike of Teachers College, Columbia University, introduced many other standardized achievement tests. Thorndike's colleagues at Teachers College helped to spread standardized achievement testing as part of the school survey movement, which assessed the quality of numerous school districts around the nation and which reached its peak in the second decade of the twentieth century. Many schools were administering standardized achievement tests in spelling, arithmetic, reading, and other subjects before the First World War. The use of widescale intelligence testing during the war, coupled with the general admiration of science and social science, helped to popularize standardized testing in the 1920s, when hundreds of different intelligence and achievement tests were produced for use in the schools. Both kinds of tests were used to sort children according to their ability and to place them into appropriate programs.[15]

Since the 1960s criticism of all kinds of standardized testing has escalated rapidly. Two points should be made about the general use of standardized testing of both intelligence and achievement. First, both were used to allocate students to different kinds of educational opportunities, in keeping with the curricular differentiation advocated by the CRSE. Second, the widespread adoption of standardized achievement tests relieved states and districts of the need to set their own explicit academic standards. In both cases educators relegated the all-important task of deciding what children should know and be able to do to the commercial testmakers.

A similar story can be told about the role of textbooks as a standardizing element in American education. Woodward, Elliott, and Nagel estimate "that from 75% to 90% of classroom instructional time is structured by textbook programs."[16] Produced for mass market sales in a highly competitive marketplace, textbooks are written to satisfy the largest buyers, especially the textbook-adoption committees in large states such as Texas and California. Because the textbooks have such an important role in determining what content is taught and because they are so widely used as a basic instructional tool, they effectively determine what children learn. How do textbook writers decide what children should know? In general the writers, some of whom are scholars and teachers, review the contents of the other textbooks in the field and the requirements of the textbook-adoption committees in a score or so of states. Through this process, the writers arrive at "content standards" that provide the framework for their product.

With the passage of the Elementary and Secondary Education Act in 1965, standardized achievement testing became securely entrenched, because the law required regular testing in schools that receive federal funding for disadvantaged students. So the tests, always important, gained an institutional foothold and became a mandated element in the program of most public schools. New programs of statewide testing were introduced in the 1970s to meet the requirements of the minimum competency movement, which demanded proof that students had mastered basic skills before graduating or being promoted. During the same era textbooks became more uniform than ever, as big companies gobbled up little companies and as a small number of textbooks in each field captured a large percentage of the market. By 1987–88, forty-five states and the District of Columbia were using some kind of statewide test; twenty-five of those entities were employing a commercially developed, nationally normed test.[17]

Many educators have criticized the proliferation of mass-market textbooks and standardized tests, but both continue to be widely used and enormously influential on what is taught in the classroom. The relevant point for this narrative is that both texts and tests are based on assumptions about what is worth knowing. Sometimes these assumptions are explicitly and thoughtfully developed, and sometimes they are derived from market research (what sells) without a lot of debate or study about what knowledge is of most worth.

The Post-Sputnik Era

In the 1960s many social and educational trends converged in ways that buffeted educational standards. First, the Soviet launching of Sputnik in 1957 created strong pressure to raise standards and enrollments in rigorous science, mathematics, and foreign language courses. The emphasis during these years was not to raise standards for *all* students, but to identify talent and improve the education of elite students. Over the years educators have worried that higher standards would discourage weak students and produce a higher dropout rate from high school. That did not happen during the post-Sputnik era. Instead, the high school graduation rate jumped from 69.5 percent in 1960 to 76.7 percent in 1964, a figure that remained stable for the next three decades; during the same period, black educational attainment increased dramatically.[18] In the post-Sputnik period, brief though it was, achievement scores on all kinds of tests showed increases, even while student enrollments were growing rapidly.

In the mid-1960s, however, a series of shockwaves hit American society. Schools, colleges, and universities were at the center of various political movements, social upheavals, and educational innovations. The civil rights revolution produced not only boycotts and demonstrations, but also an increase in the numbers of black students who graduated high school and entered college. Youthful protesters against the Vietnam war also demanded lower entrance requirements into college, more student freedom to choose courses, and more "relevant" courses. "New math," produced by curriculum reformers during the post-Sputnik period, was widely introduced into the schools, and the "open education" and radical school movements criticized traditional methods and standards.[19]

Responses to these changes were complex and varied in different cities, regions, and states. But certain trends emerged. Frustrated by their inability to change the "system," radical school reformers eventually shifted their efforts to private schools, opening a network of "free schools." Although the part of the open education movement that built schools without walls faded away, the pedagogical progressives who insisted on teaching children through contextual experiences (projects, activities, real-life experiences) survived unscathed. The new math failed, rejected by uncomprehending parents and teachers; its failure contributed to a "back to basics" movement and the spread of minimum competency testing in dozens of states.

What is thought of as "the sixties" in education probably spanned the period from 1965 to 1975. At the end of this period, college entrance requirements were markedly lower than they had been in the early 1960s (fewer colleges required knowledge of a foreign language, for example), and many students had shifted from the academic curriculum to nonacademic tracks. In one influential study, Clifford Adelman of the U.S. Department of Education analyzed high school transcripts from 1964 to 1981 and concluded that students were spending less time in academic courses; that the curriculum had become "diffused and fragmented" during that period; that enrollment in the "general track" had jumped "from 12.0% in the late 1960s to 42.5% in the late 1970s"; and that the general track had become "the dominant student track in high school. . . ." Neither vocational nor academic, the general track consisted of courses such as driver education, remedial studies, training for adulthood, health education, typing, and home economics.[20]

With the easing of high school graduation and college entrance requirements, the standards that remained were those embedded in the commercial textbooks and tests as well as in the major college entrance examinations (the SAT and the ACT). In reality, there are multiple standards, depending on which curriculum "track" students are enrolled in, whether they plan to go to college, and whether they apply to a selective college or university. Students who intend to apply to one of a relatively small number of highly selective colleges or universities are educated to very high standards; they will certainly be in the academic track, they are likely to take advanced placement examinations, and they know that they must take certain courses and demonstrate high achievement. At the other extreme, students who are not planning to go to college are likely to encounter standards geared to minimum competency, which they may demonstrate by checking off the correct box on a test of basic skills and by tests of simple recall. In between are students who intend to go to an unselective college or university, one that takes almost all applicants; the students—and their teachers—know that they will be accepted into the college of their choice regardless of how much or how little they work in school and of how much or how little they have learned.

A Nation at Risk

Education standards became a national issue in 1975, when the College Board pointed out that SAT scores had fallen steadily and sharply since 1963. In the first analysis of the causes of the decline, Harnischfeger and Wiley concluded that the decline was real and that the same pattern of decline occurred in every other standardized testing program. They found that achievement had been rising steadily until the mid-1960s when the declines began, that the declines were largest in the upper grades, that the overall decline was greatest in verbal tests, and that the number of high scores on the SAT verbal test had fallen sharply. There were exceptions (for example, on the ACT science test), but the score decline appeared to be a broad and consistent phenomenon. Although they thought that television and changes in the family may have had contributory effects, Harnischfeger and Wiley nonetheless concluded that "the strongest explanatory power seems to come from curricular changes. Our gross data indicate a considerable enrollment decline in academic courses. These course enrollment declines parallel closely the test score decline patterns."[21]

The College Board's own study commission reported in 1977 that diversification of the pool of test-takers had caused the initial score declines, which had then accelerated as a result of social and educational changes. The panel speculated that the effects of television and changes in the family may have been causes and that disruptive events such as the war in Vietnam, political assassinations, and Watergate may have contributed to "a decade of distraction." But the report also identified practices in schools that undermined academic performance, such as the assignment of less homework, dilution of the academic curriculum, tolerance of absenteeism, lower enrollments in rigorous courses, social promotion, and grade inflation. It seemed that high schools had lowered expectations for almost all students as a way to accommodate the needs of a more diverse student body.[22]

Concerns about low achievement produced calls for change. In 1979 a commission appointed by President Carter reported that "Americans' incompetence in foreign languages is nothing short of scandalous, and it is becoming worse." The commission found that "only 15 percent of American high school students now study a foreign language—down from 24 percent in 1965." It noted too that only one out of twenty high school students pursued even a second year of foreign language study, and only 8 percent of colleges and universities required a foreign language for admission, down from 34 percent in 1966.[23] Another report, prepared at President Carter's request in 1980, assessed the adequacy of science and engineering education at every level. The report warned of "a current trend toward virtual scientific and technological illiteracy." It complained about "a general lowering of standards and expectations," overemphasis on basic skills, low enrollments in advanced mathematics and science courses, and a lowering of college entry requirements.[24]

Then in the 1980s a veritable deluge of reports—prepared by local, state, and national organizations; panels; commissions; and task forces, as well as studies by scholars—all recommended ways to improve different aspects of education.

Several states began to take stock of their education systems, and none was as active as the fifteen-member Southern Regional Education Board (SREB). In 1981 a special task force of SREB issued a statement called *The Need for Quality,* which noted with concern a slackening of academic quality. "The heritage of the Sixties, when high schools reacted to the general demand for 'relevance' by expanding the curriculum with electives, continues to characterize the current array of high school courses, from movie making to driver education," the statement said. The emphasis on minimum competencies, the SREB feared, "introduces the danger of minimums becoming norms." Instead of reaching only for minimums, "the overall concern must be to challenge all students to attain higher levels of achievement." Even the colleges had succumbed to a climate of lowered expectations, by dropping their admission requirements. The task force called for higher standards for teachers and students and a more rigorous high school curriculum, as well as higher salaries for teachers.[25]

In 1983 several major studies appeared, but the blockbuster that dwarfed all others in influence and media attention was *A Nation at Risk*, prepared by the National Commission on Excellence in Education at the request of U.S. Secretary of Education Terrell Bell. The rhetoric of the report was dramatic; it warned that "the educational foundations of our society are presently being eroded by a rising tide of mediocrity that threatens our future as a Nation and a people. . . .If an unfriendly foreign power had attempted to impose on America the mediocre educational performance that exists today, we might well have viewed it as an act of war. . . .We have, in effect, been committing an act of unthinking, unilateral educational disarmament."[26]

A Nation at Risk called for action across the nation against complacency and mediocrity. It complained that Americans were content with low expectations in education, that they did not strive for excellence nor push to meet high standards. In direct, jargon-free language, the report summarized the data about low educational achievement, declining test scores, and the growing cost of remediation in higher education and business. Whether in school, college, or adult life, too many were "doing the minimum work necessary for the moment, then coasting through life on what may have been learned in its first quarter."[27] It pointed out, echoing the Adelman study, that the high school curriculum had become a diffuse smorgasbord, from which students could pick and choose at will. Consequently, students had "migrated" from academic and vocational programs into "general track" courses, and enrollments were unacceptably low in challenging courses in science, mathematics, and foreign languages. The overall picture was of an educational system where high school graduation and college entrance requirements and expectations for students were uniformly minimal. The commission recommended higher standards for students and teachers, a core curriculum for all, higher standards for high school graduation and college entrance, a longer school day and year, and higher salaries for teachers.[28]

The response to *A Nation at Risk* was unprecedented. In 1984 the U.S. Department of Education summarized the extraordinary press attention, public interest, and state-level reforms encouraged by that single report. Hundreds of state-level task forces addressed education issues, seeking ways to raise standards, improve textbooks, lengthen the school day or year, or improve the teaching profession. Business groups and universities became actively involved in collaborative programs to strengthen primary and secondary education. Some of this activity predated *A Nation at Risk.* All of it gained visibility and momentum as a result of the attention lavished on the report.[29]

In the decade that followed, the southern states became leaders in education reform. They increased teachers' salaries, lowered class size, raised standards for entry to the teaching profession, increased per-pupil spending on education, increased high school graduation requirements, introduced high school exit examinations, increased college admission requirements, and encouraged students to participate in the College Board's Advanced Placement program. The efforts to raise high school graduation and college entrance requirements prompted fears that dropouts would increase and that fewer minority students would enter college. These fears proved unfounded. School attendance rates remained stable or rose; high school graduation rates went up for all ethnic groups; more high school students enrolled in courses in mathematics, science, and foreign languages; college admission test scores went up, even though a larger proportion of high school seniors were taking the tests; and the number of students taking advanced placement courses doubled in the 1980s. College enrollments for students of all races grew significantly during the 1980s. When minimum requirements for college were strengthened, students reacted accordingly. For example, an SREB report published in 1993 found that "in South Carolina, more than 80 percent of college freshmen now meet all of the prerequisites, compared to only 47 percent of those who entered the year before the requirements went into effect."[30]

Acknowledging the Need to Improve Achievement

Recognizing that prescribing more years of study was good but not sufficient, education and political leaders began to think more about the question of standards and outcomes (what students have learned). The southern governors made their campaign for education reform a high priority for the National Governors' Association. Three of the most active southern governors were Lamar Alexander of Tennessee, Richard Riley of South Carolina, and Bill Clinton of Arkansas. The governors agreed that what mattered most was whether students were actually learning more, but that the governors would not get better results unless they set clear standards for *what students should know and be able to do* and identified or created good assessments to find out whether students were making progress toward the standards. The governors agreed that states should press for higher educational achievement while reducing the regulatory burdens on schools. "The Governors are ready for some old-fashioned horse-trading. We'll regulate less, if schools and school districts will produce better results," Alexander, chairman of the National Governors' Association, wrote in the 1986 annual report, *Time for Results*.[31]

Educational leaders in many other states took seriously the need to improve student achievement. In 1983 California elected a new state superintendent, Bill Honig, who pledged to raise standards and improve public education. While fighting for increased funding for public schools, Honig started a process of revising the curriculum in each subject field. He recognized that the starting point for reform is agreement on what to teach; panels of teachers and scholars were convened to rewrite the state's curriculum frameworks, which serve as guidelines for textbook publishers, testmakers and teachers. Because California has 11 percent of the nation's schoolchildren and is an "adoption" state (that is, the state chooses textbooks for kindergarten through grade eight), the frameworks offered the state a way to influence the national textbook market. Honig also revised state testing, encouraging the development of assessments based on the state's newly revised curricula rather than on national norms. In effect, Honig shaped a coherent program of systemic reform by setting new curriculum standards, procuring a new generation of textbooks and technology, and developing new tests.

In Washington, Secretary of Education William Bennett used his bully pulpit to campaign for "the three Cs": content, character, and choice. He criticized the tendency in schools to focus only on skills, and he regularly issued reports that called on schools to emphasize great books and important ideas in history, literature, and philosophy. He even sketched out a model school curriculum by describing his ideal school, "James Madison High School," where all youngsters take a rich diet of English, social studies, mathematics, science, foreign language, physical education, and fine arts.[32]

The critique of vacuousness was expanded by two surprise best-selling books that appeared almost simultaneously in 1987: Allan Bloom's *The Closing of the American Mind* and E. D. Hirsch, Jr.'s *Cultural Literacy.*[33] Bloom's book was a searing critique of higher education, and Hirsch's was a plea for Americans to recognize the importance of specific knowledge—the facts, ideas, names, dates, and information that is widely known and used in the culture. Hirsch argued that the lack of a common curriculum (or core knowledge) severely disadvantaged those who were newcomers to the society; to succeed in the culture, they needed access to the language, the idioms, and the ideas that educated people take for granted. Both books enjoyed popular success but were disdained by professional educators. Bloom's book was the opening blow in what eventually was recognized as a cultural war on the campuses between advocates and critics of "political correctness." Leaders of public education ignored Hirsch, and he set about writing a grade-by-grade "core knowledge" curriculum, which identified the specific facts and concepts that all students should know.

The sum of all this diverse activity was a growing political consensus about the importance of paying attention to what and whether students were learning. It was neither a conservative nor a liberal consensus. Some worried that students were not learning enough; some that they were not exposed to "the best that has been thought and known." Others worried about the yawning gaps in achievement that divided rich and poor, white and nonwhite, advantaged and disadvantaged.

With this consensus forming, the discussion in many states shifted to the need for better information about student achievement. The states had a good idea of what they were spending but not of how well their students were learning. In 1986 eight southern states (Arkansas, Florida, Louisiana, North Carolina, South Carolina, Tennessee, Virginia, and West Virginia) administered the tests of the National Assessment of Educational Progress (NAEP) to a representative sample of their students.[34] They wanted "the most current and reliable measure of how their students' achievement in reading and/or writing compares to truly national and regional results." They also wanted to establish benchmarks "to gauge their students' relative achievement levels. . . ." Winfred L. Godwin, the president of the SREB, explained the southern states' interest in assessment: "The obvious question is—How will we know that we are making progress? Many measures of progress will be important, but none will surpass student achievement."[35]

In 1987 a study group led by Lamar Alexander and H. Thomas James, president of the Spencer Foundation, proposed an expansion of NAEP to include state-by-state comparisons (Hillary Rodham Clinton was a member of the study group). Explicit in this recommendation was recognition that "state and local school administrators are encountering a rising public demand for thorough information on the quality of their schools, allowing comparison with data from other states and districts. . . ."[36] Implicit in this recommendation was the suggestion that school districts ought to be allowed to participate directly in NAEP to learn how their students were doing compared with other districts. Congress authorized trial state assessments for 1990, 1992, and 1994 but showed little interest in expanding the assessment to the district level. Even the state-by-state assessment was controversial, because many educators saw no value in the comparisons and recoiled against the drift toward a national test.

The state-level activity by policymakers and elected officials reflected a somewhat commonsense understanding that the effort to improve education must begin with an agreement about what children are expected to learn, that is, content standards. Traditionally, this agreement had been expressed in Carnegie units. But the education reformers of the 1980s moved beyond Carnegie units to ascertain what children were expected to know and be able to do. And wherever there was standard setting, there was also new interest in finding some reliable means of measuring student progress toward meeting the content standards, thus increasing the search for a test or an assessment that would permit comparisons across states, districts, and even schools.

Moving toward National Standards

As many states wrestled with the difficult process of defining their standards, two events in 1989 prepared the way for the debate on national standards that would occupy the education agenda of the Bush and Clinton administrations. The first occurred when the National Council of Teachers of Mathematics (NCTM), responding to the criticisms expressed in *A Nation at Risk* and related reports about the needs of mathematics and science education, published national standards. The second occurred when President Bush and the governors of the fifty states agreed to establish national goals for education.

The NCTM standards emerged from a successful consensus process that included many classroom teachers and the nation's leading mathematics educators. Their goal was to transform mathematics education so that all students, not just those who are college bound, are able to develop mathematical power and to apply mathematical thinking. Mathematics teachers enthusiastically embraced the new standards, and they had a dramatic impact on the field. Although full implementation of the standards requires sweeping change—the revision of instructional methods, teacher education, professional development, textbooks, technology, and assessment—within three years after their release, significant changes could be seen in every one of these areas. At the very time that governors and other political leaders wondered about the feasibility of voluntary national standards, there were the NCTM standards as an example for emulation.

While the NCTM was drafting, revising, and publishing its standards, education moved to the front burner as a national issue. In the fall of 1989, after Bush and the governors agreed that there should be goals, the White House and the National Governors' Association engaged in intensive negotiations to develop those goals, which the president announced in his 1990 State of the Union address. The goals are:

In the year 2000,
1. All children in America will start school ready to learn.
2. The high school graduation rate will increase to at least 90 percent.
3. American students will leave grades four, eight, and twelve having demonstrated competency in challenging subject matter including English, mathematics, science, history, and geography; and every school in America will ensure that all students learn to use their minds well, so they may be prepared for responsible citizenship, further learning, and productive employment in our modern economy.
4. U.S. students will be first in the world in science and mathematics achievement.

5. Every adult American will be literate and possess the knowledge and skills necessary to compete in a global economy and exercise the rights and responsibilities of citizenship.

6. Every school in America will be free of drugs and violence and will offer a safe, disciplined environment conducive to learning.[37]

Once the goals were announced, the president and the governors agreed to create the National Education Goals Panel to monitor yearly progress. It quickly became apparent that the panel had no way to monitor progress toward goals three and four without some clear definition of the "challenging" subject matter to be learned and the "competency" to be demonstrated. These goals implied the need for some kind of national standards and national testing. Logic suggested the need for national standards, but the political and practical obstacles were formidable. How would the standards be set? Who would set them? Would they be voluntary or mandatory? What would be the role of the federal government? The authority to set curricula and standards had traditionally rested with the thousands of quasi-independent school districts, and the states (including the District of Colombia), and each was jealous of its prerogatives. There was also genuine doubt about the ability of the federal government or a politically appointed national body to establish high education standards. The logic of the goals implied new arrangements, but at the outset, no one knew what those might be nor whether national standards could be established without also creating an intrusive federal bureaucracy.

3

Achievement:
A Review of
the Evidence

 IN 1975 THE PUBLIC LEARNED that SAT scores had been falling steadily for a dozen years. This revelation set off a rising tide of anxiety about the state of educational achievement as well as a debate about its causes. Some attributed it to a lowering of academic standards in the schools. Others blamed it on television and changes in society. Still others saw it as the result of democratization, which increased the number of minority students staying in high school longer and applying to college.

This chapter reviews the debate about educational achievement by examining a variety of measures, recognizing that each has its strengths and its limitations. Considered here are the SAT, the National Assessment of Educational Progress (NAEP), international comparisons of student achievement, and student course-taking patterns.

The difficulty in assessing the quality of American education—now or in the past—is that no single measure of achievement accurately reflects changes in student performance before the early 1970s. Although the press and the public want to know whether schools are "better" or "worse" than they used to be, there is no reliable source of data that allows valid judgments about whether children today achieve at higher or lower levels than their age-mates of the 1940s or 1950s. That may not even be a useful question. The more important question is whether students today are learning as much as they can or should to prepare for postsecondary education and demanding technical careers. Changes in technology, the workplace, and the economy, as well as the sheer complexity of social and civic issues, make it clear that professionals, technicians, and citizens will need more knowledge and skills in the future than they did in the past.

The SAT has major limitations as a gauge of the quality of American education. Except for its mathematics section, it does not test what students have studied in high school. Because it is a college entrance examination, it does not test a representative sample of students. Although the SAT is a stable measure, the population taking the test has changed over the years, which affects the average score.

The second major source of test data, NAEP, does test a representative sample of American students at ages 9, 13, and 17 (or lately, grades four, eight, and twelve). NAEP launched its testing program in 1969–70, several years after SAT scores began to decline. In some subjects, NAEP testing began even later; testing in mathematics, for example, did not begin until 1973, nearly a decade after the onset of the SAT score decline.

A further problem with using either college entrance examinations or NAEP scores to assess overall student performance is their lack of external performance standards. NAEP scores in 1990, for example, can be compared with those in 1970, but there is no way to judge the adequacy of student performance in either year. The NAEP scores reflect what students know, not what they *should* know. The SAT (used in combination with high school grades) is generally considered a valid test for predicting how students will perform in their first year of college, but it cannot be said with any assurance what the averages *should* be; they are a relative, not an external, measure of student performance. The difference is illustrated by the story of the man who finds an old jacket in the attic. He brings it downstairs, puts it on, and says to his wife, "Look, this jacket fits me as well now as it did twenty years ago." And she replies, caustically, "You were fat twenty years ago, too."

Similarly, learning that student performance is as good in 1990 as it was in 1970 is of little value unless there is some external standard by which to decide: "Is that good enough?" "Was it good enough in 1970?" One way to answer such questions is to refer to the international assessments of student achievement, which measure the performance of U.S. students in comparison with their peers in other countries. Another way, recently initiated by the independent, bipartisan policy board that governs NAEP, is to establish achievement levels to describe the kind of academic performance expected of students who are "advanced," "proficient," "basic," or "below basic."

This review of student achievement data also considers course-taking patterns—the extent to which American students take certain subjects and the changes that have occurred over the years. Course-taking patterns reveal a good deal about whether schools are providing equality of opportunity and indicate the expectations that schools express to students. Because the number of course titles reported by American public schools since the 1960s has proliferated, however, determining what content lies behind course titles and what students have actually studied is not always easy. Nonetheless, transcript studies add a useful dimension to the portrait of academic achievement.

In the debate about achievement, the SAT has loomed large because it represents a year-to-year judgment on most of the nation's college-bound students. Although College Board officials annually caution that the SAT is not a barometer for American education, their disclaimer is ignored in the press coverage. The occasional declines and upturns of a point or two inspire despair or jubilation about the condition of the schools. Some of the commentary is utterly misleading. For example, efforts to compare states according to their SAT scores are virtually useless because of different student participation rates. In some states, more than 50 percent of graduating seniors take the SAT; in others, fewer than 10 percent do, and they are an elite group. Thus, students in Arkansas and Mississippi receive extremely high SAT scores, far above the national averages, because only 4 to 6 percent of high school graduates in those states take the test (students in the South and Midwest tend to take the ACT rather than the SAT); the SAT scores from Arkansas and Mississippi are much higher than those of Massachusetts and New York, where close to 80 percent of the graduates take the test. Comparing Mississippi and Massachusetts on the basis of their SAT scores is meaningless and misleading.

What is meaningful is for a state to raise the percentage of its students who take college entrance or advanced placement examinations and to increase its scores from year to year.

If the SAT is not a barometer for American education, neither are the norm-referenced, standardized tests that the public schools of every state give. This point was made by two small but widely publicized studies prepared by Dr. John Jacob Cannell, a West Virginia physician who discovered that all fifty states were "above the national average" on normed, standardized tests administered in the elementary grades.[1] The media described this situation as "the Lake Wobegon effect," shorthand for pervasive test-score inflation. In his second study, Cannell found that "more than 90 percent of the 15,000 elementary school districts, and 80 percent of the secondary school districts in the nation are scoring 'above the national norm' on 'standardized achievement tests,' instead of the expected 50 percent." Cannell contended that test security was lax and that "teaching to the test" was so widespread that it amounted to cheating.[2]

Recent studies have called into question the quality of many standardized tests, thus underlining the negative consequences of teaching to the test. An analysis of the six most widely used standardized mathematics tests concluded that "97% of the questions tested low-level conceptual knowledge and 95% tested low-level thinking." This study, funded by the National Science Foundation, held that science tests "were somewhat better but still low on high-level knowledge and thinking."[3] When teachers are required to use tests of low-level skills, and when test scores are used to make judgments about the ability of both teachers and students, teachers tend to teach what is tested. When tests of low-level skills dominate instruction, teachers feel compelled to reinforce superficial learning rather than understanding. Students learn how to give the right answer but not how to explain why they answered as they did. Nor are they able to solve unfamiliar problems. For these reasons, many educators have sought to deemphasize the importance of norm-referenced, standardized tests and to replace them with performance-based measures.

In the early 1990s the ongoing debate about the condition of education took a new turn when some researchers questioned whether a decline had actually occurred and insisted that the education system was performing "better than ever."[4] This group of researchers, who call themselves revisionists, have corrected intemperate criticism of American education by emphasizing its genuine accomplishments, such as high rates of participation and completion. Unfortunately, their efforts to prove that American education is better than ever have promoted other misconceptions. It is not good enough, for example, to assert that the schools educate as well today as they did in 1970, because many students—especially those from racial minorities and low-income backgrounds—were poorly educated in 1970. That standard of performance was not good enough in 1970, and it should not be good enough a generation later.[5] Although the achievement gaps among racial groups have narrowed somewhat, they are still substantial. The challenge today is to educate the entire rising generation and to educate it at least as well as its peers in other modern societies. Pursuing this goal involves admitting that the standards of 1960 or 1970 are inadequate to the requirements of the present or the future. By contrast, one of the revisionists openly worried about the danger of "overeducation" and asserted that as a society "we must continue to produce an uneducated social class" that will "sweep the streets, unclog sewers, scrub toilets, pick up trash, bus tables or mop floors— no matter what the wages."[6]

A similar debate took place in the early 1950s, when critics complained about the quality of public education and educationists responded that it was better than ever. At that time, Arthur Bestor, a leading critic, said that the defenders of present-day policy "quote criticisms of earlier date to show that discontent in the past was as great as it is today. The logic is that of Looking-Glass Land, where, the Red Queen explained to Alice, 'it takes all the running you can do, to keep in the same place. . . .' In every other area of American life progress is measured in terms of defects overcome. Only the professional educationists take pride in the fact that, though they run several times as hard, they can always be found by their critics in pretty much the same spot." Bestor might have been addressing the revisionists of the 1990s when he wrote

> No serious critic of modern American education is asserting that the public schools enjoyed a golden age in the past. It is the shortcomings of the schools today that concern us. If we are to have improvement, we must learn to make comparisons, not with the wretchedly inadequate public schools of earlier generations, but with the very best schools, public or private, American or foreign, past or present, of which we can obtain any knowledge. The failure of virtually all professional educationists

to make such comparisons is one of their gravest derelictions of duty. Their measuring-rod seems always to be what poor schools used to do, never what good schools have done, can do, and ought to do.

The present effectiveness of the schools, measured against the best that can possibly be achieved, is the only valid measure of our educational accomplishment. If some other nation designs a better military plane, our aeronautical engineers do not point smugly to the fact that our own aircraft are better than they were in 1920 or 1930 or 1940.[7]

What is the state of educational achievement? Was there a decline? If so, was it a necessary consequence of expanding educational opportunity? As soon as such questions are asked, other questions arise: Should Americans be satisfied with current levels of academic performance? How should student performance be assessed? Should concerned citizens support changes in the educational system, or should they adopt the aphorism, "if it ain't broke, don't fix it"? Does the educational system need fixing or not?

The Scholastic Aptitude Test

The SAT is a standardized, multiple-choice test with verbal and mathematical sections, used (in combination with high school grades) to predict students' readiness for college-level academic work. Scores on the SAT range from 200 to 800. Beginning in 1964 average SAT scores dropped steadily for about fifteen years. Verbal scores fell from a high of 478 in 1963 down to the 420s by the late 1970s and hovered there; they stood at 423 in 1994. Mathematics scores dropped from a high of 502 in 1963 to a low of 466 in 1980, and then moved up to 479 by 1994, about where they had been in 1974 (figure 3-1).[8]

Although the rise and fall of the mean score was well reported, little attention was paid to the puzzling decrease of high-scoring students on the verbal portion of the test. In 1972, the first year that fully comparable figures were available for graduating seniors, 116,585 students, or 11.4 percent of the test-takers, scored above 600 on the verbal test.[9] By 1983 that number had fallen to 66,292, or 6.9 percent of the total. The number and proportion of high-scoring students remained fairly stable throughout the 1980s and early 1990s,

Figure 3-1. Verbal and Mathematical SAT Mean Scores, 1967–94

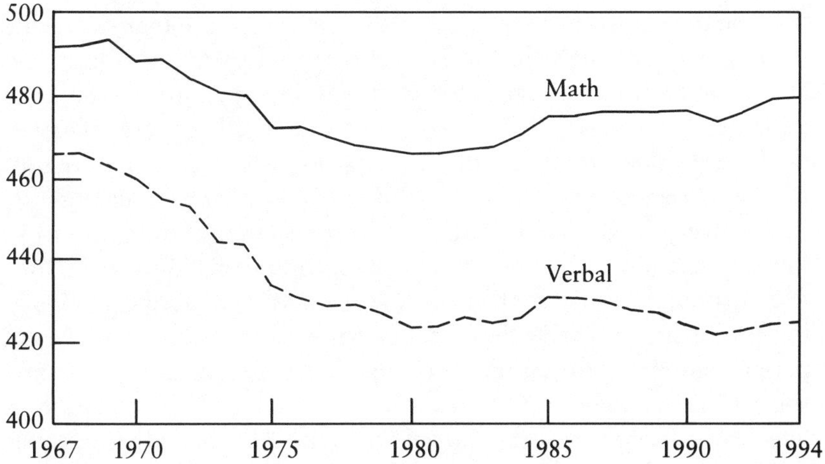

Source: The College Board. The scores for 1967–1971 are estimates because some students took the test more than once.

reaching 79,606, or 7.6 percent of the total, in 1994. The performance of high-scoring students on the mathematics portion of the test was a different story. In 1972, 182,602 students, or 17.9 percent of the test-takers, scored above 600. The number dropped as low as 143,566 (or 14.4 percent) in 1981, but by the late 1980s the high-scoring mathematics students were as numerous as they had been in 1972; and by 1994, 198,479, or 18.9 percent of the test-takers, scored above 600. Those who analyzed the SAT data were hard-pressed to explain why the proportion of high-scoring students fell precipitously on the verbal test but fully rebounded on the mathematics test.[10]

Other standardized measures of academic achievement registered declines during the same period, but none attracted as much attention as the SAT. No other national test was as well known; millions of people could remember their own SAT scores. Even though the students who take this test are not representative of all students, they do represent an important segment of the younger generation. In 1975 they included about one-third of the nation's graduating seniors, and two-thirds of all those bound for college; by 1994 the SAT test-takers included 42 percent of the nation's high school graduates and more than 90 percent of those entering four-year institutions.[11] A large drop in the scores of such a substantial proportion of the nation's students is significant even if they are not representative of all students.

The debate over the SAT score decline is of more than academic interest because one's diagnosis of the cause determines one's view about the nature of the problem and whether anything can be done about it. To those who attributed the decline mostly to diversification of the test-taking pool, the decline was not a problem but a victory for democracy in education, to be welcomed rather than deplored.[12] If, however, the decline resulted not from democratization, but from low expectations, tracking of students into undemanding programs, and curricular diffusion, then educators could take specific actions to improve achievement. If the first analysis is correct, then schools and parents should not even try to change what are actually heartening social trends; if the second analysis is correct, then schools and parents have within their power the capacity to make changes and bring about different results, so that more students graduate high school better prepared for the future.

After nearly two decades of debate, it appears clear that a score decline did begin in the mid-1960s and ended for students in the upper grades about 1980. The decline was registered not only on the SAT but on some NAEP tests as well. In a report prepared for the Congressional Budget Office, Daniel Koretz of the Rand Corporation concluded "that the overall drop in achievement" entailing "sizable declines in higher-level skills, such as inference and problem-solving, is beyond question."[13] In 1992 he offered the following generalizations about the score declines:

- Achievement, at least as measured by tests, clearly declined during the 1960s and 1970s.

- The apparent decline was in fact exaggerated by demographic and other factors, but the real decline was considerable nonetheless.

- Minority students, particularly African Americans, gained relative to non-Hispanic whites.

- Trends since the end of the decline are less clear, but the evidence does not consistently show gains that fully offset the earlier decline.[14]

The extent to which SAT scores were affected by the changing composition of the test-taking pool can never be ascertained for two reasons: first, because there is little reliable information about individual SAT test-takers before 1972 (when students first answered a self-descriptive questionnaire); and, second, because the ethnic composition of the SAT test-takers was not fully reported until 1976. Therefore, no one can be certain how the test-taking population changed at the very time that the scores were declining.

The College Board's own study in 1977 attributes fully half of the decline from 1963 to 1977 to changes in the test-taking pool, but Koretz later concluded that changes in the ethnic composition of the test-takers accounted for no more than one-tenth to one-fifth of the decline and that the addition of test-takers with lower levels of ability also "contributed appreciably to the decline."[15]

Although they do not dispute that changes in the composition of the test-taking pool depressed the SAT scores, Charles Murray and R. J. Herrnstein found that a large part of the decline occurred entirely among white students. They disagree both with those who see the SAT decline as a victory for "democratization" and with those who see it as proof that the schools are worse than ever. They contend that today's average high school students are about as well educated as ever, although they also note that "this does not mean that they are well educated by absolute standards, nor that they are well educated enough to meet the challenges from ever-stronger competitors overseas, only that things are no worse in the United States than they used to be." They attribute the sharp decrease in the number and proportion of high verbal scores on the SAT to the erosion of standards in the high schools' college track, which they call the "mediocritization" of education. Mathematical scores rebounded more than verbal scores, they believe, because of the integrity of mathematics as a discipline; unlike the courses that teach verbal skills, such as language arts and social studies, "there are limits to the amount of fudging that can be done with the course content" of calculus, geometry, algebra, and trigonometry.[16]

Murray and Herrnstein found that the decline of white scores mirrored the overall SAT decline, which led them to dispute the idea that "democratization" was the primary cause of the score decline. They hold that the white SAT pool did not change substantially during the years when the scores fell. They assert that "from 1963 to 1976, during the steepest part of the SAT decline, the white SAT population

Figure 3-2.   Percentage of All 17-Year-Olds Graduating from
High School and of Graduates Going on to College, 1920–94

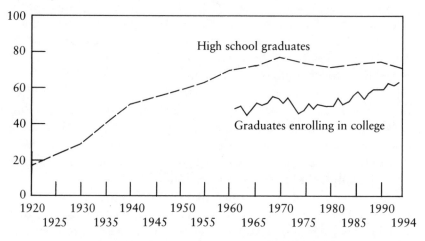

Percentage

Source: National Center for Education Statistics, *Digest of Education Statistics, 1994*, pp. 108, 188.

probably remained at least as selective as ever. It may have become more selective." They conclude that "neither race, class, parental education, nor gender can explain" the SAT decline.[17]

The addition of low-scoring students to the SAT-taking pool surely lowered average scores, but the composition of the pool did not change as dramatically as many believe. It is often assumed that scores fell because more and more young people were graduating from high school, taking the SAT, and going to college. But that is not what happened. From 1964 to 1994 the high school graduation rate hovered around 75 percent (figure 3-2).[18] The proportion of high school graduates who immediately enrolled in college did not flatten out like the high school graduation rate, but neither did it rise in a steady line. About half of all high school graduates went on to college between 1964 and 1984; some years the proportion was as high as 55.4 percent (1968), and some years as low as 46.6 percent (1973).[19] The percentage of high school students who took the SAT held steady at about one-third from 1972 to 1983 (from 1975 to 1979 the percentage of SAT-takers actually dropped to less than one-third).[20] It was only *after* 1983–84, after the score decline had ended, that the rate of college-going moved decisively upward (reaching 62.4 percent of high school graduates in 1991), and the percentage of students who

Figure 3-3. Percentage of High School Graduates Who Take the SAT and of SAT-Takers Who Are Members of Minority Groups, Compared with Mean Combined Verbal and Math Scores, 1967–94

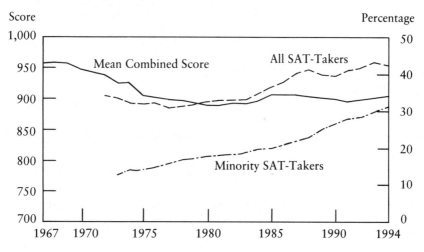

Source: The College Board.

took the SAT grew from 33 percent in the early 1980s to 42 percent in 1994.[21]

In other words, the score decline cannot be adequately explained by a large increase in the proportion of students graduating high school, taking the SAT, and going to college. In fact, during the 1970s, at the very time that scores fell fastest, high school graduation rates were stable, the percentage of students taking the test changed little and even declined, and the percentage of students going to college fluctuated but changed little. It was not until the mid-1980s, *after* SAT scores had reached their lowest point and begun a modest improvement that the proportion of students who were taking the SAT and enrolling in college increased decisively.

Compositional change surely contributed to the decline, but probably not as much as was first believed. The most dramatic compositional change in the SAT test-taking pool occurred *after* 1980, when the proportion of test-takers from ethnic minority groups expanded more than it had in the late 1960s and early 1970s. SAT-taking by ethnic minorities grew sharply, from an estimated 13 percent in 1973, to 18 percent in 1980, and then to 31 percent in 1994 (figure 3.3). Even with the addition of large numbers of new immigrants from

Latin America and Asia whose native language was not English, the scores remained stable. They moved up and down a few points in the 1980s, but they did not plummet. During the 1980s verbal scores remained stable and mathematical scores rose substantially on the SAT, even though the percentage of students, including ethnic minorities, taking the SAT increased greatly. This phenomenon should encourage reconsideration of the causes of the original SAT score decline.[22]

After years of debate about the rise and fall of SAT scores, the College Board has found a way to raise scores overnight. Beginning in 1995 the SAT scores will be "recentered." Originally, 500 was the average on a scale that ranged from 200 to 800. Since a new de facto average had been established over a long period, the board decided to convert current scores (423 verbal and 479 math in 1994) so that a score of 500 will once again become the average on both parts of the test.[23]

National Assessment of Educational Progress

NAEP is a federally financed, congressionally authorized testing program that is supervised by the National Center for Education Statistics (the statistical agency of the U.S. Department of Education). Launched in the mid-1960s, with support from the Carnegie Foundation and the Ford Foundation, NAEP was created to improve the capacity of the U.S. Office of Education to report on the condition and progress of education. U.S. Commissioner of Education Francis Keppel urged the development of NAEP on grounds that the Office of Education had collected data for nearly a century on enrollments, facilities, and spending but not on what students had learned.

Early opponents of NAEP, including many chief state school officers, feared that it would pave the way to a national curriculum, a national testing program, and federal control of local schools, and that it would become a barrier to curricular change and a weapon with which to flog the schools. To deflect such charges, NAEP was initially designed to prevent comparisons of individual students, schools, and even states. It would test national samples of students at ages 9, 13, and 17 (as well as young adults), and it would report only national and regional results. Furthermore, NAEP was designed to use matrix sampling, which means that each student takes only part of each assessment, and no assessment is administered to all students. Under this original design, reporting scores for individuals, schools, districts, or states would have been impossible. To allay fears of a federally imposed curriculum, the contents of each assessment were developed by a consensus process, involving extensive reviews by educators, subject-matter specialists, testing experts, and lay persons.

As demands for accountability rose in the 1980s, state school superintendents abandoned their opposition to state comparisons. Many education leaders expressed interest in using NAEP as a model for state or local testing programs because of its reputation as a reliable and valid measure of educational quality, something for which many districts and states yearned. Because the NAEP scores had no consequences for anyone, teachers had no reason to teach to it, and because its contents were kept secure, there was no cheating or giving the same test more than once. In 1986 eight southern states administered a NAEP-based test to develop state-by-state comparisons, and in 1990 Congress authorized trial state assessments.[24] But Congress continued to bar use of NAEP tests for comparing individuals, schools, or districts.

In 1969–70, the first national assessments were administered in science, writing, and citizenship. In subsequent years, other subjects—including art, music, reading, mathematics, literature, geography, career development, social studies, U.S. history, basic life skills, consumer skills, and computer competence—were assessed. In the absence of a national test that all children take, NAEP became known as "the nation's report card."

Unlike the SAT, which tests a self-selected population among the college bound, the NAEP tests scientifically chosen national samples that are comparable from year to year. As a longitudinal measure of achievement, however, NAEP has one significant limitation: it did not begin its assessments until several years after the SAT scores began to decline. Thus, NAEP does not provide evidence for the crucial years of the 1960s when scores started slipping. Nor can it identify those factors most responsible for the quality of student performance. Although NAEP gathers a great deal of information about student behavior and attitudes as well as classroom practices, it does not ascertain either cause or correlation of student scores (for example, high-scoring students on the whole do more homework than do low-scoring students, but it is not clear whether doing more homework causes an increase in scores or whether students with high scores choose to

Table 3-1.   Percentage of Students at or above 1992 NAEP
Mathematics Scale Score Levels, by Race/Ethnicity and Grade

Scale Score	8th Grade White	8th Grade Asian	12th Grade Black	12th Grade Hispanic
200	99	99	100	100
250	79	84	78	84
300	25	39	22	30
350	1	4	1	2

Source: Ina V.S. Mullis and others, NAEP 1992 Mathematics Report Card for the Nation and the States (NCES 1993) pp. 265–66.

do more homework or tend to go to schools that require more home-work).

Perhaps the best news to emerge from NAEP during its years of reporting is the narrowing of the gap between white students and students who are African American or Hispanic. In science, mathematics, and reading, large gains by black and Hispanic students have substantially reduced the gap between racial groups (as measured on NAEP's 500-point scale). In mathematics, a 40-point spread between white and black 17-year-olds in 1973 was reduced to a 26-point difference by 1992. A 53-point gap in reading between white and black 17-year-olds in 1971 fell to 37 points by 1992. Similarly, a 40-point difference between white and Hispanic 17-year-olds in reading in 1975 was reduced to a 26-point difference in 1992; similar gains were reported for 13-year-old Hispanic students in science and mathematics.[25]

The gap has narrowed, but it remains large. Table 3-1, based on the 1992 NAEP mathematics assessment, demonstrates the extent of the differences among racial groups. At each proficiency level, the scores of white students in the eighth grade are similar to those of black and Hispanic twelfth-grade students. Eliminating the large disparities among students from different racial groups is one of the most important challenges facing American education.

In addition to significant racial and ethnic disparities, NAEP has documented gender disparities. In science boys have significantly higher scores than do girls at ages 13 and 17. In mathematics boys and girls show no significant differences in achievement at ages 9 and 13, but boys have significantly higher scores at age 17. In reading and writing girls have higher scores than do boys at all three ages. In 1992 there was a ten-point difference favoring 17-year-old boys in science achievement and a four-point difference favoring them in mathemat-

Figure 3-4.   Percentile Distributions of NAEP Mathematics Proficiency
by Grade, 1990 and 1992

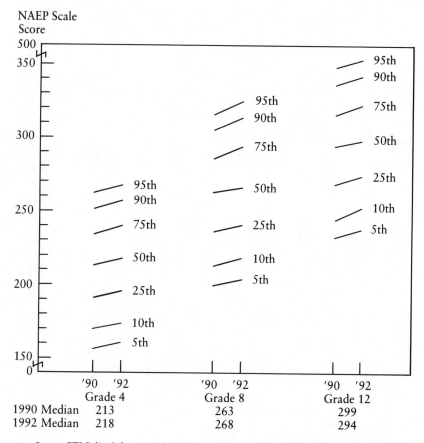

NAEP Scale
Score

	'90 '92	'90 '92	'90 '92
	Grade 4	Grade 8	Grade 12
1990 Median	213	263	299
1992 Median	218	268	294

Source: ETS Policy Information Center, *ETS Policy Notes*, vol. 5 (Summer 1993), p. 5.

ics. A twelve-point difference favored 17-year-old girls in reading, and a seventeen-point difference favored them in writing.[26]

NAEP data make it possible to examine variations in achievement from one grade level to another, as well as the large areas of overlap among students in grades four years apart. For example, data, also drawn from the 1992 NAEP mathematics assessment, show that high-performing fourth graders score higher than about half of all eighth graders and even some twelfth graders (figure 3-4). In addition, figure 3-4 indicates that "students progress more between grades 4 and 8 than they do between grades 8 and 12."[27] One possible reason for

Figure 3-5.   NAEP Trend Lines in Average Achievement in Science, Mathematics, Reading, and Writing, 1970–92

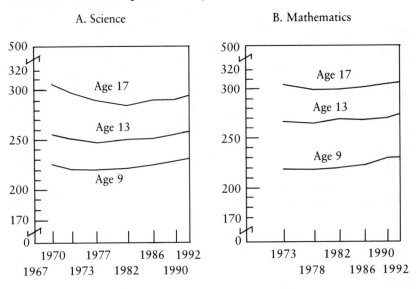

A. Science

B. Mathematics

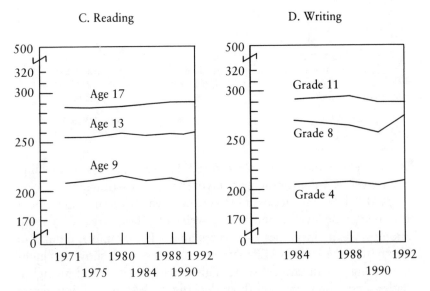

C. Reading

D. Writing

Source: Ina V.S. Mullis and others, *NAEP 1992 Trends in Academic Progress* (National Center for Education Statistics 1994), p. 5.

this latter difference is that most students in grades four through eight pursue a common curriculum, while students in the upper grades tend to be tracked into differentiated curricula.

NAEP trend lines from 1970 to 1992 showed significant improvement in some subject areas for some age groups. Science was the first subject to be assessed in 1970. Student performance in science declined during the 1970s and rebounded during the 1980s; by 1992, 9-year-old students had improved significantly, 13-year-old students were about the same, and 17-year-old students were significantly behind the performance recorded in 1970. Scores in mathematics were somewhat higher in 1992 than they had been in 1973, significantly so for 9- and 13-year-old students. Reading scores were significantly improved for 13- and 17-year old students and were "at least as high, if not higher, than in 1971," when reading was first assessed. Writing scores were markedly improved for eighth graders between 1984 and 1992, but not for fourth and eleventh graders (figure 3-5).[28]

The trends on the whole were encouraging. Most of the improvement in student performance occurred after 1984, very likely as a result of the state-level reforms enacted after the publication of *A Nation at Risk*. But NAEP added a cautionary note in its 1990 trend summary, concluding that although "students are learning facts and skills, few show the capacity for complex reasoning and problem solving. . . . The few gains that have occurred were primarily in lower-level skills and basic concepts."[29]

Consider NAEP commentaries about student achievement in the leading subject areas:

Science

The report on the 1986 assessment acknowledged an upturn in achievement but commented gloomily on the poor quality of student performance, which it described as "distressingly low." The achievement of eighth graders was described as "quite disturbing. Without a better foundation in their middle-school years, students will likely be unprepared to take more advanced courses as they progress through high school." Furthermore, the report said, "a majority of 17-year-olds are poorly equipped for informed citizenship and productive performance in the workplace, let alone postsecondary studies in science. . . ."[30]

In its reports NAEP established certain "proficiency levels" to describe what students know and can do. In the 1990 science assessment, for example, the scale ranged from Level 200 ("Understands Simple Scientific Principles"), to Level 250 ("Applies General Scientific Information"), to Level 300 ("Analyzes Scientific Procedures and Data"), to Level 350 ("Integrates Specialized Scientific Information").

The best way to understand the NAEP levels is to see some examples of questions asked at each level. The following is an example of a Level 250 item that 50 percent of fourth graders, 74 percent of eighth graders, and 87 percent of seniors in 1990 answered correctly.

Juan thinks that water will evaporate faster in a warm place than in a cool one. He has two identical bowls and a bucket of water. He wants to do an experiment to find out if he is correct. Which of the following should he do?

a. Place two bowls with the same amount of water in a warm place.

b. Place a bowl of water in a cool place and a bowl with twice the amount of water in a warm place.

c. Place a bowl of water in a cool place and a bowl with half of the amount of water in a warm place.

*d. Place a bowl of water in a cool place and a bowl with the same amount of water in a warm place."

Next is an example of a Level 300 question, answered correctly in 1990 by 35 percent of fourth graders, 51 percent of eighth graders, and 70 percent of twelfth graders.

In the United States, each day the Sun rises in the

a. north and sets in the south

b. south and sets in the north

c. west and sets in the east

*d. east and sets in the west

An example of a Level 350 question, which 46 percent of twelfth graders in 1990 answered correctly, is:

An object is hung on a string so that it can swing back and forth. To find out if the weight of an object affects the amount of time it takes to swing back and forth 10 times, which of the following should be changed for each timing measurement?

*a. The weight of the object

b. The length of the swing

c. The angle through which the object swings

d. The distance the object swings

e. The number of swings the object makes

In 1990, 84 percent of high school seniors achieved Level 250, fewer than half (45 percent) reached Level 300, and only 9 percent attained Level 350. "Considering the technological needs of today's society," NAEP observed of these results, "a disproportionately low percentage of these students possess in-depth scientific knowledge or the ability to accomplish even relatively straightforward tasks requiring application or thinking skills." In addition, the report found that—despite the progress made in the past two decades—"large performance discrepancies [persisted] for Black and Hispanic students and students attending disadvantaged urban schools as well as a gender gap that appears to emerge as part of school science education."[31] In all of its reports on science achievement, NAEP repeatedly stressed that more students should be taking science continuously for more years, that the teaching of science needed to be dramatically improved, and that science proficiency in the schools continued to be unacceptably low. In 1992, more 9- and 13-year-olds reached the 250 proficiency level, and 47 percent of 17-year-olds reached the 300 proficiency level. But the gaps between racial-ethnic groups remained large; 55 percent of white 17-year-olds attained Level 300, compared with 14 percent of black 17-year-olds and 23 percent of Hispanic 17-year-olds.[32]

Mathematics

The first assessment of mathematics was administered in 1973. The next assessment, in 1978, registered a decline in achievement, but assessments in the 1980s indicated a recovery. By 1992 the trend lines showed significant improvement for 9- and 13-year-olds and a full recovery to 1973 levels for 17-year-olds. Consider the quality of performance recorded in the 1973 assessment. Eighteen percent of 9-year-olds, 56 percent of 13-year-olds, and 81 percent of 17-year-olds answered correctly the question "What does 2/3 of 9 equal?" When asked to "express 9/100 as a percent," 43 percent of 13-year-olds could do so, as could 61 percent of 17-year-olds. Only 52 percent of 17-year-olds were able to estimate the square root of a two-digit number; only 27 percent were able to compute one-half of a mixed fraction. Only 45 percent of the 17-year-olds could calculate a certain percent of a given number in a word problem.[33]

The problem that follows is an example of a Level 300 problem in the 1986 assessment that less than 1 percent of 9-year-olds, about 16 percent of 13-year-olds, and about half of 17-year-olds were able to solve:

Which of the following is true about 87% of 10?

a. It is greater than 10.

**b. It is less than 10.*

c. It is equal to 10.

d. Can't tell.

e. I don't know.

At level 350, the most advanced level, a typical question was:

Christine borrowed $850 for one year from the Friendly Finance Company. If she paid 12% simple interest on the loan, what was the total amount she repaid?

Answer:_____ ($952)

In 1986 no 9-year-olds, less than 0.5 percent of 13-year-olds, and 6.4 percent of 17-year-olds could answer a Level 350 question correctly. Based on the 1986 assessment, NAEP concluded that the gains of the 1980s "have been confined primarily to lower-order skills. . . . Most students, even at age 17, do not possess the breadth and depth of mathematics proficiency needed for advanced study in secondary school mathematics." Furthermore, the performance of 17-year-olds was described as "dismal," with only 6 percent able to solve multistep

Table 3-2. National Overall Average Mathematics NAEP Achievement Levels, Grades 4, 8, and 12, 1990 and 1992

Grade	Years	Percentage of students at or above			Percentage below basic
		Advanced	Proficient	Basic	
4	1992	2	18	61	39
	1990	1	13	54	46
8	1992	4	25	63	37
	1990	2	20	58	42
12	1992	2	16	64	36
	1990	2	13	59	41

Source: Ina V. S. Mullis and others, *NAEP 1992 Mathematics Report Card for the Nation and the States* (National Center for Education Statistics, 1993), p. 64.

problems, "especially if they involved understanding algebra or geometry."[34]

In 1990 NAEP adopted a new reporting format. In addition to the proficiency scales that describe what students know and can do, NAEP began reporting "achievement levels" that gauge what students *should* know and be able to do. The purpose was to establish standards for what students should know at a given age or grade, not just to measure what they did know. The new policy was promulgated by the National Assessment Governing Board, the congressionally mandated, bipartisan, policymaking panel that oversees the National Assessment. The achievement levels were defined as "basic" (partial mastery of fundamental knowledge and skills), "proficient" (solid academic performance), and "advanced" (superior performance).

Whether gauged by proficiency levels or achievement levels, student performance on the 1990 mathematics assessment was far from satisfactory. Table 3-2 shows that more than 40 percent at each age level scored "below basic," while 20 percent or less reached "proficient"—the level that the governing board said *all* youngsters should reach. When viewed by proficiency levels, the 1990 results were no better. NAEP reported that only two-thirds of eighth graders "had a grasp of typical fifth-grade content." Moreover, among high school seniors, "less than half appeared to have a firm grasp of seventh-grade content," and only 5 percent of seniors "attained a level of performance characterized by algebra and geometry—when most have had coursework in these subjects. . . ." In 1992, as table 3-2 demonstrates, significant improvements were recorded at each age level, but too many students continue to score below the "basic" achievement level.[35]

In 1993 the NAEP released a special report, titled *Can Students Do Mathematical Problem-Solving?*, which gauged students' ability to answer open-ended questions. This test was prepared to meet the requirements of the National Council of Teachers of Mathematics, which had steadily pressed for including open-ended, problem-solving questions in NAEP tests. In the 1992 national mathematics assessment, one-third of the questions were either "regular constructed-response questions," that is, short-answer questions; or "extended constructed-response tasks," which required students to explain how they solved problems by writing, giving examples, or drawing diagrams. The first objective was to see how well students could solve problems; the second was to try out an approach to testing ("performance assessment") that was broadly seen as superior to multiple-choice testing. On the regular constructed-response questions, fourth graders averaged 42 percent correct; eighth graders, 53 percent; and twelfth graders, 40 percent. The extended constructed-response tasks were answered satisfactorily (or better) by 16 percent of fourth graders, 8 percent of eighth graders, and 9 percent of seniors. The gap between white students and minority students on the problem-solving questions was larger than on the multiple-choice questions.[36]

At all three grade levels, students had more difficulty with open-ended questions than with multiple-choice questions. The extended tasks, which required students to explain how they reached their solutions, were particularly frustrating for students:

- From approximately one-third to two-thirds of the students provided incorrect responses to these extended questions, indicating little evidence of understanding the mathematical concepts involved or even the question being asked.

- Substantial percentages of students, sometime as many as one-fourth, simply left their papers blank.

- Most students who did seem to understand the problems had difficulty explaining their work.

- It is encouraging, however, that some students—from 1 to 16 percent—provided *extended* responses to each one of the tasks.[37]

What kinds of questions were asked? This is an example of a regular constructed-response question:

Jill needs to earn $45.00 for a class trip. She earns $2.00 each day on Mondays, Tuesdays, and Wednesdays, and $3.00 each day on Thursdays, Fridays, and Saturdays. She does not work on Sundays. How many weeks will it take her to earn $45.00?

This question was answered correctly (three weeks) by 22 percent of fourth graders and 59 percent of eighth graders.

The following is an extended constructed-response question for fourth-graders:

Think carefully about the following question. Write a complete answer. You may use drawings, words, and numbers to explain your answer. Be sure to show all of your work.

Jose ate 1/2 of a pizza.
Ella ate 1/2 of another pizza.
Jose said that he ate more pizza than Ella, but Ella said they both ate the same amount. Use words and pictures to show that Jose could be right.

Fifty-six percent of the students either did not answer or answered incorrectly. Eight percent offered satisfactory answers showing that they recognized that the two pizzas might be of different sizes; only 16 percent provided drawings of two different-sized pizzas, each divided in half, with an explanation such as "Jose could be right because his pizza could be bigger than Ella's."[38]

Two important findings resulted from this pioneering effort to break free from total reliance on the multiple-choice question. First, the constructed-response questions provide more information about what students understand (and fail to understand) than do multiple-choice questions. Second, these kinds of questions could be successfully incorporated into a national assessment and reliably scored by trained readers.

Reading

The trend lines in reading from 1971 to 1992 are a bright note: 13- and 17-year-old students performed at significantly higher levels in 1992 than they did in the early 1970s. White and black youngsters at all three age levels and 17-year-old Hispanic students improved their reading proficiency significantly during that period. Although boys' reading achievement at ages 9 and 17 improved substantially, girls continued to register significantly higher reading achievement than boys at all three age levels.[39]

Could reading achievement be better? Of course. A majority of students do minimal homework, and students' out-of-school reading diminishes as they progress through school. When asked in 1992 how much time they spent on homework for all subjects (which is positively associated with high performance in reading), 34 percent of 17-year-olds said either that they had no homework or that they did not do it, and another 29 percent spent less than one hour a day on homework. Only 12 percent spent more than two hours on homework each day, and 25 percent did one to two hours. When asked if they read daily for fun, 56 percent of 9-year-olds did, compared with 37 percent of 13-year-olds and only 27 percent of 17-year-olds. When asked how many pages they read in school and for homework, 46 percent of 17-year-olds reported reading ten or fewer pages a day.[40]

History

NAEP administered its first assessment of U.S. history in 1986 to 17-year-old students. Students were generally familiar with major personalities in American history; most could identify Thomas Edison and Alexander Graham Bell, George Washington and Thomas Jefferson. Even though they were taking a course in American history, most did not know what the Missouri Compromise was, nor could they identify Senator Joseph McCarthy, Reconstruction, the Dred Scott decision, the Progressive movement, Magna Carta, Jim Crow laws, the Articles of Confederation, or the Scopes trial. Two-thirds of the students did not know that the Civil War occurred between 1850 and 1900.[41] When the assessment was repeated two years later, little change was noted, and NAEP concluded that "across the grades, most students have a limited grasp of U.S. history."[42]

In sum, NAEP reports from 1970 to 1992 provide a partial confirmation of the SAT score decline of the 1970s. The scores in mathematics fell during the 1970s and regained ground in the 1980s on both the SAT and NAEP. Although the SAT declines were steepest and most prolonged in the verbal test, NAEP reading scores remained stable or improved from 1971 to 1992. The match between the mathematics tested on the SAT and NAEP is probably closer than the match between the NAEP reading test and the SAT verbal test. Why the difference in performance between these two measures? The NAEP reading test emphasizes basic reading skills; the SAT verbal test focuses mainly on reasoning skills (antonyms, synonyms, and analogies) and advanced vocabulary questions. The strong showing of American students on NAEP reading tests and the persistent weak showing on the SAT verbal test may reflect the differences in the two tests, as well as the fact that American classrooms tend to promote the basic reading skills tested by NAEP.

International Assessments

In the 1960s the United States began to participate in international assessments of student achievement in various fields, administered by either the International Association for the Evaluation of Educational Achievement or the Educational Testing Service.[43] Such international assessments allow comparison of American students' skills and knowledge with those of their contemporaries in other nations; this measure provides a valuable contrast to the SAT and NAEP, in which American students are compared only with other American students. One of the valuable lessons that researchers have drawn from the international surveys is "that U.S. pupils could attain a much higher level of achievement in science and mathematics than they currently do."[44]

Policymakers have used the results of international assessments to find out whether American students are learning as much or as well as students in other countries. The educators who design and administer the surveys see them as a way to encourage participating nations "to examine the structure, practices, and curricula of their educational systems, and as a consequence, to envision the possibility of rethinking curriculum content and the ways in which students are taught."[45] The results of the assessments have been used to identify the kind of performance that is *possible* and to explore the likely relationships between student achievement and school variables. The subjects most frequently assessed are mathematics and science. These are especially worthy targets for international surveys because they are taught in every nation and are least subject to linguistic and cultural differences; in addition, the importance of these studies is widely recognized for postsecondary education, technical careers, and participation in a technologically advanced society.

Although more than thirty countries took part in at least one of the assessments of mathematics and science, the United States participated in all of them. The results of the early international assessments were reported in scholarly and pedagogical journals; with so many nations involved, analysis was slow, unwieldy, and usually underfunded. Researchers labored to refine methods of conducting large-scale survey research. Not much attention was paid to the policy implications of the assessments until the publication of *A Nation at Risk*, which pointed out that "international comparisons of student achievement, completed a decade ago, reveal that on 19 academic tests American students were never first or second and, in comparison with other industrialized nations, were last seven times."[46] After they were highlighted as evidence of the low quality of American education, the international assessments became—like SAT scores—a focus of media attention, reported in the language of sporting events, with headlines proclaiming which country was first and where the United States placed. The sponsors of the international assessments warn repeatedly that the surveys are not an intellectual olympics or an academic horse race, but to no avail; such cautions usually are neither reported nor heeded.[47]

Nonetheless, U.S. students performed poorly in the international assessments, seldom rising above the median, often scoring near the bottom. Only in an international literacy survey—a subject stressed in American schools—did American students perform very well.

- The First International Mathematics Study, carried out in the mid-1960s, tested 13-year-olds and high school seniors in twelve countries. American 13-year-olds scored significantly lower than students in nine other educational systems, ahead of only one. On a test given only to seniors enrolled in a mathematics course, the U.S. students scored last, behind those in eleven other nations; on a test given to seniors not enrolled in a mathematics course, the United States also scored last, behind seven other countries.[48]

- The First International Science Study was administered in the late 1960s and early 1970s to 10-year-olds (from sixteen educational systems), and to 14-year-olds and students in the last year of secondary school (from eighteen educational systems). Among 10-year-olds only the Japanese scored higher than the Americans, and five systems scored lower. (The score differences with the other participating educational systems were not statistically significant.) Among 14-year-olds, five systems scored higher than the Americans; and three were significantly lower. Among students in the last year of secondary school, Americans scored last of eleven systems.[49]

- The Second International Mathematics Study (1981–82) tested students in fifteen systems. It assessed 13-year-olds and high school seniors who had already taken at least two years of algebra and one year of geometry. American 13-year-olds (eighth graders) placed at or near the median on most tests. The American seniors, however, placed at or near the bottom in number systems, algebra, geometry, and calculus. Furthermore, "*average* Japanese students achieved higher than the top 5% of the U.S. students in college preparatory mathematics," and "the algebra achievement of our most able students (the top 1%) was lower than that of the top 1% of any other country."[50]

- The Second International Science Study (1983–86) surveyed 10-year-olds from fifteen systems; 14-year-olds from seventeen systems; and students in the last year of secondary school from fourteen systems. American 10-year-olds scored at the median, and American 14-year-olds in the bottom quarter. The American seniors were an elite group enrolled in a second year science course; about 6 percent of U.S. high school seniors take a second year of biology, 4 percent take a second year of chemistry, and 1.5 percent study a second year of physics. Yet American seniors scored at or near the bottom in biology, chemistry, and physics.[51]

- The International Assessment of Educational Progress in Mathematics and Science (1988) tested 13-year-olds in six countries (one of them was Canada, which administered the test in seven provinces as separate systems). Of the twelve educational systems, eight had significantly higher scores than the U.S. students in science; in mathematics, students in ten systems scored significantly higher than the U.S. students. Assessment specialists Robert L. Linn and Stephen B. Dunbar described this assessment as "particularly sobering in that the exercises were all developed specifically for U.S. students as part of the NAEP. Thus the poor showing of U.S. students cannot be dismissed because the exercises were more in line with the curriculum of another country."[52] On an attitude survey of test-takers, the Korean students—who received the highest mean scores in mathematics—scored lowest when asked if they were good at mathematics, while the American youngsters—with the lowest mean scores—scored highest when asked the same question.[53]

- The Second International Assessment of Educational Progress in Mathematics and Science (1990–91) tested 9- and 13-year-olds in twenty countries. Of fifteen countries in which comprehensive populations were tested, U.S. 13-year-olds placed in the bottom quarter in both subjects. U.S. 9-year-olds placed near the bottom of ten countries in mathematics, but third in science, close behind Korea and Taiwan.[54]

The performance of American students on other international assessments has produced varied results. In an international assessment of geography for 13-year-olds in 1991, Americans placed in the middle among nine nations.[55] But in an international assessment of basic reading skills in thirty-two countries, American 9-year-olds ranked second (behind Finland), demonstrating " consistently high performance on all items," and 13-year-olds scored in the top third.[56] Reading is one area of the curriculum that receives strong emphasis in American schools, and this attention paid off in the international reading assessment. In this survey, 9- and 13-year-old American students had the highest level of television-watching of any country in the survey; 21.3 percent of American 9-year-olds watch more than five hours of television each day, as do 11.4 percent of the 14-year-olds. American 9-year-olds also watched television the highest average number of hours each day (three), while the older group shared this dubious honor (at two and a half hours daily) with 14-year-olds of several other countries. Like many NAEP reports, the international literacy survey found that reading achievement declines as television-watching increases.[57]

Although researchers, journalists, and others scour the international assessments for clues to explain low or high student achievement, it may not be possible to draw valid conclusions based on aggregate, cross-sectional country data. An international assessment does not provide as much information as does a longitudinal, individual-level survey, for example, or a study of planned variation (where large numbers of students use different educational methods in a controlled experiment). Mean scores on an international assessment can be correlated with certain patterns, but there is no way to say whether the particular behaviors, patterns, or programs that were studied are responsible for a given level of student achievement; it may be that the most important variables were not identified or analyzed.

Many criticisms have been leveled at the technical quality of the international assessments.[58] A rigorous review by experts at the National Center for Education Statistics faulted the sampling procedures and response rates in many of the international surveys but nonetheless concluded that "there is one consistent message. Students from the United States, regardless of grade level, generally lag behind many of their counterparts from other developed countries in both mathematics and science achievement." Despite the technical flaws of the international surveys of educational achievement, "certain trends appear to be clear":

- The more students are taught, the more they learn, and the better they perform on the tests. There are significant differences in the content of instruction among countries at common levels of schooling.

- Use of a differentiated curriculum based on early tracking is negatively associated with student performance on the international assessments and also reduces opportunities for some students to be exposed to more advanced curriculum.

- The school affects learning in some subject areas more than in others.

- Countries committed to keeping students enrolled in secondary school score less well on the international surveys, but they spread more knowledge across a larger population. Japan is an exception. Even with high retention rates at the secondary level,

Japanese students perform very well on the mathematics and science achievement surveys.

- Generally the "best students" in the United States do less well on the international surveys when compared with the "best students" from other countries.[59]

The international assessments demonstrate that students tend to learn what they *have* studied and that they cannot learn what they *have not* studied. If this point seems obvious, it nonetheless is important advice in a nation where many youngsters choose whether or not to study basic academic courses; where many students are "tracked" into programs that deny them access to courses necessary either for college or a technical career; where students in many schools are taught arithmetic again and again until the high school years, instead of being introduced to higher-order mathematical thinking drawn from statistics, probability, geometry, algebra, and other areas.

The international studies are the source of the concept "opportunity to learn." Analysts realized that students could not learn material that they had never studied, so they wrote about the curriculum as a "distributor of opportunity to learn." They developed ways to quantify the opportunity to learn as a measure of the student's actual exposure to topics and content that were tested. When comparative scholars write about "opportunity to learn," they mean "Did the student have a chance to learn the material? Was he or she taught it?" One major review of the Second International Mathematics Study found four different kinds of mathematics courses taught in eighth grade in the United States—"remedial," "typical," "enriched," and "algebra." The amount of algebra taught and learned in each of these types differed considerably. This curricular differentiation "between schools, and especially between classes within schools, has set boundaries on what each individual can achieve by his or her own efforts. . . ." The study concluded that, "under current policies, large proportions of U.S. students are being deprived of opportunities to participate in the best mathematics programs that schools have to offer."[60]

Reviewers of the international surveys concluded that "students learned what they were taught, and those from countries with more demanding curriculum learned more of the kinds of items tested in the survey, and performed better. . . ." These surveys "also revealed something that many Americans had not supposed possible—that students can be taught complex mathematics at a relatively early age."[61] Eighth graders in Japan received the highest scores on the Second International Mathematics Study, and researchers noted that "teacher coverage (opportunity-to-learn) of these topics in Japan was among the highest of any country. . . ." U.S. eighth graders received low scores in geometry, a subject that most of them had not been taught.[62]

The differences between students in Japan and the United States could be accounted for almost entirely by the differences in curriculum. Because the Japanese mathematics curriculum is structured, coherent, and rigorous, Japanese students have much greater opportunity to learn challenging material. Of the concepts represented by forty-five calculus questions on the test, for example, twenty-four were taught in Japan before twelfth grade, but only four in the United States.[63]

One group of researchers called for "a fundamental revision" of the American curriculum, beginning in the early grades of the elementary school. The current curriculum has too much arithmetic and too much repetition of topics, this group maintained. Furthermore, too many students are tracked into mathematics curricula that "offer little intellectual challenge, seriously limit their chances for success in many fields of study . . . and greatly restrict their career choices in today's society."[64]

American students, it seems, are disadvantaged by low expectations and by a diffuse, unstructured curriculum that inappropriately allocates opportunity.[65] What the international assessments seem to suggest is that students learn more when expectations are high, when all students are expected to learn, and when the content of the curriculum is well planned, challenging, and coherent.

Course-Taking Patterns

Test scores are not the only objective gauges of educational performance. Course-taking patterns are no less important (and may be even more important), because they may reveal whether children are even exposed to what they need to know to participate successfully in a demanding, technologically advanced economy. If one consistent message can be found in the studies of test score data, whether from the SAT, ACT, NAEP, or international assessments, it is that students perform best when they have taken a challenging program of studies. Students who take a full program of history, geography, English, mathematics, science, foreign language, and the arts are best prepared for whatever lies ahead in their lives. In other words, a liberal education—one that opens the mind to new worlds and liberates the individual from ignorance—remains not only the best education for free men and women, but the best preparation for the future, whether one chooses to enter higher education or the work force.

Time is an important variable in education. William H. Schmidt, who conducted a study of high school course taking, concluded that "the more courses and time spent in a given curricular area, the better the resulting achievement in that area." He discovered "major differences . . . in the quantity-of-schooling that high school students receive in various areas of the academic curriculum." Students who attend the same school may "by their own choice or through the influence of counsellors, be exposed to radically different curricula." Much of the variation in time spent in various studies was attributable "to differences among schools—a likely consequence of differences in course offerings." Schmidt found the largest achievement differences in mathematics, where an additional two years of mathematics in high school could raise student achievement by 16 percentiles.[66]

The College Board echoed these findings in its own studies of course-taking patterns; it concluded that certain courses function as "gatekeepers" for college entrance and determine whether poor and minority students prepare for college. The College Board identified algebra and geometry as the critical gatekeepers. It noted that white students were about twice as likely to take geometry as black and Hispanic students, and that high-income students were twice as likely to take geometry as low-income students. About 80 percent of the students who took geometry enrolled in college, regardless of whether they were black, Hispanic, or white: *"The gap between minorities and whites virtually disappears among students who took geometry."* Based on its analyses of the relationship between what students study and their college attendance and graduation, the College Board recommended "that schools consider the strategy of requiring mastery of algebra and geometry of all students and that schools develop a plan to encourage college aspirations in all students."[67]

High school graduation requirements and college admission requirements set clear expectations for students. In the absence of graduation requirements (that is, expectations set by the school), social
class differences in achievement will likely grow stronger, because the
children of the best-educated parents tend to take the courses necessary for college entry in response to their parents' expectations, while
children whose parents are not well educated are less likely to be
prodded to raise their aspirations. It is unfortunate that requirements
for graduation and college admission deal only with the last four
years of high school. The years spent in elementary and junior high
school are no less critical in establishing the foundation for success in
high school, college, and career.

Although many educators look nostalgically to the schools of the
1950s as exemplars of academic rigor, a recent historical investigation
suggests that schools of that era were rigorous only for a minority.
David Angus and Jeffrey Mirel conclude, after reviewing course-taking patterns in this century, that academic courses taken "declined
significantly from the late 1920s until some time in the late 1960s or
early 1970s." From the 1930s on, educators worked on the assumption that every expansion of the high school enrollment required an
expansion of the curriculum; and that every enrollment expansion
increased the number of low-ability students, who were directed into
less-demanding courses and a nonacademic track. The authors point
out that the late 1960s and early 1970s were notable for "the reorganization of full-year courses into courses of a half-year or less, the
increase of mandated requirements in such non-academic fields as
health and physical education, and the granting of full academic credit
toward graduation for such courses."[68] In other words, the special
contribution of this era was that, for the first time, students across
the nation received academic credit for physical education, yearbook,
and other nonacademic, extracurricular activities.

*So, the challenge to those who seek to improve education by raising
standards is not to go back to the schools of their childhood, but to
create schools that never were: schools where all children are expected
to learn, schools where expectations are high for all students.*

One of the principal obstacles to a common curriculum is the
practice of tracking, which spread throughout American education
with the introduction of intelligence testing after the First World War.
Once educators were given the technology to sort students on the

basis of their intelligence or aptitude, they proceeded to use it because sorting, or tracking, seemed both educationally effective and administratively efficient. The leaders of progressive education supported tracking because it promised to put each student into the curriculum that was appropriate to his or her needs. Of course, tracking fragmented the academic curriculum, but that was of no concern to progressive educators, many of whom saw the academic curriculum as an exercise in mental gymnastics, appropriate only for the college-bound minority.

As noted in chapter 2, Clifford Adelman of the U.S. Department of Education studied high school transcripts and found that students were spending less time on academic courses and more time on "personal service and development" courses. He concluded that the general track—which was neither academic nor vocational—had become the dominant student track in high school. The theme of his report to the National Commission on Excellence in Education was that "the secondary school curriculum has become diffused and fragmented over the past 15 years, as have college courses and degrees. . . ."[69]

Another study by analysts in the U.S. Department of Education compared high school seniors of 1972 and 1980, and it too found a marked decline in the percentage of students enrolled in the academic curriculum. The typical 1980 senior had taken more mathematics courses than the typical 1972 senior, but during this short period "there was a sevenfold increase in the number of seniors who had taken high school remedial mathematics courses (from 4 to 30 percent) as well as a large increase for remedial English courses (from 6 to 31 percent)." The study also found "a sharp increase (from 50 to 72 percent) in seniors who thought their school should have placed more emphasis on basic academic subjects." Class size grew smaller from 1972 to 1980. Although the proportion of black and Hispanic students increased from 12 to 18 percent, the retention rate remained the same (75 percent).[70]

The same tests of vocabulary, reading, and mathematics were administered to 1972 and 1980 seniors. Over the eight-year period, the mean verbal test score fell by one-fifth of a standard deviation and the mean mathematics test score fell by one-sixth of a standard deviation, which were about the same sizes as the declines in SAT scores during the same period. These score declines could not be attributed to compositional change, because "the decline in vocabulary scores (but not reading scores) was only about one-third as large for minority-group students as it was for white students. Moreover, the estimated decline in vocabulary scores (but not reading scores) was less than one-half as large for students from low SES [socioeconomic status] backgrounds as for those from high SES backgrounds." Similarly, the gap in average mathematics scores between white and minority students narrowed.[71]

Seniors in the class of 1980 reported that they did less homework than the class of 1972. In 1980 only 24.5 percent of seniors spent at least five hours a week on homework, compared with 35.2 percent of seniors in the class of 1972. Even though seniors in 1980 had weaker performance and did less homework than the class of 1972, they had higher grades, and the proportion of seniors who received an A average increased by one-third. Even more striking was that the seniors of 1980 had higher self-esteem than the seniors of 1972, and a larger percentage (48 percent versus 41 percent) thought that they "definitely" had the ability to complete college. The seniors of 1980 were doing worse on objective measures than their predecessors of 1972, but they felt better about themselves and their academic competence.[72]

Curricular differentiation is a major source of educational inequity. Large racial and socioeconomic differences occur among academic, vocational, and general tracks. Tracking usually begins in the elementary grades in an effort to "meet the needs" of students who enter school with differing levels of ability and then continues into secondary schools where "low-ability" students are funneled into nonacademic tracks. Black, Hispanic, and low-income students are disproportionately assigned to low-ability groups and nonacademic tracks, where they are denied access to educational opportunities afforded to students in the academic track. Jeannie Oakes, who has studied extensively the effects of curricular tracking, has written that "the processes and outcomes of tracking are complex, subtle, often informal, and incremental. Although the decisions are usually well-intentioned, considerable evidence suggests that tracking, especially at secondary schools, fails to increase learning generally and has the unfortunate consequence of widening the achievement gaps between students judged to be more and less able."[73] In other words, tracking is a primary means by which schools allocate access to knowledge and restrict access to "programs, teachers, resources, curricular goals, and instructional activities . . . in ways that disadvantage low-income students. . . ."[74] This invidious differentiation legitimates providing different educational opportunities and lower expectations to certain groups of students; it actually *widens* the gap between advantaged and disadvantaged students. The educational philosophy on which this widespread practice is based can be traced directly to the Cardinal Principles of Secondary Education, described in chapter 2, which distorted and retreated from democratic principles in education.

One of the central recommendations of *A Nation at Risk* was that *all* students should meet higher graduation requirements, which the National Commission on Excellence in Education called "the new basics": four years of English, three years each of mathematics, science, and social studies, and one-half year of computer science (plus two years of foreign language for the college bound). In response to the report's recommendations, forty-two states raised their high school graduation requirements, and forty-seven mandated student testing standards.[75]

The most important effect of the state-level reforms of the 1980s can be seen in the dramatic changes in high school course-taking patterns from 1982 to 1992. At the end of these ten years, students across the board—whites, blacks, Hispanics, Asians, American Indians, males, and females—were taking more academic courses. In addition, more graduates of 1992 had taken more rigorous courses in mathematics and science than their peers of a decade earlier (table 3-3).

Foreign language enrollments rose as well. In 1992, 58 percent of all graduates earned two or more credits in foreign language study, compared with 33 percent of the class of 1982. From 1982 to 1992 the percentage of students who studied a foreign language for four years doubled, from 5.2 percent to 10.6 percent. Among college-bound students, the study of foreign language for at least two years increased as well, from 55 percent in 1982 to 73 percent in 1982.[76]

The gains of this ten-year period are clear. Enrollments in advanced courses in foreign language, mathematics, and science went up substantially for every group of students. Course-taking in English and social studies is harder to quantify because of the wide variety of course titles, as well as uncertainty about the likely content and rigor of different courses.

Considering that ten years is a relatively short time to change ingrained patterns of behavior, remarkable progress was made in

Table 3-3. Changes in Course-Taking Patterns for Science and
Mathematics from 1982 to 1992, by Race, Ethnicity, and Gender
Percentage

Category	Algebra 2	Geom.	Trig.	Calc.	Bio.	Chem.	Physics
All							
1982	36.9	48.4	12.2	4.3	78.7	31.6	13.5
1992	56.1	70.4	21.1	10.1	93.0	55.5	24.7
White							
1982	40.5	53.9	13.8	5.0	80.1	34.7	15.3
1992	59.2	72.6	22.5	10.7	93.5	58.0	25.9
Black							
1982	26.2	30.3	6.3	1.4	75.3	22.5	6.8
1992	40.9	60.4	13.0	6.9	92.2	45.9	17.6
Hispanic							
1982	22.5	29.0	6.8	1.6	73.2	16.7	5.5
1992	46.9	62.9	15.2	4.7	91.2	42.6	15.7
Asian							
1982	55.0	64.3	25.7	13.1	83.5	51.9	35.8
1992	60.8	77.1	31.3	20.1	93.4	67.4	41.6
Male							
1982	37.5	48.3	13.3	4.7	76.5	32.4	17.9
1992	54.0	69.0	21.4	10.3	91.9	54.2	28.2
Female							
1982	36.3	48.5	11.2	4.0	80.6	30.9	9.4
1992	58.1	71.7	20.8	9.8	94.2	56.8	21.4

Source: National Center for Education Statistics, *The Condition of Education: 1994* (U.S. Department of Education 1994), pp. 242–43.

raising academic expectations for American students. The state-level reforms of the 1980s and increased high school graduation requirements in particular made a meaningful difference for most students.

Another way to see the striking changes is to review the progress toward meeting the curricular program of the new basics. In 1982 only 1.9 percent of high school graduates had taken the full diet of the new basics, including the two years of foreign language recommended for the college bound. By 1992 that percentage had grown to 23.3 (table 3-4). The proportion of graduates who took the new basics plus half a year of computer science but not foreign language— the curricular program recommended for all students—increased from 2.1 percent in 1982 to 29.4 percent in 1992. Leaving aside both computer science (which need not be offered as a separate course) and foreign language study (which should not be left out), the gains are even more striking: 46.8 percent of the class of 1992 took the

Table 3-4. Changes in Course-Taking Patterns for All High School
Graduates, Selected Years

Percentage

Courses taken*	1982	1987	1990	1992
4 English, 3 social studies, 3 science, 3 math, ½ computer science, 2 foreign language	1.6	12.0	17.3	23.3
4 English, 3 social studies, 3 math, ½ computer science	2.1	16.3	22.7	29.4
4 English, 3 social studies, 3 science, 3 math, 2 foreign language	8.8	20.9	30.6	36.9
4 English, 3 social studies, 3 science, 3 math	12.7	28.6	39.9	46.8
4 English, 3 social studies, 2 science, 2 math	29.2	54.6	66.8	72.8

Source: National Center for Education Statistics, *The Condition of Education: 1994* (U.S. Department of Education 1994), pp. 240–44.

requisite courses in English, science, mathematics, and social studies, compared with 12.7 percent of the class of 1982. During the ten years the percentage of graduates who took both advanced algebra and geometry grew from 29 percent to 50 percent, and the percentage who took both biology and chemistry increased from 29 percent to 54 percent.[77]

In the most rigorous program, the one that included a course in computer science and at least two years of foreign language, every demographic group except American Indians registered a large increase during the ten-year period. By 1992, 23.7 percent of white students, 21.9 percent of black students, 20 percent of Hispanic students, and 29.4 percent of Asian students were enrolled in the most demanding academic program. The largest enrollment gains were recorded by females and Asian students. By 1992, 25.5 percent of young women were enrolled in this program, compared with 21 percent of young men.[78]

The gains made in the decade following the release of *A Nation at Risk* were truly impressive. Higher expectations produced higher enrollments in advanced courses. Students' aspirations for higher education increased, as did the percentage of students enrolling in college (from 50.6 percent of all high school graduates in 1982 to 61.9 percent in 1992).[79] A cautionary note, however: In the absence of comparable content standards and assessments, there is no way to know how rigorous were the courses in mathematics and science that students had taken, even those with the same titles. Researchers have pointed out that "the *quality* and the *content* of the time spent are as important as the *quantity*."[80] Comparable assessments are needed to determine the extent to which increased course taking translates into higher student achievement.

The impressive gains in academic course taking were cause for satisfaction, but not for complacency. By 1992 nearly half the nation's seniors had risen to the challenge posed a decade earlier by the National Commission on Excellence in Education. Among high school seniors in 1992, 43 percent were in the academic track (compared with 37.9 percent in 1982), 11.7 percent were in the vocational track (compared with 26.9 percent in 1982), and 45.3 percent were in the general track (compared with 35.2 percent in 1982). Although participation in both the academic and general tracks had increased, the largest number of students was enrolled in the general track, which is neither academic nor vocational. In Catholic schools, which had always stressed a core curriculum, 73.5 percent of seniors were in the academic track. In public schools, which enroll nearly 90 percent of all students, 40 percent of seniors were in the academic track, while 47 percent were in the general track.[81]

Overall, a review of student achievement on the SAT, NAEP, and international assessments, as well as course-taking patterns, suggests that test scores declined in the late 1960s and throughout the 1970s; that the decline ended around 1980; that average achievement improved during the 1980s, probably because higher graduation requirements spurred a significant increase in academic course taking among all groups of students; and that the achievement gap between majority and minority students is narrowing. The changes observed during the past generation indicate that student achievement goes up or down in response to expectations and standards. The state, the school district, the schools, teachers, parents, peers, colleges, employers, the community, and the media, each in their own way, send a message to students about the kind of behavior and performance that is expected of them. Most students respond accordingly.

4

Seeds of Reform

 AT THE HEART OF AMERICAN education is a paradox. On the one hand, public school classrooms across the country display a striking uniformity of course offerings, teaching methods, textbooks, tests, staffing patterns, and organizational structures. A person who was dropped into an unidentified classroom somewhere in the United States would very likely have no idea in which state or region it was located. On the other hand, the highly decentralized nature of American education has complicated any effort to forge a clear national consensus about what schools are supposed to do and what students are supposed to learn. In response to legislation and court decisions, the schools are expected to meet many needs and to serve multiple agendas; in so doing, they make compromises and accept responsibilities that create a high degree of similarity among all schools. (For most of the twentieth century, American schools have operated on the assumption that their mission was to meet the needs of the whole child, eschewing priorities among the child's many needs.) But in trying to be all things to all people, they lose not only their distinctiveness, but their focus as educational agencies.

This lack of clarity about the purpose of schooling leaves the educational enterprise vulnerable to transient trends as well as to interest groups that seek to define education in ways that advance this or that special cause. Many of the heated controversies of the twentieth century can be seen as episodes in a struggle among various groups to broaden or narrow the national consensus about the purpose of American education. If the schools are to regain their efficacy as *educational* institutions, their *educational* purposes must be given highest priority. Perhaps the best way to replace the weak consensus around the idea that the schools should be all things to all people is to develop a strong national consensus that teaching and learning should be the schools' highest priorities.

In the second half of the twentieth century, several attempts were made to use federal funds as a lever to redefine the schools' purpose. First, during the brief post-Sputnik period in the late 1950s and early 1960s, the nation's schools were urged to identify their best students and encourage them to take rigorous courses in the sciences and foreign languages. Then, in the mid-1960s, the civil rights revolution shifted the focus of educators from meritocracy to egalitarianism, from a talent search to a search for equity. The measure of success was no longer the accomplishments of the gifted few, but the ability of schools to lower their dropout rate, desegregate their classes, and retain students of all different backgrounds through high school graduation and even into postsecondary education. By the 1980s, however, the federal government joined with the states in efforts to raise educational standards, not just for the elite and talented, but for all students. Informed by the egalitarianism of the 1960s, the reformers of the 1980s asked the schools to do what they had never done before: to educate *all* students well, without regard to social class or background.

The will to confront this daunting task emerged as the result of an ideological sea change in American education. A new consensus formed around the importance of focusing on educational quality, and not just on the number of students who entered and graduated. This new consensus was shaped by a tall stack of commission reports; by presidents and governors who realized that education was important for the future of the nation; by business leaders who were concerned about the quality of the work force and the international competitiveness of the nation; by passionate, eloquent educators such as Mortimer Adler, William Bennett, Ernest Boyer, Albert Shanker, and Theodore Sizer, who, through their writing and advocacy, drew attention to the need for education reform; by minority educators such as Ronald Edmonds who insisted that the principles of effective schools, which succeeded in raising the educational achievement of minority children, were replicable; and by heroic practitioners such as Marva Collins, Jaime Escalante, and Deborah Meier, who were celebrated in the national media for their success in difficult circumstances.[1]

Although some who helped to create the new consensus would have difficulty recognizing the others as colleagues in a joint undertaking, these disparate partners nonetheless challenged a deeply rooted educational tradition of utilitarianism and anti-intellectualism, of curricular tracking and low expectations. But not only pedagogical stars, corporate leaders, and elected officials saw the need for change in the nation's schools. By the mid-1980s scholars, educators, university leaders, employers, parents, and others joined in criticizing the status quo. Some found the vastly unequal opportunities and uneven outcomes for students unacceptable; others objected to low standards. Some criticized tracking and asked why black and Hispanic students were so frequently underrepresented in college preparatory classes. Some complained about the growth of remedial programs at the college level, even in highly selective institutions. Employers objected to the costs of providing basic or remedial education to new employees who had high school diplomas but poor literacy and numeracy skills. College professors worried about the poor high school preparation of entering students. These different critiques of education tumbled together, joining into an insistent demand for higher standards for *all* students.

There was opposition, to be sure. Any number of thoughtful educators and researchers feared that the seductive call of high standards for all was a screen for something else, something they considered nefarious, such as a national curriculum, a national test, a trend toward standardization of what was taught and learned, an effort to stifle innovative education, a well-disguised scheme to replace equity with meritocracy, an attempt by powerful elites to gain control of the nation's educational system, or even a purposeful diversion of attention from demands by schools for more money.

Yet for all the doubts and fears of critics, the movement to establish higher standards for all pushed forward. Some educators endorsed standards as a means to promote equity, by narrowing the achievement gaps among different groups of students. Others supported standards as a means to promote excellence, by encouraging higher achievement from all students. These two goals—equity and excellence—are often presented as opposites, a necessary tradeoff, with one subverting the other. Yet proponents of the standards movement argued that equity and excellence need not be at odds; that the very act of defining high expectations for all students and fashioning means to enable students to meet those expectations could promote both equity and excellence; and that neither equity nor excellence could be attained without standards for what is taught and learned.

Certain events affected the intellectual debate decisively—the discovery of the SAT score decline in 1975, the publication in 1983 of *A Nation at Risk,* and the agreement in 1989 between the president and the governors to establish national goals for education. These high-profile events captured the headlines, but no less influential in shaping the national discussion were the scholarly contributions of various individuals, the advocacy activities of subject-matter organizations, and the policies of state and national leaders. For their own diverse reasons, a wide range of people and groups converged to frame the debate about how to improve the educational achievement of American students.

The New Cognitive Science

For most of the twentieth century, educational psychology was influenced mainly by associationist and behaviorist principles, in which learning was considered to be the consequence of the right chain of associations and behaviors, reinforced by practice and reward. For many years this view of learning validated the teaching of skills through repetitive drill and practice and the teaching of knowledge through rote memorization; appropriate rewards reinforced appropriate behavior; and learning was measured by quick responses on multiple-choice tests. Students were not permitted to learn problem-solving skills until after they had mastered the "basics" through drill and memory work.

Starting in the late 1950s, the traditional ways of teaching and testing were challenged by what came to be known as "the new cognitive science." Educational psychologists began to change their focus from measuring the *results* of learning to studying the *process* of learning. Cognitive psychologists questioned the mechanistic assumptions then widespread in American schools. They complained that behavioristic pedagogy did not encourage thinking or understanding; that students quickly forgot the answers that they had memorized; that such instruction disregarded reasoning, analyzing, problem solving, and other higher-order skills; and that multiple-choice tests subverted good instruction and critical thinking skills. Furthermore, separating the "basics" from higher-order thinking was wrong, because learning to read, write, and do arithmetic requires inference and reasoning; worse, "thinking and reasoning became not the heart of education but hoped-for capstones that many students never reached."[2]

Pioneers in the emerging field of cognitive science began to construct a new theory of learning, one whose goal was to understand *how* children learn and to use that understanding to improve systematically both instruction and assessment. They sought nothing less than a paradigm shift in the way children were taught and tested. Behind the paradigm shift was recognition, first, that American education was changing from a system of selection (that is, a system in which most students gained only basic literacy, while a small elite was selected for high-quality education) to a system that was expected to educate everyone; second, that modern life requires higher levels of competence from more people than life did in the past; and third, that most current educational tests had serious limitations. Robert Glaser of the University of Pittsburgh, a leader of the field, wrote in 1981:

> It seems clear that we are over the threshold in the transition from education as a highly selective enterprise to one that is focused on developing an entire population of educated people. . . .There is now less emphasis on selecting individuals for available educational opportunities and more on helping them to succeed in these opportunities. . . . We are now also aware that we have not come close to assessing the limits of effective instruction and that we need to begin to do this. The requirement now is to design a helping society in which we devise means for providing educational opportunities for all in equitable ways.[3]

Whereas tests had been used in the past to restrict access to education, Glaser noted that tests in the future should be used to provide information "that is oriented toward instructional decision rather than prediction. Tests in a helping society are not mere indexes which predict that the individual child will adjust to the school or which relieve the school from assisting the student to achieve as much as possible. The test and the instructional decision should be an integral event."[4]

This was a fundamental recasting of the way schools should work and called for a radical reconsideration of both instruction and testing, as well as of the linkage between them. For most of the twentieth century, tests were used to sort students according to their ability and to assign them to different tracks (academic, vocational, or general) or to admit them to advanced courses. Glaser suggested that tests should be used to improve instruction, not to parcel out opportunities for further education. He proposed that they should be designed to find out not only what students *had* learned, but why students *had not* learned what was taught; by understanding student errors and misconceptions, he held, teachers could improve instruction and reduce failure.

Researchers analyzed how children learn, the strategies that students use to solve problems, the ways that children organize and apply what they know, and the nature of the errors that students make in solving problems. Working directly with young learners, researchers studied their conceptual grasp of problems as well as the ways that they failed to understand basic principles. When children are asked to solve a problem, researchers found, they usually apply rules; when the rule is wrong or incompletely understood, the problem will be incorrectly solved. Observing children performing tasks or solving problems offered clues to children's misconceptions, as well as to the thinking processes of successful students. From this kind of research, they began to understand the ways by which novice learners could become proficient.

Certain principles have evolved from the new study of cognitive science. First, students do not simply "receive" new knowledge, they "construct" it based on their own experience, previous knowledge, and understanding. Teachers who know what the students' preconceptions are can help them understand new ideas and replace misconceptions. Second, students' previous knowledge is critically important: the more they know, the more they can learn. Schools have to build on what students already know, but schools also have to expand students' experiences and knowledge to increase their capacity for new learning. Third, assessment must be designed both to find out whether students *understand* what they have learned and to enable them to demonstrate what they know (for example, through essays, portfolios of their work, projects, and other kinds of "exhibitions" of proficiency). Fourth, students learn best by applying knowledge, skills, and problem solving to real situations ("situated learning") and when they work actively with other students and think out loud about how to solve problems ("metacognition"). This suggests the value of cooperative learning groups, where students work together to solve challenging problems by comparing notes, questioning each other, and explaining their decisions. Fifth, cognitive scientists recognized that learning is "domain-specific," because each subject-matter field has its own cognitive strategies. "Critical thinking skills" cannot be taught in isolation; knowledge of the subject matter is necessary (for example, learning how to solve algebra problems does not much improve one's ability to solve geometry or chemistry problems).[5]

Robert Glaser predicted that achievement testing in the twenty-first century "will not provide merely a score, a label, a grade level, or a percentile," but would be "a method of indexing stages of competence through indicators of the development of knowledge, skill, and cognitive process." Such assessments would be integrated with instruction and would show to student and teacher the errors and misconceptions "which need instructional attention." The object of assessment, in other words, would be to improve instruction and learning, not just to produce a grade or a ranking.[6]

Glaser's colleague Lauren Resnick took on the challenge of reforming the way the nation assesses its students. Resnick had conducted studies of how children learn mathematics and, with her husband, Daniel Resnick, had written several essays on the historical relationship between curriculum and assessment. Convinced that changing the way children were tested was the key to changing curriculum and instruction, Resnick joined in partnership with Marc Tucker of the National Center for Education and the Economy to found the New Standards Project, whose goal was to design a national examination system. Funded by major foundations in 1991, the New

Standards Project created a partnership with nearly a score of states to explore new ways to test student performance.

Behind the New Standards Project was a logical argument: what is tested determines what is taught. Lauren and Daniel Resnick believed that the United States in the nineteenth century had "developed two educational systems—one designed for an elite, the other for the mass of our population." While elites learned high-level skills such as reasoning and problem solving, the mass system "was intended to teach routine skills: simple computation, reading predictable texts, reciting civic or religious codes." The current system remained wedded to its origins, they maintained, and standards were far too low, even for students in the college preparatory track. What was needed now for a technologically sophisticated economy, they held, was "a significant new educational agenda . . . a thinking-oriented curriculum for all. . . .While it is not new to include thinking, problem-solving, and reasoning in *some* students' school curriculum, it is new to include it in *everyone's* curriculum."[7]

The Resnicks' analysis was radical indeed. They maintained that "a thinking curriculum" for all was impossible so long as the schools continued to rely exclusively on standardized, multiple-choice tests. Such tests are based on behavioristic principles of learning; they break learning into little bits of decontextualized knowledge, which students produce on request but do not necessarily know how to use outside the classroom. When teachers try to raise test scores by teaching to this kind of test, instruction becomes focused on meeting the demands of the test. Thus, teaching to a multiple-choice test that was developed without regard to the school's curriculum not only gives the test too much power, but corrupts instruction and devalues thoughtful, reflective study.

The only way to change the current system's low expectations and to introduce a thinking curriculum, the Resnicks held, is to change the means of assessing students. They argued for an examination system that is tied to the curriculum, "for which teachers can legitimately prepare students, and for which students can study."[8] Most current tests, they noted, are designed to be divorced from the curriculum: it is considered cheating for teachers to prepare children for standardized tests, and college admission tests are supposed to be "curriculum-free." Although standardized tests (whose contents are a secret until the test is given) may serve adequately for accountability purposes (to monitor the school's performance), they cannot simultaneously motivate students and improve instruction, the Resnicks said. In place of current tests, they recommended external examinations "coupled with publicized syllabi," jointly developed by teachers and scholars.[9] Other nations, such as Germany and France, offer a well-established precedent for such tests.

Lauren Resnick, Tucker, and the New Standards Project maintained that current tests should be replaced by *performance assessments* based on high standards. Performance assessment, also called authentic assessment, might consist of portfolios and projects or other means by which students could demonstrate that they understood and could apply what they had studied. With a well-designed assessment, the teacher and student would find out what the student has and has not learned. Performance assessment is intended not just to produce a test score, but to improve teaching, curriculum, and learning. Teachers could prepare students for the assessment, and students could take it again and again until they were able to show that they had learned what was taught.

From a strategic point of view, Resnick argued that the federal role should be limited to providing financial support for "broadly specified national standards," such as the mathematics standards created by the National Council for Mathematics Teachers. These national standards should be sufficiently broad so that states and localities can "craft curricula and assessments . . . suitable to their own communities." In addition, Resnick opposed federal support for "central national tests—even strongly performance oriented ones—intended for administration to all children in the nation at particular grade-levels. . . ."[10] Whether mandatory or voluntary, she maintained, a federally controlled test was undesirable because teachers would have little or no opportunity to influence it. She argued that both tests and curricula "need to engage the energies of those closest to instruction" and need to leave room for substantial local variation.

The project worked closely with teachers to develop tasks for performance assessments of fourth and eighth graders. This process was meant not only to create the assessment, but also to give teachers a sense of ownership. Resnick contended that the project would succeed only if the new higher standards were internalized "by teachers at first, and eventually by students."[11] In 1992 the New Standards Project piloted performance tasks with 10,000 fourth graders; in 1993 the project tried out additional tasks with 50,000 fourth and eighth graders. Hundreds of teachers convened during the summer to score the student responses and to determine their ability to score them with reliability and consistency.

Seventy performance tasks were administered to fourth graders in the 1993 trial, including the following. It is called "Checker Tournament."

> Marc, Ana, Julia and Daniel decide to have a checker tournament at school. They want to be sure that each of them gets a chance to play each of the others one time. They ask you to make a schedule for the tournament. Here is the information you need to make a plan that works:
>
> - They want to finish the tournament in one week. They can play from Monday to Friday.
>
> - They will play only at lunchtime. There is enough time during lunch period to play one game of checkers.
>
> - The students have two checker sets, so two games can be going on at once.
>
> - Marc can't play checkers on the days he is a lunch helper (Mondays and Wednesdays)
>
> - Each player must play every other player once.
>
> Make a schedule for the tournament. Your schedule should make it easy for everyone to see who plays whom each day.[12]

Students were allowed forty-five minutes to complete the task, but the teacher could offer more time if needed. Teachers from participating states developed a scoring "rubric" from 0 to 4, to represent different levels of achievement. The purpose of this activity was to demonstrate that the idea itself could work—that teachers could create tasks requiring thinking and problem solving, that the tasks could be scored with a high degree of agreement among scorers, and that such assessments, regularly administered, had the potential to change both what was taught and how it was taught.

As the national debate on standards and assessments progressed, the New Standards Project offered its program to states as an alternative to a federally sponsored and controlled testing system. The states that supported the project intended to use its examinations in different ways: some planned to use it as their state examination; some intended to revise their state examinations to conform to the principles of the New Standards Project; others planned to integrate the New Standards Project examination into their state testing program.

It remains to be seen whether the New Standards Project can achieve its goal of creating a national examination system with high standards and local variation. It is a gargantuan task, and one fraught with unresolved technical problems. What it has already done, however, largely through the effective research and advocacy of Lauren Resnick, is to give legitimacy to the value of performance assessments as a way to encourage thoughtfulness and understanding, high standards for *all* children, external examinations tied directly to the curriculum, and the involvement of teachers in a central role (not just as teacher representatives on a committee of experts).

Comparative Cultural Analysis

In 1980 Harold W. Stevenson, a research psychologist at the University of Michigan, began a series of cross-national studies, working with colleagues in Taiwan and Japan and later also in China, to examine achievement in mathematics and reading at the first- and fifth-grade levels. The work of Stevenson and his associates appeared just as state and national leaders wanted to know what "world-class" standards were and how American students compared with their peers in other countries. In contrast to the international assessments, which provide rankings but little insight into why students perform well or poorly, Stevenson's group developed an extremely sophisticated causal analysis that identified the reasons for good and poor achievement.

Stevenson's cross-national studies were enormously influential for several reasons. His findings were published in widely circulated and respected magazines such as *Science* and *Scientific American,* where they were immediately noticed by the national press. They offered a clear and understandable interpretation of achievement differences between American and Asian students. Stevenson's sophisticated research methods avoided the conceptual weaknesses of international assessments, which had recurrent problems with sampling and with finding the right match between what was taught and what was tested.

Stevenson's studies were carefully constructed, longitudinal, and in-depth. In contrast to the international assessments, which are a snap-shot of a single performance, Stevenson used a combination of testing; interviews with students, teachers and parents; and classroom obser-vations to monitor performance over time and to understand differ-ential performance.

Working with scholars from the other nations, Stevenson selected students and schools in Minneapolis, Sendai, Japan, and Taipei, Tai-wan, from similar socioeconomic backgrounds.[13] The researchers ex-amined textbooks and constructed tests of material that was actually taught, making sure that the content and language of the tests were culturally appropriate. They administered the tests to thousands of students, then selected random samples for in-depth testing and in-terviews. They spent hundreds of hours observing in classrooms and interviewing teachers, children, and parents.[14]

What they found was that schoolchildren in Asia performed better academically than those in the United States, and that the academic gap grew larger between first and fifth grades. American students performed best in reading in first grade, but Asian students caught up by fifth grade. In mathematics the differences among first graders from the different nations were small. By fifth grade, however, American students were far behind students from Japan and Taiwan. In fact, "the highest average score of an American fifth-grade classroom was below that of the Japanese fifth-grade classroom with the lowest av-erage score. In addition, only one Chinese classroom showed an av-erage score lower than the American classroom with the highest av-erage score. Equally remarkable is the fact that the lowest average score for a *fifth-grade* American classroom was only slightly higher than the average score for the best *first-grade* Chinese classroom."[15]

The research team returned to Minneapolis, Taipei, and Sendai in 1990 and 1991 to test fifth graders and to find eleventh graders who had been part of their original study in 1980. They found that the achievement gap in mathematics was consistent among fifth grad-ers throughout the decade. "Japanese children were consistently su-perior to the American children, and the difference between the per-formance of the Chinese and American children was greater in 1990 than in 1980. The gap is large: for example, only 4.1% of the Chinese children and 10.3% of the Japanese children in 1990 had scores as low as those of the average American child." Among eleventh graders, the disparities continued to be large: "Only 14.5% of the Chinese and 8.0% of the Japanese students received scores below the average score of the American students." When the researchers compared the scores of the top 10 percent of students from each location, they found that the performance of the top Minneapolis students—in both the fifth and eleventh grades—"was more similar to that of the average Taipei and Sendai students than it was to the top students in those cities."[16]

What accounted for these large differences in mathematics achievement? Stevenson pointed out that American students do very well, better than their Asian peers, on tests of general information. In mathematics, "where performance is highly dependent on academic instruction," however, Americans fall behind.[17] Stevenson identified several factors that contribute to poor academic performance by American students.

First, *American students spent less time in academic activities, either in school or at home.* In the American classrooms, 64.5 percent of the time was devoted to academic activities in fifth grade, compared with 91.5 percent in Taiwanese classrooms, and 87.4 percent in Japanese classrooms. This translated into 19.6 hours of instruction a week in Minneapolis, 40.4 hours in Taipei, and 32.6 hours in Sendai. "In both grades 1 and 5, American children spent less than 20 percent of their time on the average studying mathematics in school. This was less than the percentage for either Chinese or Japanese children." In the fifth grade, Asian children spent equal amounts of time on reading and mathematics, but American children spent twice as much time on reading (40 percent) as on mathematics (17 percent). In some American classrooms, "no time was devoted to work in mathematics, during the approximately 40 randomly selected hours when an observer was present."[18] A curious finding about use of time in school was that American students were out of the classroom 18.4 percent of the time that they were to be observed; absence from the classroom during the observation period almost never occurred in the Asian schools. At home, fifth graders in Minneapolis spent 46 minutes each day on schoolwork, compared with 57 minutes by Japanese students, and 114 minutes by Chinese students.

Second, *American teachers usually worked in isolation, while Asian teachers collaborated to improve their teaching.* In Asian countries, which have a national curriculum, teachers work together more frequently as a group than they do in the United States, because "they are all teaching the same lesson at about the same time. More experienced teachers help newer ones. Head teachers in each grade organize meetings to discuss technique and to devise lesson plans and handouts. The group may spend hours designing a single lesson or discussing how to frame questions that will produce the greatest understanding from their pupils." By contrast, most American teachers work alone, "with few opportunities for professional interaction or consultation." Lacking a national curriculum or guidelines, "American schools typically develop their own agenda. In any year the curriculum may not be consistent within a city or even within a single school. Adding further to the diversity in the curricula among American classrooms is the fact that teachers are free to proceed through textbooks at any rate they wish, skipping the parts they do not find especially interesting or useful." When the researchers asked teachers in Beijing and Chicago what they considered the most important characteristics of a good teacher, the most common response in Beijing was "clarity," while the most common response in Chicago was "sensitivity to the needs of the individual."[19]

Third, *American parents were very satisfied with their children's schools and their children's performance, while Asian parents were not.* One of the most striking findings of the first study was that American mothers were very pleased with their children's school: 91 percent rated it either "excellent" or "good;" only 42 percent of Chinese mothers and 39 percent of Japanese mothers gave their children's school similar ratings. When asked whether they were satisfied with their children's current academic performance, more than 40 percent of American mothers were "very satisfied;" fewer than 6 percent of Chinese and Japanese mothers were.[20] Stevenson speculated that the high level of satisfaction among American mothers stemmed from a lack of information; he had expected that the many press reports in the 1980s about American students' poor performance on international assessments would have caused "diminished satisfaction by American mothers." But, he found, that was not the case; "if anything, somewhat more American mothers said they were 'very satisfied' with their children's performance in 1990 compared with 1980." Stevenson concluded that American parents are very satisfied because "they seldom receive clear, explicit information about their children's standing in academic subjects." The positive attitudes of American parents were shared by their children, who "expressed confidence that they were doing as well in school as their parents and teachers wanted. Asian students were less sure." Stevenson observed, "in view of the persistence of such positive attitudes and of the continued poor performance of American students, one must wonder about the degree of popular support that exists generally in the United States for extensive changes in elementary and secondary education."[21]

Fourth, *American students and their parents attributed academic success to ability; Asian students and their parents attributed academic success to effort.* One of the most important findings to emerge from Stevenson's cross-national studies was what he learned about "parental beliefs." American mothers believe that *ability* contributes most to students' performance in school, while Asian mothers believe that *effort* contributes most to academic success. Stevenson noted that "parents who emphasize ability as the most important requisite for success may be less disposed to stress the need to work hard than would parents who believe success is largely dependent on effort."[22] When they interviewed eleventh graders and their teachers in 1990–91, his team asked, "Here are some factors that may influence students' performance in mathematics: a good teacher, innate intelligence, home environment, and studying hard. Which do you think is the most important factor?" The majority of Asian students thought that studying hard was most important, but only 27 percent of American students agreed. Most American students (54 percent) thought that the most important factor was a good teacher. When teachers were asked the same question, 93 percent of Japanese teachers but only 26 percent of American teachers said studying hard. Two-fifths of American teachers—41 percent—said "innate intelligence."[23]

Stevenson identified a fundamental cause of poor student achievement: American students, their parents, and—to some extent—even their teachers believe that innate intelligence, not hard work, is the primary determinant of success in school. These attitudes, which demean the value of studying and effort, are reinforced by tests of aptitude or ability, such as IQ tests and the SAT. Although the College Board changed the name of the SAT in 1993 from the "Scholastic Aptitude Test" to simply the "SAT," it originated as a test of aptitude for college work, whose purpose was to predict whether students were likely to do well in college. This is markedly different from a test of achievement, in which students are tested on what they have studied rather than on their general abilities or intelligence or skills.

Knowing that American educators tend to disregard comparisons with Japan, on grounds that Japanese students are under too much academic pressure and that Americans therefore have nothing to learn from the Japanese approach to education, Stevenson interviewed eleventh-grade students in both countries and found that "American students reported the most frequent feelings of stress, academic anxiety, and aggression" and "the most common source of stress was school."[24] To those who assumed that Asian students were "smarter" than American students, Stevenson explained that there was no difference in cognitive functioning among the children in the three nations.[25] Furthermore, Stevenson found that the Americans' scores on tests of general information exceeded those of Asian children and concluded: "Thus, throughout their schooling American students proved to be as capable as or even more capable than the Asian students when they were tested with items not based on the school curriculum."[26]

Stevenson's research demonstrated that "the achievement gap is real, that it is persistent, and that it is unlikely to diminish until, among other things, there are marked changes in the attitudes and beliefs of American parents and students about education."[27] Perhaps most corrosive to academic achievement in the United States is the widely held belief that innate ability counts for more than effort. Students who believe this are not likely to study hard; parents who believe this are not likely to encourage their children to keep trying; teachers who believe this are less likely to set high expectations for their students, except for those who are identifiably "smart." Perhaps most disturbing among his findings is that American students and parents are generally satisfied with the current level of academic performance.[28]

That high level of satisfaction reflects the fact that parents and their children have no external standards by which to gauge the quality of academic achievement, and consequently neither parents nor students are accurately informed about whether student achievement is good enough and how it compares to standards of achievement in other modern societies.

Economic Analysis

While psychologists such as Robert Glaser and Lauren Resnick decried the influence of behaviorism in instruction and testing, economists maintained that the American educational system had thrown

out behaviorism where it mattered most: in the incentives and sanctions connected to working and studying hard in school. Economists
argued, first, that education was more important than ever; second,
that American students had little motivation to work hard in school;
and third, that students would not take school seriously unless they
knew that their grades and their effort in school would affect employment decisions and their admission to college.

Economists saw that the American economy was going through
a major restructuring because of new technologies, new ways of or-
ganizing work, and new international competition. They predicted
that jobs for unskilled and semiskilled workers would virtually vanish
and that everyone in the United States would need a much higher
level of general education. Peter Drucker maintained that "knowledge
has become the key resource for all work. . . .The only long-term
policy which promises success is for developed countries *to convert
manufacturing from being labor based into being knowledge based.*"
The greatest employment need of the future, he foresaw, would be
for technicians who "possess a substantial amount of formal knowledge, formal education, and the capacity for continuous learning."[29]
Lester Thurow held that "in the twenty first century, the education
and skills of the work force will end up being the dominant competitive weapon" among nations. Success, he claimed, would go to the
nation having a "work force skilled from top to bottom."[30]

In a review of American competitiveness, economists Martin Neil
Baily, Gary Burtless, and Robert E. Litan recommended a strategy of
national education standards and assessments. They held that "the
nation ought to specify core elements that must be included in all
secondary curriculums, and it must develop specific standards identified with 'sufficient,' 'good,' and 'superior' knowledge of each subject." Furthermore, they said, "students should be required to demonstrate mastery of the core subjects on nationally recognized tests."
These tests, they believed, had to be mandatory or they would lose
their meaning.[31] One widely publicized report, *America's Choice:
High Skills or Low Wages!*, declared that the United States was not
producing "a highly educated workforce" because it lacked "a clear
standard of achievement and few students are motivated to work hard
in school." Students see "little or no relationship between how well
they do in school and what kind of job they can get after school."
The report recommended that "a new educational performance standard should be set for all students, to be met by age 16. This standard

should be established nationally and benchmarked to the highest in the world."[32] The report stressed the importance of educating the non-college-bound for high performance workplaces. As a result *America's Choice* stimulated interest in several states and in Washington in strengthening the school-to-work transition. The primary author of the report was Marc Tucker, director of the National Center for Education and the Economy and co-director with Lauren Resnick of the New Standards Project.

America's Choice, like many other major reports and studies of the late 1980s and early 1990s, reflected the influence of John Bishop, a labor economist at Cornell University.[33] Bishop—a former director of the Center for Research on Youth Employability and associate director for research in the National Center for Research in Vocational Education—had initially concentrated on the effectiveness of schooling in preparing young people for the labor market. In the mid-1980s Bishop reviewed data from NAEP surveys and international assessments and asked why American students learned so little and what could be done about it. Bishop argued that the nation's standard of living depended in large part on having a well-educated work force. He noted that cognitive skills contribute to productivity because "they *help the worker learn new tasks more quickly.* . . .The quality of education is not the only determinant of a worker's productivity and a nation's competitiveness and standard of living, but it is probably the most important determinant that is under the control of government."[34]

The key to American students' poor performance, Bishop held, is apathy and lack of motivation. The typical high school student spends only eighteen to twenty-two hours each week on instruction and study, compared with twenty-four hours each week on television and another ten in a part-time job. Teachers cannot demand much because many students are passive and uninterested in learning. He pointed to several research studies that documented student apathy, citing Theodore Sizer's observation that "no more important finding has emerged from . . . our study than that the American high school student, *as student,* is all too often docile, compliant, and without initiative."[35] Bishop argued that:

> The fundamental cause of the problem is our uncritical acceptance of institutional arrangements that do not adequately recognize and reinforce student effort and achievement. During the

1960s and 1970s we adopted practices and curricula that hid a failure to teach, that protected adolescents from the consequences of failing to learn, and that prevented many of those who did learn from reaping the fruits of their labor. Although there are benefits to staying in school, *most students realize few benefits from working hard while in school.* The lack of incentives for effort is a consequence of three phenomena:

- The labor market fails to reward effort and achievement in high school.

- The peer group actively discourages academic effort.

- Admission to selective colleges is not based on an absolute or external standard of achievement in high school subjects. It is based instead on aptitude tests which do not assess the high school curriculum and on such measures of student performance as class rank and grade point averages, which are defined relative to classmates' performances, not relative to an external standard.

Bishop maintained that high school grades have "essentially no impact" on a student's ability to get a job or on wage rates because employers seldom ask prospective employees about grades or for a high school transcript. It is not because cognitive skills are unimportant; in fact, higher test scores in reading, mathematics, science, and problem solving "are strongly related to productivity on the job." Employers' unwillingness to check grades, he says, "probably reflects the low reliability of self-reported data, the difficulties of verifying it, and the fear of EEO [Equal Employment Opportunities Commission] challenges to such questions." Students are quick to recognize that hard work in school is not rewarded in the labor market. Nor are the schools prepared to respond when employers do ask for transcripts. Bishop cited the case of an insurance company in Ohio that sent 1,200 requests (with the job applicants' permission) for high school records, but received only 93 responses from the schools.

And what incentives are there for the college bound to study? If they plan to go to a selective college, their chances are determined partially by grades, but also by a college admission test that measures their "aptitude," not what they have learned in high school. If they are among the majority who plan to go to a nonselective college, then all that matters is that they have a diploma and perhaps took certain courses; their grades do not matter. This indifference to effort and learning, Bishop observed, seems to be "a peculiarly American phenomenon." In Germany school marks determine who gets the best apprenticeships. In Australia, Canada, Japan, and many European countries, examinations are based on the curriculum, and students' performance on these examinations determines whether they will enter a university, which field they will study, and whether they will get a good job. Because the examination has consequences and is based directly on what is taught in school, students work hard to master what is taught in school. "National exams are the yardstick, so achievement tends to be measured relative to everyone else's in the nation and not just relative to the child's classmates," Bishop explained.

Another cause of low motivation, Bishop said, is "peer pressure against studying hard." Students are in a zero-sum competition with their classmates for good grades; their achievement is "not being measured against an absolute, external standard. . . .When students try hard to excel, they set themselves apart, cause rivalries and may make things worse for friends. *When we set up a zero competition among friends, we should not be surprised when they decide not to compete.* All work groups have ways of sanctioning 'rate busters.' " Bishop contrasted the zero-sum competition for grades and class rank with the awarding of scout merit badges, where scouts are recognized for reaching a fixed standard of competence, and there is no limit on how many can gain recognition. And he contrasted students' apathy in the classroom with their energetic involvement in sports activities, where team members have "shared goals, shared successes and external measures of achievement." On the sports field, team spirit is a strong motivation; in the classroom, success is "purely personal." Furthermore, because few students ever win recognition for academic accomplishments (and they are usually the same students year after year), many others simply give up trying.

Bishop concluded that the key to higher performance is to recognize and reward effort and achievement. To do this employers must request high school transcripts and factor academic achievement into hiring decisions. Schools should encourage cooperative learning groups, with competition between evenly matched teams rather than individuals. All students should have a "competency profile," which records their academic, vocational, artistic, and extracurricular accomplishments. Every student who works hard should have a good chance for recognition. All of these measures should be available to help students find jobs. For the college bound, less emphasis should be placed on relative measures (such as grading on the curve or class rank) and more on absolute standards, such as Advanced Placement examinations.[36]

Albert Shanker, president of the American Federation of Teachers, frequently invoked Bishop's analysis in his weekly column in the *New York Times,* where he advocated high national standards and a national examination system with real consequences for college admission and employment. "National standards and exams go hand in hand," he wrote. "Critics here say that testing kids won't make them work harder, but in [other] countries, the national tests have important consequences. Kids know they need to work hard because test scores determine whether or not they get into university or what kind of job they get. This sounds harsh, but it is fairer than our system. Everybody knows exactly what is required to succeed, so students can work toward this goal and teachers can help them."[37]

To other economists, if not to educators, Bishop's prescriptions were self-evident. Robert J. Samuelson, a columnist for the Washington Post and *Newsweek,* pointed out that "the main reason that most American students don't do as well as they might is that they don't work very hard." Samuelson argued that only rewards and sanctions would induce students to work harder: "Tougher standards matter only if they affect students directly. The federal government might require students applying for federal college aid (about half those going to college) to pass a qualifying test. The message would be: If you don't learn in high school, you won't go to college on public money. For other students, we could encourage employers to use national tests and high school transcripts for hiring decisions. The message: The better you do in high school, the better job you may get." But Samuelson acknowledged that the chance of anyone actually adopting such remedies was remote: "Congress has repeatedly refused to impose a meaningful academic requirement on federal college aid. And civil rights laws deter employers from using general tests or high school records. Companies are supposed to use tests directly related to specific jobs. Anything that merely indicates general competence or diligence is legally suspect."[38]

The poor motivation of American students has been the subject of several studies, which analyze the informal understandings between uninterested students and discouraged teachers. The authors of *The Shopping Mall High School* depicted comprehensive high schools in which teachers and students typically reach tacit arrangements to keep the peace. "Some want to learn or teach. Others want to get through courses with as little effort as possible. Still others are wholly uncommitted," they wrote.[39] The authors of *Selling Students Short* described the "bargain" between teachers and students to limit academic demands:

> In most high schools there exists a complex, tacit conspiracy to avoid sustained, rigorous, demanding academic inquiry. A 'bargain' of sorts is struck that demands little academically of either teachers or students. . . .When set at a low level, the bargain's essential features include: relatively little concern for academic content; a willingness to tolerate, if not encourage, diversion from the specified knowledge to be presented or discussed; the substitution of genial banter and conversation for concentrated academic exercises; improvisational instructional adaptation to student preference for or indifference toward specific subject matter or pedagogical techniques; the 'negotiation' of class content, assignments, and standards.

These attitudes, the authors concluded, are not confined to urban schools where performance is lowest but are common "to the vast majority of high schools," affecting perhaps as much as 70 percent of secondary classrooms.[40]

The continued indifference of employers and most colleges to high school grades has profoundly undermined not only the students' willingness to work in school but the authority of their teachers, who cannot either reward or punish students, according to economist James E. Rosenbaum of Northwestern University. Changes in values and legal rulings mean that sanctions such as expulsion and nonpromotion are seldom used. Because employers regularly ignore student grades, the teachers' main measure of performance, teachers are like "lion-tamers without a whip," who cannot make demands on students. Teachers and students tacitly agree to demand little of each other (if you don't bother me, I won't bother you). Consequently, "American high schools have dramatically lowered standards for graduation, and the high school credential is no longer a meaningful signal of academic achievement." Students know they need a diploma but, because employers seem uninterested in what students studied, "they do not see any reason to learn what is taught in school." The best ways to improve the quality of the young work force, Rosenbaum argued, are to increase "student incentives and teacher authority."[41]

In contrast to the situation in the United States, Japan has established a school-to-work transition that strengthens the teachers' authority and encourages students to study conscientiously in school. Japanese employers not only send notices of job openings to schools, but they also ask schools to nominate students for these jobs. Rosenbaum noted that "while over 75% of Japanese high-school seniors used schools' job placement activities to find jobs, fewer than 10% of US seniors used their school's placement services." Unlike schools in Japan, which help their students whether they are going to college or to work, most American schools spend more effort on college placement, helping students to meet recruiters and sending out transcripts to college. Few high schools have contacts with employers, and many do not even know whether their graduates got jobs.

American students, Rosenbaum said, are pragmatic: "If they believe that school achievement affects their future careers, they will work in school." But in fact, they know that "grades and test scores have little effect on which youths get jobs, better jobs, or better wages."[42] Rosenbaum holds that it is up to employers to restore incentives and teacher authority by taking into account grades, test scores, and school recommendations when making hiring decisions. Schools can help employers do this by creating transcripts that make sense to employers; for example, schools might give separate grades for effort and for achievement, so that hard-working students in the bottom half of the class do not give up but instead gain recognition for their diligence. He argues for closer ties between schools and employers; students need to know that their future employability will be affected by their performance in school and their teachers' recommendations.

Bishop, Rosenbaum, and other economists maintain that students respond to the rewards, sanctions, and consequences that follow their behavior in school. Absent these, students know that what happens in school does not matter to their future.

Economists who have examined the performance of American schools seem to agree that educational standards must be higher than ever before in American history, not only for those bound for college, but for all students. These economists recognize the profound changes wrought by new technologies, by the new competition among nations for markets and products, and by the restructuring of the workplace from a hierarchical, top-down, factory model, to a model in which workers are expected to collaborate, innovate, and make decisions. They see standards and examinations as part of an incentive and signaling system. Evidence of student performance—both grades and test scores—should become part of the student's record, which would affect decisions about college entry and employment. Effort and achievement should be rewarded. Schools and employers should work closely together. Colleges should establish clear standards for incoming students, taking into account grades and courses taken. Such a system would establish the importance of learning, make teaching a powerful and honored profession, and motivate students to work hard for valued and attainable rewards.

Subject-Matter Reform

In 1990, when the president and the governors established national education goals, the third goal decreed that all students should be able to demonstrate competency in English, mathematics, science, history, and geography. What the president and the governors did not know was that in only one of the subject fields listed—mathematics—were educators ready to say what children should learn and teachers should teach. In no other field was there general agreement on what should be taught, and in no field, including mathematics, was there any widely accepted test that schools could use to ascertain how well students are performing.

Part of the problem was that all of the fields, for different reasons, were torn by factionalism, in revolt against the status quo, or suffering from years of neglect. Science educators, for example, had been unhappy for years because of the neglect of science in the schools. Unquestionably a subject that is necessary for understanding fast-paced technological change, science was nonetheless not given its due in the school curriculum. Little time was allotted for science in the elementary grades; it had no guaranteed place in the junior high years; and it was locked into a pattern in the high school that guaranteed diminishing enrollments each year (most students took a year of biology, half the students took a year of chemistry, and about 10 percent enrolled in physics).

Several well-established professional organizations—such as the National Science Teachers Association and the American Association for the Advancement of Science—agreed on the poor condition of the subject in American schools. They agreed too that students needed to spend more time doing "hands-on" science (meaning experiments and projects, as opposed to textbook study) and that they needed better-equipped laboratories and better-educated teachers. Yet the science organizations had not agreed on content standards, and without content standards, there could be no meaningful examinations at a state or national level, or any popular consensus that science should be taught in every grade to everyone, not just the college bound.

The other three fields—history, geography, and English—were in even worse shape. Since the creation of the "social studies" field in 1916, both history and geography had been in retreat as school subjects. Over the decades, the social studies had evolved into a nondisciplinary mélange of the social sciences, civics, and sociopersonal engineering. Every attempt to define the field tended to devolve into pedagogical jargon about such activities as decisionmaking, developing self-esteem, "group problem solving," "social mathematics,"[43] "valuing self and others," and "understandings and attitudes."[44]

History, once considered the core of the social studies, eventually became only one among many competing courses in the social studies curriculum. Some state departments of education, rather than drop history outright, renamed it "cultural heritage," suggesting that study of the past has value only when it pertains to someone's ancestors.[45] A 1986 survey, funded by the National Endowment for the Humanities, concluded that sizable numbers of high school juniors had little knowledge of important events in American history.[46] This was not surprising, because the time allotted to history had diminished as the social studies field expanded. Typically, most students study American history in the fifth, eighth, and eleventh grades; about half study world history for one year in high school.

In 1987 the state of California took the unusual step of making history the central focus of the social studies in almost every grade (by adding three years of world history to three years of American history and increasing historical activities in the elementary grades).[47] In 1988 the Bradley Commission on History in Schools, a panel composed of historians and teachers, proposed "that the kindergarten through grade six social studies curriculum be history-centered" and that four years of American and world history should be required of students between grades seven and twelve.[48] Yet efforts to revive history as a study that could be pursued with delight by students of all ages have been stymied by the social studies field, which controls key supervisory positions in state departments of education and has a strong professional association (the National Council for the Social Studies). Although a professional organization (the National Council for History Education) was created in 1990 to support history in the schools, students in grades four, eight, and twelve are unlikely to be able to demonstrate competency in history unless it is taught more frequently than it is now, by teachers who have actually studied history (in California and New York teachers can be certified to teach social studies without ever having taken a college course in history).

Geography is in even more trouble than history because it virtually disappeared from the school curriculum after the ascent of the social studies. A major course of study in many other countries, geography in the United States became little more than an add-on, a time for map study, seldom taught by teachers who had studied the discipline of geography. In 1984 the National Council for Geographic Education and the Association of American Geographers published guidelines for geographic education, which included content standards for elementary and secondary schools, but few schools had teachers trained to teach the subject.[49] It was the energetic activities of the National Geographic Society that revived geography. The society not only spent millions of dollars on teacher training, but also lobbied to include geography as a core academic subject in the national goals. In the 1980s the society commissioned surveys that revealed geographic ignorance, initiated a NAEP survey of high school seniors' geographic knowledge, and sponsored a Gallup Poll, which found that "Americans' geographic literacy has gotten worse in the last 40 years" and that American 18-to-24-year-olds knew less geography than their peers in eight other nations.[50] When the U.S. Department of Education began making grants to professional organizations for standard setting in 1991–92, the partisans of geography were well organized and well prepared to reach consensus about what children should learn. Although those in the field were ready to agree on standards, the dominant position of the social studies and the very small number of trained geography teachers offered little assurance that geography would find a regular place in the school curriculum.

English encounters problems different from those of any other school subject. Well ensconced in the schools and with many well-educated teachers, English is nonetheless rife with ideological and political dissension. In the elementary schools decades of struggle over reading methods continued unabated, as champions of phonics and advocates of "whole-language learning" struggle with one another. In the middle and high schools, the once traditional curriculum based on great literary works of Britain and the United States became embroiled in fractious battles over multiculturalism and "the canon." Long before the debate over multiculturalism arose, many members of the field preferred to call it "language arts" rather than English, to avoid implying that they preferred one language over another. During the 1960s and 1970s, side battles broke out over issues such as the teaching of spelling, punctuation, and grammar, a practice that seems to allot higher status to a "standard" version of the language and that might (some leaders of the field believe) discourage students by calling attention to their errors. These ideological struggles continued to rage during the 1980s, and it was by no means certain that the field could agree long enough to set standards (that act itself being not only dubious but possibly dangerous to leaders in the field, who feared that a standard implied that some version of language study would be privileged over all others).[51]

Alone among all the subjects described in the national education goals, the field of mathematics had adopted standards. The mathematics field had several strengths: a major professional organization, the National Council of Teachers of Mathematics (NCTM), that was a staunch proponent of reform; experienced leaders who had been working to change the teaching of mathematics for more than twenty years; and a minimal number of divisive controversies. Although members of the profession differed over how to teach mathematics, differences about defining the field itself were insignificant.

The disastrous fate of the "new math" in the 1960s energized the NCTM as a political force. Supported by the federal government and designed for students in the college-preparatory track, the new math was based on the belief that the best way to teach the subject was to teach its structure and its unifying ideas. Enthusiasm initially greeted these innovations, but as they spread to elementary schools and non-college-bound classes, resistance grew. Critics, including parents and teachers, complained that the new math was too abstract, too formal, too theoretical.[52] By the mid-1970s the new math had been swept away by a "back-to-basics" movement, supported by minimum competency testing, which restored traditional computation with whole numbers.

The new-math debacle produced much soul-searching among mathematics teachers and professors and more than a few reports. Leaders of the field recognized that future efforts to reform mathematics would have to target all children, not just the college bound, and would have to stress *application* of concepts, not just theory and concepts. In a report that has been called "a turning point in the collective consciousness of the professional mathematics community,"[53] a prestigious commission of mathematics educators recommended in 1975 that "concrete experiences be an integral part of the acquisition of abstract ideas" and that "the opportunity be provided for students to apply mathematics in as wide a realm as possible. . . ."[54] The commission recommended the use of calculators in the classroom and the ouster of norm-referenced standardized testing. Well aware that most teachers were restricting their teaching only to what was tested, the commission sought a better match between the tests used and the kind of instruction offered. If the test was a fill-in-the-blanks sort, then the instruction would be equally limited.

In 1980, still trying to dislodge the back-to-basics movement, the NCTM issued *An Agenda for Action: Recommendations for School Mathematics of the 1980s*. Expanding on the 1975 report, the NCTM recommended that "problem solving be the focus of school mathematics in the 1980s," that basic skills "be defined to encompass more than computational facility," that calculators and computers be made widely available, that "stringent standards of both effectiveness and efficiency be applied to the teaching of mathematics," that more mathematics study be required "for all students" in a flexible curriculum with many options, and that mathematics programs be evaluated by a broader range of measures than conventional testing.[55] By problem solving, the NCTM meant something more than the conventional "word problems" found in most textbooks; it proposed that students should encounter real-world problems in unfamiliar settings that would require them to apply mathematical skills and concepts.

The NCTM believed that students spent far too much time on computation, drill, and rote memory work. The organization wanted students to be taught to think mathematically, instead of using mathematics in an automatic, formulaic manner. Yet the leaders of the NCTM—including Shirley A. Hill of the University of Missouri,

F. Joe Crosswhite of Ohio State University, John A. Dossey of Illinois State University, Shirley M. Frye of the Scottsdale, Arizona, school district, and Thomas A. Romberg of the University of Wisconsin— had a serious problem: dislodging an approach that was well entrenched in the schools and replacing it with a vision of what they thought mathematics education should be.

In 1984, building on the momentum and public attention that followed the publication of *A Nation at Risk,* a national conference of mathematics educators conceived a strategy to implement the vision. They recommended, first, the development of "guidelines" for every grade from kindergarten through the sophomore year of college, and second, the establishment of a national steering committee to monitor reform at the federal, state, and local levels. The proposed guidelines eventually became the NCTM standards for curriculum and evaluation; the proposed steering committee was created in 1985 by the prestigious National Research Council in Washington, D.C., and was called the Mathematical Sciences Education Board (MSEB). In the following years MSEB served as a lobby for mathematics education in the nation's capital.

The mathematics leaders immediately recognized that the proposed content standards could be a lever for changing teaching methods, testing, teacher training, computer software, and textbooks. The standards, they agreed, "should include a detailed outline of the suggested mathematical topics to be taught at each grade, an estimate of the time to be spent on each topic, options for including topics, options for sequencing topics, the way topics should be organized for instruction, possible materials for instruction, the instructional methods which teachers might use for those materials, and suggested standards for student performance following instruction."[56]

By 1986 the NCTM had organized a Commission on Standards for School Mathematics. The following year, writing teams composed of teachers, supervisors, mathematicians, teacher educators, and researchers reviewed curriculum documents from leading states and other nations and began drafting standards for curriculum and evaluation. Ten thousand copies of a draft statement of standards were circulated for review to teachers, parents, business leaders, and others. The writing teams met again to revise the draft in 1988, and in 1989 the NCTM standards for curriculum and evaluation were published.[57]

The goal of the standards was not just to reform the teaching of mathematics, but to revolutionize it. The traditional approach was to teach mathematics as "a collection of fixed concepts and skills to be taught and mastered in a certain strict order." The new NCTM standards discarded this approach and substituted for it the idea of mathematics as a dynamic discipline, one in which problem solving and meaning take precedence over computation, in which students are expected to solve open-ended problems that have more than one right answer, and in which the strategies that students use to solve problems are more important than the answers they reach.[58] To be mathematically literate, students must be able to "make conjectures, abstract properties from problem situations, explain their reasoning, follow arguments, validate assertions, and communicate results in a meaningful form."[59]

Grounded in the new cognitive psychology, the NCTM standards promoted the idea that students had to use and apply knowledge actively in order to learn it well, as opposed to the behaviorist emphasis on direct instruction and recitation of formal rules. Romberg, a leading mathematics researcher who served as chair of the NCTM Commission on Standards, derided what was taught in schools as "shopkeeper arithmetic," good enough for the nineteenth century but completely inadequate for the demands of the information age.[60] "Information is the new capital and the new raw material. Communication is the new means of production," Romberg wrote in 1988. "Today our society needs individuals who can continue to learn and adapt to changing circumstances and produce new knowledge. Knowledge is seen as constructive, teaching as guiding, and learning as occurring through active participation."[61]

The NCTM engaged in vigorous efforts to disseminate its standards. It promoted them in numerous publications, videotapes, and workshops; it won the endorsement of other major professional education associations; it mailed a summary of the standards to every principal and school board president in the country; it worked with organized coalitions of mathematics teachers in many states. Furthermore, NCTM received strong endorsements from the National Science Foundation and the U.S. Department of Education, which lent additional prestige and funding to implementation of the standards.

Although the NCTM standards called for radical changes in the teaching and testing of mathematics, they received remarkable acceptance in a short period of time. Only three years after their release, they were being used in at least forty states as the basis for curriculum revision; they were embraced by many schools of education as standards for preparing new teachers; **and** they influenced the methodology of several national tests, including the SAT and the NAEP, which added mathematics problems with open-ended answers. The NCTM standards served as a model of a successful nongovernmental consensus process for the U.S. Department of Education, when it provided funding in 1991–92 for other discipline-based professional organizations to develop voluntary national standards in various subject areas.

The NCTM standards arrived at the right moment. They appealed to those who were concerned about both equity and excellence. They sought to teach mathematics to all students, including those who had previously been tracked away from demanding courses, but they also aimed to make mathematics more challenging by introducing concepts drawn from algebra, geometry, statistics, and probability as early as the elementary grades. Although some teachers and supervisors undoubtedly grumbled about the proposed changes and harbored misgivings about their utility, the NCTM standards achieved remarkable support from different ends of the political and ideological spectrum.

The greatest triumph of the NCTM was in winning acceptance for the idea of standards. Its greatest problems lie ahead, because the efficacy of the standards are, as yet, untested and unevaluated; no one can say with certainty that students taught by the new methods will learn more mathematics or perform at higher levels. Furthermore, the NCTM has not developed performance standards, no clear definition of expectations for student achievement. It has criticized current multiple-choice tests as inappropriate to the new standards, but as yet nothing has been developed to take their place. One NCTM leader reminded his colleagues that it would be necessary to demonstrate that "today's students can outperform their counterparts of years ago." Zalman Usiskin, director of the University of Chicago School Mathematics Project, warned, "we need some attention to the problems of grading students. . . .After the early elementary grades, teachers need to obtain a relatively impartial way of assigning grades to students. The newer assessment rhetoric needs to be fitted into the reality of a very important aspect of the job of many teachers; the requirement that they come up with defensible grades periodically during the year. . . ." Usiskin also offered a note of caution about the rush to abolish multiple-choice tests:

Let us drop this overstated rhetoric about all the old tests being bad. Those tests were used because they are quite effective in fitting a particular mathematical model of performance—a single number that has some value to predict future performance. Until it can be shown that the alternate assessment techniques do a better job at prediction, let us not knock what is there. The mathematics education community has forgotten that it is poor performance on the old tests that rallied the public behind our desire to change. We cannot very well pick up the banner but then say the tests are no measure of performance. We cannot have it both ways.[62]

Ultimately, the success or failure of the NCTM standards will depend not on whether they work in theory, but on whether they can produce higher levels of learning in the nation's classrooms. If, as Usiskin warned, there is no way to demonstrate the superiority of the new standards and the new methods, they will be subject to the same criticism that derailed the new math.

State-Level Systemic Reform

Many of the principles eventually adopted by those across the country seeking national standards and assessments in the 1990s were first developed in California under the leadership of Bill Honig. In 1982 Honig was elected superintendent of public instruction in California. He had given up his career as a lawyer to become a teacher in an inner-city elementary school and was later appointed to the state board of education. When he decided to run for state superintendent, the only requirement for high school graduation in California was two years of physical education; of the few courses that local school districts required for graduation, more than 40 percent were nonacademic. (A Stanford University study released in 1984 found that high school students were assigned to four different tracks. About 10 percent were in an honors track, about 35 percent were in the college preparatory track, 10–15 percent were in a remedial track, and nearly 45 percent were in the general track. The general track students had the weakest, most incoherent curriculum, with the most nonacademic electives. A sample transcript of a general track student included courses in typing, cultural awareness, homemaking, beginning restaurant management, food for singles, exploring childhood, and clothing.[63])

In his campaign, Honig pledged to champion traditional education by increasing graduation requirements and developing a strong academic curriculum for all students. By traditional education, he did not mean a focus on minimal competencies or "back-to-basics," but one that gave all students the advantages of a rigorous curriculum in the academic disciplines (English, history, a foreign language, mathematics, science, the fine arts, health, and physical education), taught by well-educated teachers in orderly and purposeful classrooms, where homework was regularly assigned and where hard work and achievement were respected. "It's the best preparation for life money can buy," Honig wrote. "If it's good enough for the sons and daughters of the nation's leaders, then the children of the middle class and of those striving to escape poverty deserve no less."[64]

The voters gave Honig a large majority and a mandate to transform the state school system. Honig's vision of what education should be and his boundless energy gave him enormous advantages in the ensuing years. After persuading the business community and the state legislature to increase funding for public education, he took specific steps to follow through on his campaign promises. In 1983 the state board of education adopted model graduation requirements, reversing years of laissez faire policy. Meanwhile, Honig began to build consensus for change by stimulating a statewide conversation among different constituencies about the deficiencies of the current system and the kind of education that was necessary to prepare the state's children for the twenty-first century.

Honig's vision of a rich core curriculum for all students had to be realized piece by piece and step by step. The state already had "curriculum frameworks," (that is, guidelines describing in general terms what was to be taught in all schools). Before Honig, the state curriculum guidelines—like those in most states—described minimum requirements in different subjects; teachers could easily ignore them, because they were unrelated to what was tested. Most tests used in the state assessed basic and minimum skills in subjects such as reading and mathematics. Honig changed all that. In what one aide has called a "Manhattan Project for curriculum,"[65] committees of teachers and scholars prepared ambitious new curriculum frameworks in every subject area.

These new state curriculum frameworks became the state's *content standards,* describing what students should learn at each grade level. They were detailed enough to provide guidance to teachers, but general enough so that teachers could use a variety of methods to convey the important concepts. The framework committees drew upon the best available research and scholarship in each field. Although each framework dealt with a particular field, they all contained certain common ideas:

- An emphasis on thinking, application, and problem solving

- High expectations for all students, instead of the tracking that had been prevalent

- A focus on the body of knowledge and the ways of knowing in each discipline, enabling every student to build a foundation for future learning

- A shift from coverage of minute details to emphasis on understanding the major ideas in each field

Curriculum development was the critical element of Honig's strategy for change, because everything else was based on what students were expected to learn. Honig knew that the new curricula would be ignored so long as norm-referenced, multiple-choice tests were the primary means of gauging student performance, so he convened teams of teachers to develop new assessments based on the new curriculum frameworks. Performance assessments were introduced to encourage the shift to problem solving and application. One of the new tests was a writing assessment, which was important in itself because multiple-choice tests discourage the teaching of writing.

The new curriculum frameworks also spurred a major reform in the textbooks, many of which were at odds with the spirit of the new frameworks. California is one of twenty-two states that adopt textbooks for kindergarten through eighth grade,[66] and it accounts for nearly 12 percent of the national market for textbooks. Honig used the power of the marketplace to demand high-quality textbooks in every field. In 1985 the state rejected many middle-school science textbooks; in 1986 it rejected every mathematics textbook. In time many textbook publishers produced first-rate textbooks and software that supported the state's new, high-standards curricula.

The curriculum frameworks also led to other important changes. Professional development was redesigned to offer teachers the skills and subject-matter knowledge that they needed to teach the new curricula. Multimedia programs were created to match the requirements of the frameworks. An accountability system was put in place, including school report cards, with specific information about student achievement and course taking in every school, so that parents and the general community would know how their children and their schools were doing. Parent guides were written and disseminated to explain the changes and to suggest ways that parents could help their children succeed in school. Honig, however, was unable to change teacher education and teacher credentialing, which were controlled by the state legislature, not the state department of education.

What Honig pioneered is now called "systemic reform." Beginning with a vision of what education ought to be, he oversaw the development of content standards and linked together all of the parts of the educational system—including new tests, new textbooks, and staff development activities to teach teachers how to teach the new materials—in support of achieving higher standards. Once the systemic changes were under way, the state department of education helped create networks of schools, each working toward a common goal, such as getting more low-income students into college or strengthening elementary science or middle-school mathematics. It is through these networks that teachers and principals take responsibility for implementing change in their own schools.

After a decade of relentless standards-based reform, California could point to some solid achievements: the dropout rate declined, the proportion of high school seniors who met the entrance requirements established by the University of California increased by one-third, and the number of Advanced Placement examinations taken (and passed) tripled. Those achievements were all the more remarkable because Honig's era of reform coincided with an increase in school enrollment, a rapid expansion of immigrant and non-English-speaking students, and a dramatic increase in the number of children living in poverty. While enrollment exploded, state funding for education declined, dropping California's expenditures well below the national average and raising class sizes well above.[67]

Honig created a model for systemic reform that influenced policymakers in the Bush and Clinton administrations as well as in other states. He demonstrated that the model begins with a belief that all children can learn at high levels. Three broad requirements are then necessary to achieve success: clear content standards, embodied in coherent statements of what students are expected to learn and do; changes in testing, professional development, textbooks, technology, and all the other parts of the education system; and a long-term commitment to build support for the reform agenda in every school, so that teachers come to feel a sense of ownership in its success.[68]

Ideas Have Consequences

From the many different perspectives, contentions, and experiences of educational reformers in the 1980s came certain ideas that shaped the national consensus about what schools should do. These ideas helped to forge a surprisingly wide agreement about the potential value of national standards and national assessments. Consensus was emerging on the following points:

- First, what students should know and be able to do must be clearly defined (content standards), so that they, their teachers, and their parents know and understand what is expected of them.

- Second, content standards should define what is to be learned, not the kind of behavior, attitudes, or personal qualities that students should display when the course is concluded. Content standards define knowledge and skills (and are measurable), not behavioral or attitudinal objectives (which are usually unmeasurable).

- Third, tests should be aligned with content standards so that students know that they will be tested on what they have been taught.

- Fourth, content standards should be used to reform examinations, textbooks, teacher training, teacher education, teacher certification, and other parts of the educational system.

- Fifth, all students should be expected to learn mathematics, science, English, history, geography, civics, the arts, and a foreign language. Although some ability grouping may be necessary for students at the extremes, curricular tracking should be discouraged or eliminated because it excludes students from the opportunity to learn the knowledge and skills that are needed for good jobs and postsecondary education.

- Sixth, teachers should encourage students to think, to apply what they have learned to novel situations, and to develop the ability to explain how they arrived at the answer to problems.

- Seventh, parents and teachers should stress the importance of effort, rather than ability, as the key to success in school.

- Eighth, tests should stress achievement (what is learned in class) rather than aptitude.

- Ninth, tests should be designed to determine whether students really understand what they have studied, rather than simply having them pick a correct answer from a series of boxes.

- Tenth, public agencies should pay more attention to results (whether students are performing at high levels) and regulate less (that is, leave schools and teachers free to do things their own way so long as they aim for high performance for all students).

These ideas became guiding principles in the growing movement to establish national standards and national assessments.

5

The Politics of Standards

THE DEBATE ABOUT NATIONAL STANDARDS and assessments happened very quickly, perhaps too quickly; even a bipartisan consensus, shaped mainly in Washington, D.C., was insufficient to guarantee that the public understood and supported the changes that were proposed. During the mid-1980s, despite well-publicized concern about educational quality, despite the bevy of commissions and task forces, no one suggested that what was needed was national standards and assessments. The National Commission on Excellence in Education, in its report *A Nation at Risk*, had recommended a core curriculum to establish clear and high expectations for all students, but it did not urge national standards or a national test. Given the nation's tradition of state and local control of education, such an idea would have seemed outlandish.

But once President Bush and the nation's governors agreed to set specific goals, with a target date (the year 2000) and detailed objectives, the logic of standards was inescapable. How, after all, could the nation ensure that students could demonstrate competency in challenging subject matter or become "first in the world" in science and mathematics without specifying in some fashion what was to be learned? It seemed equally obvious that some kind of test would be needed to determine whether and how well students had learned the challenging subject matter.

Agreeing on the desirability of standards was far easier, however, than establishing them. When the president, the governors, and their aides shaped the national education goals in 1989 and 1990, they did not realize, for example, that educators were divided about what competency is and how it should be demonstrated, about which subjects should be taught to which students, and about the value of challenging students with higher standards. Nor did the president and the governors understand the extent to which a generation of criticism of standardized testing had undermined faith in its validity. As a result there was no widely accepted test that could be used to ascertain whether American students had achieved the competency that the goals called for.

Moreover, what seemed logically obvious was not necessarily politically possible. In poll after poll, the American public insisted that it approved of national standards in education, even of a single national test. Yet at the same time, politicians and policymakers believed that it was politically unacceptable to propose a national curriculum. National standards implied that the nation would somehow work together to improve achievement; but a national curriculum implied that bureaucrats in Washington would tell teachers what to teach and might impose divisive ideas or deadening conformity on every classroom. Thus, the political terrain was treacherous, demanding an embrace of national standards and a simultaneous disavowal of a national curriculum.

The issue was further complicated by the active participation of the full array of education interest groups devoted to monitoring federal policies and funding. Any new piece of federal legislation that has the potential to affect all schools energizes groups that want to advance their agenda and avoid losing ground to others. Advocates and lobbyists carefully parsed the language of the goals, for it provided an opening for groups seeking more instructional time, new programs, and federal funding. Subject-matter groups battled for the right to control content standards. The disciplines listed in the goals—mathematics, science, history, geography, and English—rejoiced because they were specifically included, while those not named (such as the arts, civics, foreign languages, economics, home economics, social studies, and physical education) lobbied the politicians to rewrite the goals to include them, which would gain them federal recognition and funding. Some groups even insisted that any effort to focus the schools' attention primarily on academic instruction was too confining. In short order, the same countervailing pressures that produced curricular diffusion in the schools were re-created in Washington. The easiest way for the politicians to respond to these pressures was to agree, as the schools had long done, that no subject was more valuable than any other subject, even though it was widely acknowledged that the failure to set priorities had vitiated the mission of the schools and undermined student achievement.

A second set of battles occurred over potential performance standards, that is, how well students would be expected to learn content and how their knowledge and skills would be tested. Most contentious was the issue of testing, and, in particular, whether any "stakes," or consequences, would be associated with tests. In other words, should student test scores influence promotion, graduation, college admissions, or entry to the work force? Again, interest groups dominated the debate, arguing over what kinds of tests were appropriate, whether it was fair to attach consequences to tests, and whether any test could reliably measure academic achievement. Those who were developing new forms of performance assessments warned against reliance on the well-established multiple-choice tests. Publishers of commercial tests warned that abandoning the tried-and-true tests was perilous and should be deferred until sometime in the distant future. Civil rights groups held that current testing methods were discriminatory. Groups opposed to testing warned that every test was flawed and that no one's future should be determined by a test. In this debate, education research mattered less than the ability of advocates to win the support of a powerful legislator or staff member.

A new kind of standard, the opportunity-to-learn (OTL) standard, was championed by advocates for low-income and minority students, who hoped to use it as a means to force equalization of resources and funding in the nation's schools. These advocates argued that it was unfair to expect such students to meet the same educational standards as those students who attended well-endowed schools. They believed that the OTL standard could become a powerful tool for financial equalization if every school district and state were required to document and justify disparities among schools as a condition for receiving federal education funds. Opposition to OTL standards came mainly from governors, who saw the standards as an invitation to the federal government to impose unfunded mandates and regulation on every aspect of schooling, as well as from some supporters of academic standards, who believed that OTL standards would serve to reduce students' responsibility for their own achievement.[1]

The same concerns for educational quality that had launched the standards movement in Washington also prompted similar activities in the states, and many became embroiled in fractious debates about outcomes-based education (OBE). In Washington the steadying influence of the National Education Goals Panel kept the discussion focused on measurable academic outcomes. But in some states, battles erupted over OBE when the state department of education wrote documents that described student "outcomes" in terms that had more to do with desirable attitudes and behaviors than with academics. Critics of OBE feared that public authorities were attempting to impose intellectual and political conformity on children. The ideological conflicts in the states about OBE demonstrated the reluctance of many in education to emphasize academic outcomes and the danger that populist hostility to OBE might turn into a full-fledged assault on academic standards as well.

Debate in Washington: AMERICA 2000

During the presidential campaign of 1988, George Bush promised to be "the education president." In the fall of 1989, President Bush convened an education summit with the nation's governors in Charlottesville, Virginia, where they agreed to establish national education goals, which the president announced in his State of the Union speech in 1990. Nearly a year went by before he recruited new leadership for the Department of Education: Lamar Alexander, former governor of Tennessee, and David Kearns, former chairman of the Xerox Corporation.

Their plan, called AMERICA 2000, announced in April 1991, was not a new federal program, but a nationwide strategy with several complementary parts. First, every community and state was encouraged to organize its own AMERICA 2000 citizens' committee to work toward the goals (eventually nearly 3,000 such groups were created). Second, a privately funded entity called the New American Schools Development Corporation was established to manage a design competition for "break-the-mold" schools. Congress was asked (and declined) to authorize $535 million to open a "new American school" in every congressional district, but the private corporation awarded grants (which did not require congressional approval) for innovative schools.

Third, school choice would be promoted through a small number of demonstration programs (Congress refused to authorize such projects). Fourth, new "world class standards" in core subject areas would be developed, along with "voluntary national tests for 4th, 8th and 12th graders," called American Achievement Tests.[2] The AMERICA 2000 plan did not say who would shape the new standards and tests. Alexander looked to the NCTM standards as a model, and he thought that the Department of Education could make grants to help other subject areas develop their own standards. He also expected that states and private testing firms would collaborate to create the new national tests. Of one thing he was sure: he did not want the federal government to control national standards and testing.

The Republican administration had little reason to expect Congress, controlled by the Democrats, to endorse AMERICA 2000, but it counted on building enough public support so that Congress would eventually back the plan's initiatives.

National Council on Education Standards and Testing

In June 1991, Alexander persuaded Congress to establish a bipartisan body called the National Council on Education Standards and Testing. The implicit purpose of the council—whose acronym, NCEST, always drew a laugh—was to create a broad bipartisan consensus about national standards and testing and to mollify Congress about being left out of the national goals process that had begun in Charlottesville. Its stated purpose was to "advise on the desirability and feasibility of national standards and tests," as well as to "recommend long-term policies, structures, and mechanisms for setting voluntary education standards and planning an appropriate system of tests."

Led by the co-chairmen of the National Education Goals Panel, Democratic Governor Roy Romer of Colorado and Republican Governor Carroll A. Campbell, Jr., of South Carolina, NCEST included administration officials, members of Congress, scholars, teachers' union leaders, and educators. In what may have been a record time for a federal entity, the council convened in mid-1991, held hearings, and issued its report in January 1992.

NCEST recommended national content standards and a national system of assessments based on the new standards, but not a single national test. "To make [national] standards meaningful, it is important that the Nation be able to measure progress toward them," it declared. In addressing one of the most controversial issues before the panel, it also recommended that states establish "school delivery standards" and performance standards for school systems, to "attest to the provision of opportunities to learn and of appropriate instructional conditions to enable all children to reach high standards." The content and performance standards were to be national, but the states were to define and control school delivery standards and the system performance standards.

National standards, NCEST said, should have the following characteristics:

- Standards must reflect high expectations, not expectations of minimal competency.

- Standards must provide focus and direction, not become a national curriculum.

- Standards must be national, not federal.

- Standards must be voluntary, not mandated by the federal government.

- Standards must be dynamic, not static.

The council's hope was "to raise the ceiling for students who are currently above average and to lift the floor for those who now experience the least success in school, including those with special needs."

In proposing a system of assessments, NCEST recognized that tests influence what is taught and that the new standards would be ignored unless they were made the basis for new tests. Accordingly, NCEST recommended both the continuation of the national sampling done by the National Assessment of Educational Progress and the development of new individual student assessments, "building on the best tests available and incorporating new methods." Both kinds of tests should be aligned with high national standards, and both should be capable of producing "useful, comparable results." The new system of assessments, NCEST said, should have the following features:

- *There should be multiple assessments, rather than a single test.* It will be up to states, individually or in groups, to adopt assessments linked to the national standards. States can design the assessments or they may acquire them.

- *Voluntary, not mandatory.* State participation in the national system of assessments would be voluntary. The federal government will not require that states adopt any particular tests.

- *Developmental—not static.* The system should be developmental. It should change and evolve over time, maintaining alignment with the national content and performance standards and incorporating improved assessment techniques as these are developed.

NCEST envisioned that states, districts, commercial publishers, and others would independently develop the new assessments based on common standards so that the results would be comparable. No one knew whether a system of multiple, independent assessments would produce comparable test scores; NCEST recognized the importance of having nationally comparable test scores but was unwilling to recommend a single national test. NCEST also concluded that the tests could eventually be used as high-stakes tests for "high-school graduation, college admission, continuing education, and certification for employment."

To coordinate the development of standards and assessments, NCEST proposed the creation of a National Education Standards and Assessment Council (NESAC), which would certify content and performance standards and "criteria for assessments." The new body would award the educational equivalent of the Good Housekeeping Seal of Approval, but its powers were otherwise limited. In fact, it would not have the power to approve or withhold approval of state assessments, only to certify "criteria for assessments."

NCEST was careful to point out that national standards and assessments were "not panaceas for the nation's educational problems." More was needed, NCEST stressed, including the development of state curriculum frameworks, professional development for teachers to learn the new standards, new technology, "new roles and responsibilities for educators," "assistance to families and communities in need," and action to reduce health problems and social barriers to learning.[3]

During NCEST's brief life, the question of "school delivery standards" ignited intense controversy. The debate about delivery standards was strongly influenced by Jonathan Kozol's best-selling book, *Savage Inequalities,* which argued passionately for equalization of resources between rich and poor schools.[4] NCEST never fully defined what it meant by delivery standards but described them in its report as "a metric for determining whether a school 'delivers' to students the 'opportunity to learn' well the material in the *content standards.*"[5] In other words, school delivery standards were meant to measure the ability of schools and districts to provide the resources, staff, and conditions for learning. Some members of NCEST argued forcefully that it would not be fair to expect students to meet high content standards so long as there were glaring inequalities among schools and school districts; they insisted that schools should have to meet high standards before requiring students to do so. Opponents of delivery standards insisted that the point of the national goals was to focus on results rather than "inputs"; they worried that delivery standards would lead to additional federal regulation of local schools and would defer for many years, perhaps indefinitely, any serious attention to educational outcomes. The members were nearly evenly divided on this contentious issue.

NCEST reached an artful compromise, proposing "*school delivery standards* developed by the states collectively from which each state could select the criteria that it finds useful for the purpose of assessing a school's capacity and performance."[6] Thus, those in favor of delivery standards could claim victory because NCEST recommended them, but those opposed could also claim victory because each state would remain free to choose the standards by which it judged its adequacy. The issue, as it happened, was far from resolved and would reemerge as the major sticking point in efforts to pass legislation, during both the Bush and Clinton administrations.

Political Divisions

On the same day in January 1992 that NCEST released its report, fifty educators, leaders of civil rights organizations, and professors of education issued a statement declaring their staunch opposition "to the development of a new national test of educational achievement as a means of establishing higher standards for students and holding schools accountable." Such a test, they argued, would be bad for students and their schools, especially if "high stakes" were attached to it. It would narrow the curriculum, cause schools to push out low-scoring students, and penalize students who attended poor schools. Any assessments, they held, should be developed at the local level, expressing the values and standards of the local community. The signatories expressed deep skepticism about creating national standards and assessments:

> We believe that any real effort to create accountability in American schools must focus equal or more attention on improving the capabilities of children to learn and schools to teach as it does on gauging educational "outcomes." Parents and taxpayers have a right to expect that accountability policies will aim to *provide* good education, rather than merely measuring schools. Given the tremendous differences between today's achievements and the goals set for America 2000, the inadequate supports for children and families in American society, and the dramatic inequalities among schools' resources, any policy to establish benchmarks for achievement without creating equity in the educational resources available to children would be a cruel hoax.[7]

Among the signers of the statement were some of the nation's leading school reformers, such as Theodore R. Sizer of Brown University; James Comer of Yale University; and John Goodlad of the University of Washington. Other prominent signatories were Marian Wright Edelman of the Children's Defense Fund, Donna Shalala of the University of Wisconsin, and Gregory Anrig of the Educational Testing Service. Two members of NCEST—Keith Geiger of the National Education Association, and Marshall Smith of Stanford University—signed both the NCEST report and the statement criticizing that report.

The statement indirectly demonstrated the difficulty of engaging in informed debate about national issues. Its primary point was to oppose a national test, but NCEST had not recommended a single national test. The statement criticized the inappropriate use of norm-referenced, standardized test scores, yet NCEST had not recommended such tests. Still, a solid core of disagreement was evident: the critics were opposed to using tests to track, promote, or otherwise determine students' educational futures. Indeed, the critics were against using tests for "assigning consequences to schools." NCEST had concluded, however, that test results might "eventually" be used to influence decisions about students' educational futures. The NCEST report also concluded that student motivation declines when school work has no bearing on decisions about entry to college or employment. The critics decried such uses of tests as punitive.

Although the public strongly supported national standards and assessments, opinion among interest groups was sharply divided. The National Governors' Association, representing the public officials with the most direct responsibility for education, favored national—but not federal—standards. The two teachers' unions parted company. The National Education Association said little about national standards but opposed national testing, standardized testing, and high-stakes testing; the American Federation of Teachers, however, endorsed national standards and national testing with consequences. The business community advocated national standards and national testing, which they believed would establish clear priorities, goals, and accountability for results. Civil rights groups were strongly opposed to both national standards and national testing, which they claimed would place an unfair burden on minority students. Educational researchers were divided. Some strongly supported standards and testing, on the grounds that expectations should be raised for all students, and that better information was needed to spur improvement; others, however, dismissed the proposal as a dangerous move that would narrow the curriculum and measure schools instead of improving them.

Even the major political parties were internally split. Committed to the principle of decentralization and local control, Republicans had traditionally opposed or sought to limit the federal presence in education; a decade earlier, President Reagan had tried unsuccessfully to abolish the newly created Department of Education. President Bush's championing of national standards and a national system of tests, even if voluntary, made many members of his party deeply uncomfortable. Some, however, were willing to support the president's plan, not only because he was their party leader, but because they believed in the importance of accountability and the principle of pursuing educational improvement by focusing on results, rather than inputs. Nonetheless, the president could not be sure of the unified support of his own party on these issues.

Unlike the Republicans, the Democrats had few qualms about federal intervention into education; they usually perceived the federal role as a guarantor of equity, especially on behalf of racial minorities, handicapped children, and others in need of special protection. But many Democrats were reluctant to make the federal government the final arbiter of national standards and assessments. One reason was frankly partisan. The Democratic majority on the House Education and Labor Committee did not want a Republican president to be able to claim credit for any education reform legislation. More important, committee Democrats were closely allied with the education lobby, most notably the politically powerful National Education Association, as well as civil rights organizations, which contended that schools needed more money and regulation, not new standards and tests. The committee majority openly disdained national standards and assessments as a reform strategy.[8] Senate Democrats, however, did not share the House committee's hostility to standards and testing. On the contrary, Senator Claiborne Pell, chairman of the Senate Education Subcommittee, was an active proponent of both; in fact, in 1988 he sponsored an amendment authorizing the Department of Education to develop a high school test of academic excellence. Needless to say, the House did not appropriate funding for such a test, nor did the Department of Education dare to incur the wrath of the House by using its discretionary funds to act on the Pell amendment.

Given the political lineup in the Congress, it was not surprising that the Democratic majority pushed the Bush administration's AMERICA 2000 aside and replaced it with its own initiative. Initially, Republicans tried to incorporate a few features of the AMERICA 2000 proposal into the Democratic bill, but in 1992 the legislation got caught up in election-year posturing by both sides. The administration insisted on features, such as parental choice and regulatory flexibility, that were objectionable to the Democratic majority; and the Democrats stripped the bill of everything that the administration wanted (even public school choice), daring Bush to veto an education bill only weeks before the election.

In the end what made the bill finally unacceptable to the Bush administration was its inclusion of school delivery standards, the very issue that had divided NCEST. NCEST had finally recommended that the states develop such standards, but the Democrats' legislation elevated them to equal importance with national content standards and, in some versions of the legislation, suggested that states would be required to meet national school delivery standards as a condition for eligibility for federal funding. Predictably, the administration worried about federal interference with state and local control of education. Secretary Alexander advised the president to veto the bill if it came to his desk, because the legislation "creates at least the beginnings of a national school board that could make day-to-day school decisions on curriculum, discipline, teacher training, textbooks, and classroom materials. . . . A federal recipe book dictating how to operate a local school board does not make schools better."[9] The bill finally died on a parliamentary maneuver in the Senate late in the 1992 session, mourned by no one. "It's no secret that nobody's really enthusiastic about this bill," acknowledged an aide to the House Education and Labor Committee.[10]

Strategy of Reform

Even though the Department of Education was unable to get any legislation passed in 1992, it nonetheless purposefully pursued a strategy of education reform based on high standards. The implicit model was California's education reform program. The department took as a starting point the idea that educational improvement should begin with an agreement on content standards that could be forged at both the national and state levels. Without such an agreement, "each part of the educational system pursues different, and sometimes contradictory, goals. As a result, the educational system as a whole is riddled with inequity, incoherence, and inefficiency." But once broad agreement is achieved on what is to be taught and learned, then everything else in the education system can be redirected toward reaching higher standards: new tests can be designed to reflect the new content; schools of education can prepare new teachers to teach the new content; in-service staff development activities can help teachers master the new content as well as better ways to teach it; new textbooks can be written to teach the new content; software can be produced based on the new content. Secretary Alexander believed that this kind of comprehensive, standards-based reform would occur without federal mandates, because people want the best for their children; he did not want to create a new federal agency to control the reform process, but chose instead to use federal dollars to initiate voluntary national standards that would then have to prove themselves in practice and win support from teachers, as the NCTM standards had done.[11]

Toward that end, the Education Department made awards in 1991 and 1992 to broad-based groups of scholars and teachers to develop voluntary national standards in science, history, the arts, civics, geography, foreign languages, and English. It also made competitive awards to states to develop curriculum frameworks (state content standards) in all of these subject areas (and in mathematics, where national standards already existed). Because of the House's hostility to testing, no effort was made to create voluntary national achievement tests (indeed, the House even refused to appropriate funds requested for new research on performance assessment).

In addition, the National Science Foundation funded an ambitious program of systemic reform at the state level, awarding large competitive grants to nearly half the states to develop new curriculum frameworks in mathematics and science and to realign the other parts of their educational system to support high standards.

Education was not a particularly important issue on the presidential campaign trail in 1992, but the candidates did address it from time to time. President Bush talked almost exclusively about choice. He never mentioned that his own Department of Education was actively promoting the development of national content standards, nor did he point out that Congress had rebuffed his own proposal to create voluntary national examinations.

By contrast, Governor Clinton talked about the importance of creating high national standards and national examinations. He pointed with pride to his record in Arkansas, where he had played an active role in revamping the state education system, insisting on higher standards and new tests for both students and teachers. And he spoke with enthusiasm about his role at the Charlottesville education summit, where he had helped to write the national goals. In every appearance before education groups, he voiced the same message: "By the year 2000, we should have national standards for what our children should know at the fourth, eighth, and 12th grades in math and science, language, geography, history, and other subjects, and we should have a *meaningful* set of national exams to measure whether they know what they're supposed to know."[12] Similarly, in his campaign document, *Putting People First,* he promised to "establish tough standards and a national examination system."[13]

Passage of Goals 2000

Once in the White House, President Clinton chose former governor Richard Riley of South Carolina as secretary of education and former governor Madeline Kunin of Vermont as deputy secretary. One of the leading educational reformers at the state level, Riley had promoted a thorough overhaul of his state's school system, increasing taxes to pay for higher standards. He believed in the value of standards, both for raising achievement and promoting equal opportunity. The prime strategist for the new administration was Undersecretary Marshall Smith, former dean of the Stanford School of Education, who had served in the Carter administration. A member of the NCEST panel, Smith was deeply versed in standards and assessments issues. As the new president had promised, the cornerstone of his education program was a bill called Goals 2000, whose primary purpose was to advance national standards and assessments. Goals 2000 did not include any proposal for a national testing system, probably in deference to opposition by key allies, such as the National Education Association, civil rights groups, and leading Democrats on the House Education and Labor Committee. Clinton's Goals 2000 legislation passed in March 1994. It has four main components:

First, it formally authorized the National Education Goals Panel and codified the national education goals after adding two new goals. (For goals, see appendix.)

Second, it created a new federal agency, the National Education Standards and Improvement Council (NESIC), which is responsible for certifying voluntary national content and performance standards; voluntary national opportunity-to-learn standards; and state standards for content, performance, and opportunity to learn, as well as state assessments. NESIC must ensure that national standards "are internationally competitive and comparable to the best in the world," and that state standards "are comparable [to] or higher in rigor and quality" than the national standards.[14]

Third, it established a grant program for participating states. The governor and state superintendent must appoint a panel to design the state's education reform plan. The panel's membership must reflect the diversity of the state by geography, race, ethnicity, gender, and disability characteristics. The committee must include representatives of the governor, the chief state school officer, the state board of education, teachers' organizations, state legislators, parents, students, teachers, administrators, community organizations, institutions of higher learning, colleges of education, business and labor organizations, organizations serving young children, rural and urban educational agencies, local school boards, state and local health and social service agencies, educational experts, private schools that receive federal funding, and, where appropriate, Indian tribes. Theoretically, states do not have to submit their plans to NESIC for approval, but under the requirements of another bill, the Elementary and Secondary Education Act, they cannot receive federal funds for elementary and secondary education unless NESIC or the secretary of education has approved their state reform plan.

Fourth, the secretary of education was authorized to award grants to one or more consortia to develop voluntary national opportunity-to-learn standards, which include "the quality and availability to all students of curricula, instructional materials and technologies, including distance learning; the capability of teachers to provide high-quality instruction to meet diverse learning needs in each content area to all students; the extent to which teachers, principals, and administrators have ready and continuing access to professional development, including the best knowledge about teaching, learning, and school improvement; the extent to which curriculum, instructional practices, and assessments are aligned to voluntary national content standards; the extent to which school facilities provide a safe and secure environment for learning and instruction and have the requisite libraries, laboratories, and other resources necessary to provide an opportunity-to-learn. . . ."[15]

Goals 2000 created an elaborate structure in which the states receive federal funds to design their own reform plans. NESIC reviews and certifies state plans and national standards. The National Education Goals Panel reviews NESIC's decisions and can overturn them by a two-thirds majority.

Although it was widely anticipated that the Goals 2000 legislation would pass quickly and easily in 1993, that did not happen. Just as the administration was preparing to release its proposed legislation in March 1993, House Democrats told the Department of Education that the bill, as drafted, was a nonstarter. The chair of the House Committee on Education and Labor, William Ford, stated that "the legislation will not come out of my committee unless service-delivery standards are equal to or slightly ahead of any testing or standards."[16] To satisfy House critics, the administration pulled back the bill, rewrote it, and released it in late April.

Still, the legislation raised four troublesome issues. Once again the school delivery standards, now renamed opportunity-to-learn standards, were the most controversial. Other significant issues included the control and composition of the federal agency charged with certifying national and state standards; the use of tests and assessments; and apportioning responsibility for standards and assessments among the federal, state, and local governments.

Opportunity-to-Learn Standards

Changing the name from school delivery standards, with its bureaucratic ring, to opportunity-to-learn standards, which sounded more idealistic, was a brilliant public relations stroke. The new name made the concept more palatable to wary legislators and the press. But what exactly did it mean? Assessment experts used the term to describe whether students had been taught the material on a test; researchers asked whether students had the "opportunity to learn" what was tested. Did the teacher teach it? Was it covered in the textbook? If so, then students had had the opportunity to learn.

Neither the Clinton administration nor many in Congress were satisfied with that limited definition. The Clinton administration proposed that a national commission be created to develop voluntary national OTL standards, which presumably would serve as a model for the states.

But some members of Congress, especially on the House side, had an even more ambitious view of OTL standards, seeing them as a lever to force equalization of resources among schools and districts, perhaps in time among states. The issue of equalization was being fought out in the courts and state legislatures in nearly two dozen states. OTL standards offered a way to hasten the process by requiring states to document every disparity among districts and schools. The bill that emerged in the House agreed that a national commission would create national opportunity-to-learn standards that would be certified by NESIC and furthermore that every state participating in Goals 2000 must include OTL standards in its school reform plan. The Senate was considerably less enthusiastic about OTL standards than was the House. The Senate bill declared that states should develop such standards but avoided turning them into covert mandates on the states.

Some commentators saw the OTL standards as the first step down the slippery slope toward federal control of education and as the basis for new unfunded mandates directed at the states. One scholar wondered whether OTL standards would "provide a vision . . . of what good practice might be" or "provide prescriptions of required practice that can be used to police the actions of teachers, administrators, and politicians. . . ."[17] Newspapers in Secretary Riley's home state of South Carolina warned that, if enacted, these new standards "would give the federal government unprecedented control over local school budgets."[18]

Others suggested that the real purpose of OTL standards was to encourage lawsuits challenging districts or states that did not meet them. Critics often referred to the standards as "opportunity-to-litigate" standards, anticipating that civil rights lawyers would use any national standards, even voluntary ones, to demand new judicial mandates for spending or to impose uniform federal regulations regarding teaching methods, class size, disciplinary codes, salaries, teacher training, and other matters that are normally decided by professional groups or state and local officials. Still others saw the OTL standards as a tool for denying federal funds to states that did not equalize spending.[19]

The National Governors' Association was the leading critic of federal OTL standards. In May 1993 Governors Romer and Campbell wrote Secretary Riley on behalf of the nation's governors to oppose the OTL standards and to complain about the extensive powers of the proposed NESIC. "Even on a voluntary basis, some of the Governors believe that this is an example of federal intrusion into an area that has historically been a responsibility of the states. Moreover, some Governors fear that the creation of a voluntary mechanism for this certification [of content and OTL standards] could create pressure for a mandatory requirement," they wrote.[20]

On the same day Governor Campbell wrote a separate letter to the secretary, observing that "throughout the [legislative] process, the pressure has always been to prescribe more and more federal requirements, and to switch performance based accountability to accountability based on inputs." He warned that the House bill "comes dangerously close to derailing our hard-won emphasis on student achievement." Worse, he wrote, the power given to NESIC "leads us inevitably toward a federalization of what has been, until now, a pact that recognized and respected the preeminent role of states in education reform."[21] Riley responded that Goals 2000 would improve teaching and learning for all students "without mandating what states and local districts must do. Community and state participation will be strictly voluntary."[22]

The governors' fears appeared justified when Democrats on the House Education and Labor Committee advanced an amendment to deny federal funding to states that did not meet OTL standards. President Clinton then wrote to the committee, asking it to forgo such amendments. "Amendments which require states, as a condition of federal support, to commit to specific corrective actions for schools that fail to meet these standards go too far," the president said. "The requirements will impede states' efforts to focus accountability on results. In addition, they will require states to commit to specific actions even before the nature of the problem is known. . . .I urge you not to support amendments that expand the definition or role of opportunity-to-learn standards."[23]

In July 1993 Romer and Campbell, on behalf of the National Governors' Association, wrote to Senator Edward Kennedy, chair of the Senate Labor and Human Resources Committee, to express the association's views about the pending legislation. Pronouncing the House bill "unacceptable," the governors urged the Senate to specify that certification of standards "will not be mandated as a condition for state participation in any federal education program," and they recommended language that would make clear that states and localities would continue to be in control of assessing their capacity to meet OTL standards. They also asked that no additional goals be added to the six national goals agreed upon in 1990.[24] The Senate was responsive to the governors' concerns, incorporating most of the association's proposals in its bill.

Shortly before the House and Senate bills went to conference, Governor Campbell wrote a strong letter to President Clinton, objecting to the prospect of OTL standards in the House versions of both Goals 2000 and the Elementary and Secondary Education Act, which was simultaneously on a fast track for passage. Campbell wrote: "Mr. President, I am saying 'enough'; let the federal government stay out of the goals/standards movement because the federal government cannot seem to contribute without wanting to control. . . .Governors and parents should not have to fight for their rights in a very complicated subject area every time Congress passes an education bill. It's not right, and it's dangerous to our system."[25]

President Clinton promptly responded that he agreed with Campbell. "The key to meaningful long-term education reform lies in clearly stated national goals coupled with maximum feasible flexibility for states and localities to devise and implement their own plans for achieving those goals," Clinton wrote. "Schools should be held accountable for results—not for complying with a discouraging maze of micromanaged bureaucratic prescriptions." The president noted that his proposal to reauthorize the Elementary and Secondary Education Act contained "no mention whatever of 'opportunity-to-learn' standards. Because I believe so strongly that every child can learn, I believe that actual student performance is the best measure of the extent to which equal opportunity to receive a world-class education has in fact been achieved." The president pledged to direct his representatives to press for final bills that respect "historic state and local prerogatives in education."[26]

The president kept his word. The final version of Goals 2000 encouraged but did not require participating states to develop OTL standards. NESIC was authorized to certify "voluntary national opportunity-to-learn standards," and several sections of the law repeatedly assured the states that implementation of such standards were voluntary and that nothing in the states' plans could be used to "mandate equalized spending per pupil for a State, local educational agency, or school; or mandate national school building standards. . . ."[27]

Composition of NESIC

At the heart of the Goals 2000 bill was a proposal for a new federal entity to certify national and state standards and assessments. Because it would have the authority to make decisions that would influence the content and quality of education across the country, to influence what American children should learn, how they should be tested, and what kinds of resources should be in every school, this body was potentially quite powerful. As a result controversy soon developed over who should appoint it and who should serve on it.

The NCEST panel had recommended the creation of such a body, which it called the National Education Standards and Assessment Council. NCEST had suggested that the new council's members be appointed by the goals panel (which would keep it bipartisan, relatively insulated from politics, and protected from capture by interest groups); and that its membership be one-third educators, one-third public officials, and one-third representatives of the general public, so that it would not be dominated by any one interest group.

In its original draft, the Clinton administration followed the NCEST guidelines by recommending an entity to be appointed by the goals panel and composed of "eminent Americans," including at least two classroom teachers. In redrafting Goals 2000 to satisfy the House Education and Labor Committee, however, the administration changed the name from NESAC to NESIC, substituting "improvement" for "assessment" and signaling that assessment would be downgraded in importance, and its members were to be appointed by the president (eight members), the Speaker of the House (four), and the Senate majority leader (four) as well as the goals panel (four). These twenty would include five professional educators; five representatives of business, labor, and postsecondary education; five public members, including representatives of "advocacy, civil rights and disability groups," or state and local education policymakers; and five education experts. It was possible, under this formula, that all twenty members could be educators, an unusual departure from the American principle of lay control of education. In the Senate bill, the council would consist of nineteen members appointed solely by the president, drawn from the same groups of educators and interest groups. Neither the House nor the Senate thought it necessary to require that the lay public—parents, employers, and others who are not professional educators—have a significant place at the table.

The legislation that ultimately passed in March 1994 created a nineteen-member council, all appointed by the president but nominated by a complex formula. (Seven were to be nominated by the secretary of education, and the other twelve by the Speaker of the House, the majority leader of the Senate, and the goals panel.) The nominees would be drawn from among professional educators, education experts, and representatives of business, labor, postsecondary institutions, the public, and advocacy groups.

The law required that at least one member must represent business, but the other eighteen might all be educators. And, "to the extent feasible," NESIC was to "reflect the diversity of the United States with regard to race, ethnicity, gender and disability characteristics" and to be "equally divided between the 2 major political parties." In addition, no fewer than one-third of NESIC's members must have "experience or background in the educational needs of children who are from low-income families, from minority backgrounds, have limited-English proficiency, or have disabilities."[28] In other words, at least seven of the council's nineteen members must be chosen from representatives of historically low-achieving populations. Left to the president was the critical decision about whether NESIC would be dominated by educators and interest groups or would have any significant representation of members of the general public. And, after all the political considerations had been taken into account, the most important question was whether this agency would have the will and ability to set high standards for American education.

National Examinations

Systemic reform in education means that the entire system, with all of its many parts, must change. The two essential components of systemic reform are standards and assessments. What happens if there are national standards without examinations? If schools continue to use the standardized, multiple-choice tests that bear no relationship to the new standards, the national standards would simply be ignored and have no influence on textbooks, teacher training, instruction, or anything else.

Two years before he became undersecretary of education in the Clinton administration, Marshall Smith advocated creating not only national standards but national examinations that would have real consequences for teachers, schools, and students, including using students' examination scores to influence their entry to college or the workplace.[29] NCEST, in its 1992 report, recommended developing a national system of examinations tied to common national standards and eventually using the test scores to make decisions about promotion, graduation, and college admission. As a candidate for president, Governor Clinton repeatedly promised to create a national examination system. Once in office, Clinton continued to speak assertively about the importance of a national examination system; in his 1994 State of the Union address, he declared that the nation should "measure every school by one high standard: Are our children learning what they need to know to compete and win in the global economy?"[30]

But the House Education and Labor Committee did not like student testing, and even the limited proposals of the Clinton administration ran into a wall of hostility. For House Democrats the issue was fairness; standards and assessments should not be imposed until the playing field had been leveled. In its original Goals 2000 bill, the administration did not lay the groundwork for a national examination system, but it did propose to give NESIC the authority to certify student examinations (presumably, these would be submitted by individual states, groups of states, or any organization that wanted its tests to get official recognition for meeting high standards). The House, however, insisted that NESIC not be allowed to certify a state's assessments until *after* the state had adopted OTL standards. The House also barred using any certified assessment system to make decisions about grade promotion, graduation, or retention of students. This prohibition raised the question why a state would even seek federal certification of its assessment system if certification meant that the test could no longer have consequences; in Arkansas, for example, students must pass a state test to be promoted, but, under the House bill, such a practice would not be allowed after the state's test won federal approval.

The most articulate critic of the House's insistence on deferring standards and assessments until OTL standards were implemented was Albert Shanker, president of the American Federation of Teachers. Shanker argued that insisting on having a level playing field before employing standards and assessments would defer the latter for a very long time, perhaps forever. He offered a metaphor. Suppose, he said, the United States were the only industrialized nation that did not participate in the Olympics. Suppose that, as a result, youngsters were not exercising or eating well and that the physical wellbeing of the nation was in question. Suppose then that legislation was introduced to have the United States enter the Olympic competition in 2000 and that Congress was asked to create a U.S. Olympic Commission to establish the rules for participation. Some critics (on the right), he imagined, would say that it was strictly a local or state matter. But "the biggest problem" would be fairness, as critics on the left would say "that some of the kids competing would not have had as many opportunities to run, jump and swim as others." Some youngsters had poor prenatal care, poor health care, and ill-equipped gyms, while others grew up with fine nutrition and health care, excellent facilities and professional coaches. At this point, imagine that Congress decides that in the interest of fairness, no domestic athletic competition would be held "until all likely contenders had had the same opportunities"; that any state or local competition in which some contenders did not have equal prenatal care or nutrition or facilities would be closed down; and that for five years there would be no losers or winners in any competition.

Shanker's metaphor suggested how unproductive it would be to defer standards and assessments until all schools offered equal education to all youngsters. "A lot of youngsters who come from tough neighborhoods have been inspired by the standards of Olympic competition, and they've overcome obstacles and created their own opportunities," Shanker observed, and added,

> Something similar would happen if we challenged disadvantaged youngsters with clear and high education standards and assessments they could study for. When held up to high standards and shown the route to something they really wanted, a lot of youngsters who now do nothing because nothing is asked of them would begin working and succeeding—at the very least, doing better than they do now. And, as the Olympics example also tell us, there would be a lot of pressure to make sure that gyms were built and coaches trained in places where they didn't exist before.[31]

Shanker's advocacy of national standards *and* testing received a sympathetic hearing among Senate Democrats. Their version of Goals 2000 allowed states to use their assessment for high-stakes purposes after only three years.

In the version of the bill that Congress finally passed, assessment continued to be a troublesome subject, surrounded by qualifications and caveats. If a state uses federal funds to develop new assessments, the assessments may be used for decisions regarding graduation, grade promotion, or retention of students only on the condition that students have been prepared in the content for which the students are being assessed. If a state wants to get its assessments approved by NESIC, however, the state cannot use its assessments for high-stakes decisions and must submit extensive technical reports on the validity and reliability of the test.[32] Because states have no incentive to win federal certification and must bear considerable cost to gain it, they may well decide to bypass federal certification altogether.

In the end it is clear that Goals 2000 does not create a national examination system. Each state will develop its own tests, based on its own standards, which may or may not be approved by NESIC. There will be no way to know whether performance standards and assessments are comparable and equally challenging in the fifty states. Perhaps the decision to create voluntary national standards was as large a step as could be expected in a short period of time, particularly in light of the strong opposition to testing among certain key interest groups, as well as the reluctance of many educators to countenance high-stakes testing.

Federal, State and Local Relations: Who Controls American Education?

Historically, education in the United States has been almost exclusively a state and local function. Federal education legislation deals mainly with special needs. The three major purposes of federal education programs and spending are to provide equity (for students with disadvantages), access to higher education, and research and statistics. Efforts to pass a general program of federal aid to education were always stymied by fears that federal aid meant federal control. These fears remained strong, for neither Republicans nor Democrats trusted the other party to control what was taught in the nation's schools. Since 1970 federal education activities have been constrained by the following statutory prohibition: "No provision of any applicable program shall be construed to authorize any department, agency, officer, or employee of the United States to exercise any direction, supervision, or control over the curriculum, program of instruction, [or] administration . . . of any educational institution . . . or over the selection of library resources, textbooks, or other printed or published instructional materials. . . ."[33]

When they began to work on national education goals in 1989, the president and governors agreed that certain responsibilities were appropriate for each level of government. The primary responsibility for education, they concurred, belonged at the state and local levels, which together paid about 93 percent of the cost of education. Most federal programs were designed to supplement state or local activities, and the participants in the summit wanted to keep it that way. In their concluding statement, they agreed that the focus in education had to shift from rules and regulation to accountability and results. "We want to swap red tape for results," they wrote.[34]

The phrase heard again and again was that the federal-state partnership would produce initiatives that were "national—not federal." NCEST recommended that the new standards be national but "voluntary, not mandated by the federal government."[35] The governors were well aware of the tendency of the federal government to use relatively small amounts of money to impose large regulatory burdens; they expected to be partners with the federal government in this new enterprise, not wards of Washington. Secretary Riley, like President Clinton and Deputy Secretary Kunin, was a former governor; he understood the governors' perspective and repeatedly assured them that Goals 2000 was entirely voluntary. Each state could choose whether or not to participate. The law itself stipulated that it could not be used as the basis for mandates nor to deny federal funding to a state. The governors nonetheless remained wary.

They had reason to be, for NESIC was designed to be a classic federal agency, whose functions and powers could be redefined and perhaps expanded by Congress in future years. After the passage of Goals 2000, Congress and the executive branch, not the governors, would control the standard-setting process. Indeed, despite the strenuous objections of the National Governors' Association, Congress added two new national goals—one calling for parent participation, the other for professional development for teachers. Although neither was controversial, their addition demonstrated how control of the goals process had shifted from the governors to the federal government and the interest groups that surrounded the legislative process.

At the state level, there was considerable uncertainty about how Goals 2000 would work in practice. The panel each participating state must create to design its education reform plan has extensive powers, including designing and implementing student access to "social services, health care, nutrition, related services, and child-care services" and devising strategies "for improved governance, accountability and management of the state's education system." What will happen if this panel adopts a plan that doubles the state education budget? Or if the panel's priorities differ from those of the state board of education? Or if local boards of education oppose the state plan? At best, the state reform panels will spark a much-needed dialogue about educational improvement; at worst, they may provoke contentious disputes over money and power with existing educational authorities.

The States Take the Lead

For their part, the states were not waiting for federal direction. A survey conducted at the end of 1992 found that most states had "willingly joined the national push toward more demanding, discipline-based content standards, defined in terms of comprehensive curriculum frameworks and innovative assessment systems."[36] Many states had obtained federal funds, either from the National Science Foundation or the Department of Education, to develop improved curriculum frameworks and assessment systems.[37] According to the survey, fifteen states were implementing new curriculum frameworks and another thirty states were planning them; eight states were implementing and twenty-five states were planning new performance standards. Thirteen states were implementing and twenty-eight states were planning new performance-based assessments.[38]

Many states embarked on ambitious reform programs during the 1980s and early 1990s, sometimes because of a court order (as in Kentucky), but more often because the governor or chief state school officer worked with the legislature, the business community, educators, and others to build a consensus for reform (as happened in California, Connecticut, Delaware, Florida, Michigan, Nebraska, Oregon, South Carolina, Texas, and Washington). The National Governors' Association became a major clearinghouse for education reform. With education the leading expenditure in state budgets, consuming an average of one-third of general funds, the governors were active proponents of reform, working to build public support for standards and assessments of student performance; to strengthen accountability (for example, by creating "report cards" for individual schools and districts); to encourage decentralization and deregulation of schools; to "restructure" the state education department, changing its mission from seeking "compliance with procedures" to emphasizing improvement of student performance; to provide choices for students, teachers, and parents (by promoting, for example, choice plans for students, as well as charter schools and magnet schools); and—with an occasional nudge from potential or actual litigation—to revamp the way schools are financed.[39]

The OBE Controversy in Pennsylvania

After the national education summit, one of the first states to revise its standards for what students should learn was Pennsylvania; it also became the setting for intense controversy about the way "standards" or "student outcomes" are defined. In 1989 the State Board of Education began to review the state school code, and committees of professionals recommended that the state's attention shift from Carnegie units—hours spent in the classroom on specific subject areas such as English and science—to "student learning outcomes," or demonstrations of what students have actually learned. By chance, a bipartisan group of Pennsylvania legislators attended a summer institute in 1990 where they heard Chester E. Finn, Jr., advocate the importance of focusing on outcomes, rather than "inputs." A former assistant secretary of education in the Reagan administration and an advisor to Tennessee Governor Lamar Alexander, Finn believed that improvement in student academic achievement should be the most important measure of a school or school system's progress and that the traditional focus on inputs, expenditures, and procedures had undermined student achievement. The legislators returned home convinced that Pennsylvania needed to adopt a strong state program based on student outcomes.

During the summer of 1991, the state department of education produced a draft of more than five hundred "student learning outcomes" that were intended to show what students should know and be able to do in the third, sixth, ninth, and twelfth grades. During the next year, that proposal encountered angry public opposition. In mid-1992 the state board pared the number of outcomes down to fifty-two. After more hearings, more protests, and more revisions, the board approved student learning outcomes in 1993. The controversy did not end there, however.

In the original proposal, the list of outcomes included some that stressed correct values, attitudes, and behaviors. For example, students were to "give examples of their own positive and negative personal impacts on the environment and assess their personal commitment to the environment." Other outcomes stated that "all students [are to] demonstrate the ability to bring about and adapt to change in their own lives" and that "all students [are to] develop personal criteria for making informed moral judgments and ethical decisions."[40] Although most people would probably agree with those values, attitudes, and behaviors, some parents did not think that the state should tell their children what to believe or deny promotion and graduation to any youngster who did not espouse state-approved beliefs. Critics of OBE wondered who would decide which behaviors were ethical. Would their children be barred from graduating if they did not have the right attitudes or self-esteem? The critics distorted the state's intentions, yet the vagueness of the outcomes, as well as the implicit political content of some of them, invited distortion and misunderstanding.

At rallies across the state, opponents warned that OBE would substitute the state for the parent. "This is truly a war," one Democratic state representative said. "Now is the time, and this is the place. No one has the right to treat your child or my child as a guinea pig." The leader of a group of conservative parents, Peg Luksik, declared, "Our children are not and never will be creatures of the state."[41] Opponents wrote angry letters to the editor, expressing such sentiments as: "I keep hearing that OBE is necessary because parents are failing to teach values in the home. This is not true! Parents are just not teaching your values." And, "As a parent, I do not want my children being taught morals and values that may differ from ours. . . . Since when is it up to the state to decide what is morally right?"[42]

Many, although not all, of these critics were conservative Christians, which allowed the defenders of OBE to castigate opponents as fringe groups from the far right.[43] But middle-of-the-road organizations also opposed the outcomes as written. For example, the Pennsylvania Business Roundtable, which supported an outcomes-based plan, objected to the proposed outcomes because they were neither clearly defined nor measurable. The business leaders offered alternative outcomes. In writing, for example, they proposed that a senior in high school should be able to write legibly; use "standard English sentences with correct sentence structure, verb forms, punctuation, capitalization, possessives, plural forms, word choice and spelling"; and use "suitable vocabulary" and "varied sentence patterns, such as simple, compound and complex. . . ."[44] The state's outcome for writing merely stated: "All students write for a variety of purposes, including to narrate, inform and persuade, in all subject areas."[45] Compared with the recommendations from the business leaders, the state's objectives were diffuse, untestable statements.

OBE sounds very much like standards, but the differences are significant. Both OBE and standards start by identifying what students should know and be able to do and then work backward to construct a curriculum that will achieve the appropriate "outcomes." But there are three main differences. First, content standards are clear and measurable. OBE outcomes are so frequently vague that they are inherently unmeasurable. Second, content standards focus on cognitive learning, while OBE outcomes may include not only cognitive learning but also affective skills, attitudes, and psychosocial behaviors. Third, content standards are usually based on traditional academic disciplines, such as history, English, science, mathematics, civics, the arts, and geography. OBE outcomes include some traditional academic disciplines but are mainly organized around interdisciplinary or nondisciplinary topics (such as "communications," "environment and ecology," "self-worth," and "adaptability to change"). Even the outcomes prescribed for academic subjects such as mathematics and science are stated in generalities that provide little or no guidance to teachers, testmakers, or textbook writers.

Compare the Pennsylvania outcome for history ("All students demonstrate an understanding of major events, cultures, groups and individuals in the historical developments of Pennsylvania, the United States and other nations, and describe themes and patterns of historical development") with content standards proposed by the groups developing national history standards. The following are samples of content standards for American history from 1754 to 1815 ("Revolution and the New Nation").

Standard 1: Students Should Know: The causes of the American Revolution, the ideas and interests involved in forging the revolutionary movement, and the reasons for the American victory.
    Students Should Be Able To: Demonstrate understanding of the causes of the American Revolution by:

• Explaining the consequences of the Seven Years War and the overhaul of English imperial policy following the Treaty of

Paris in 1763, demonstrating the connections between the antecedent and consequent events. . . .

- Comparing the arguments advanced by defenders and opponents of the new imperial policy on the traditional rights of English people and the legitimacy of asking the colonies to pay a share of the costs of empire. . . .

- Reconstructing the chronology of the critical events leading to the outbreak of armed conflict between the American colonies and England. . . .

- Analyzing the connection between political and religious ideas and economic interests in bringing about Revolution. . . .

- Reconstructing the arguments among Patriots and Loyalists about independence and drawing conclusions about how the decision to declare independence was reached.[46]

These content standards are specific enough to provide guidance to teachers, textbook writers, and testmakers as well as to students. They are clear and measurable, but they do not dictate how teachers are to teach, they do not contain a single right answer, and they do not promulgate a state-approved version of truth. By contrast, the OBE outcome is too general to provide guidance or to raise standards; it is so broad that it cannot be considered a content standard.

When a Public Agenda survey asked parents about outcomes-based education, focus groups in Minneapolis and Des Moines expressed "a surprising degree of frustration and even ridicule." A parent in Des Moines said, "Outcomes-based education? That's sort of on the idea where the students are all in the classroom, and they decide the way it's going to be and [assign] their own grades." A parent in Minneapolis said, "They have this outcomes-based education. I never did fully understand it, but when I got my son's report card, I was fully confused. It just had columns and check marks of 'has not fully accomplished' or 'needs work accomplishing.' I had no idea where he was at, what level he was at. What *was* he accomplishing? It was a real arbitrary thing—the opinion of the teacher. *She* couldn't even tell us where he was at. It was real vague, without those boundaries and concrete measures that say, 'Yes, he can do fractions, or he knows his multiplication tables.' All of that was totally lost."[47]

OBE in Other States

Conflicts over OBE occurred in more than a dozen other states, including Georgia, Iowa, Ohio, Virginia, and Washington. Critics reacted negatively to language that seemed unexceptional to pedagogues, who had been trained to express their concern for "the whole child" (not just her academic development) and who were accustomed to using impenetrable jargon. Washington abandoned a goal that asked students "to demonstrate that they would be responsible and caring members" of society. James Cooper, the dean of the University of Virginia school of education, commented that "people couldn't show where math was going to be learned directly, where science concepts were going to be learned. They were all interwoven in there, but it was hard to explain it and hard to make the general public understand it."[48]

Albert Shanker wrote that "the problem is not with measuring outcomes instead of inputs; it is with the particular outcomes that OBE reformers propose to measure." "While other industrialized countries call for solving simultaneous linear equations algebraically and by graph or analyzing the causes of the Civil War," he noted, proposed outcomes in Pennsylvania included such outcomes as "all students know and use, when appropriate, community health resources," and "all students know and demonstrate a comprehensive understanding of families, their historical development, and the cultural, economic, social and political factors affecting them." Shanker pointed out that among Ohio's twenty-four outcomes were calls for high school graduates to "function as a responsible family member"; "maintain physical, emotional and social well-being"; and "establish priorities to balance multiple life roles."[49]

Probably the greatest danger OBE poses is not to students, but to the prospects for creating real standards. Indeed, the controversy over OBE in Pennsylvania fueled opposition in other states to efforts to raise standards. In Connecticut, a proposal by a state commission to create an "outcome-based, world-class educational system" was defeated in the Legislature as a result of fierce and misleading criticism. When the commission held that "all children can learn" the critics understood that to mean that bright students would be held back until the slowest students met the new standards. When the commission talked about raising standards for all, the critics asserted that what was really afoot was an egalitarian scheme to "dumb down" the schools by eliminating grades, standardized tests, and individual competition. In a fruitless effort to derail the critics, the commission struck all references to "outcomes-based education" from its proposals. A commission member said, "in Fairfield County, we have a great deal of passion being stirred up through a terrifying vision that is being called outcome-based education. And it is a terrifying vision, even though nothing like it is being proposed; it is the Devil. We have simply got to recognize that that name has been tarnished and lost."[50] In many other states the critics were unable or unwilling to discriminate between vague, affective outcomes and clear academic standards. As a result, even thoughtful efforts to set academic standards—such as those in Kentucky—were jeopardized.

If any benefit derived from the battle over OBE in Pennsylvania, it was that the controversy there stopped or delayed the spread of OBE in other states and forced educators to think seriously about the differences between OBE and content standards. Virginia abandoned plans to adopt a "common core of learning" after Governor Douglas Wilder said that he would not support "value-based education." Georgia backed away from plans to develop learning outcomes. The governor of Minnesota, which had already embraced OBE, announced "I want all the soft goals out; I want the hard, definable, measurable goals in." A superintendent in Ohio warned that "politicians better not use anything with the term 'outcome' in it, because that is a key word that will really send people into orbit." In Kansas the legislature specified that outcomes "related to student academic achievement are the most important and should be emphasized over any others."[51] The Michigan legislature passed a law mandating the development of a state "model core academic curriculum," which "shall not include attitudes, beliefs, or value systems that are not essential in the legal, economic, and social structure of our society and to the personal and social responsibility of citizens of our society."[52]

The most decisive response to the battle over OBE came from the National Education Goals Panel, which reported on progress toward reaching the national goals. The panel declared that "voluntary national content standards should address only the core academic areas as stated in the National Education Goals" and not "non-academic areas such as values, beliefs, student attitudes and behaviors." And it added that "voluntary national content standards must not be compromised or watered down for any reason. The Panel believes that our focus should be on helping each student reach higher levels of academic achievement."[53]

A different set of difficulties confronted those states that were first to create new assessments based on high standards. They quickly learned how painful it would be to leave behind the familiar norm-referenced assessment system. In the past, half the students were usually above the norm, by design; as teachers learned to teach to the test, even more than half the students scored above the norm. This apparent success encouraged parental complacency. As states began to replace norm-referenced, multiple-choice tests with rigorous new assessments, student performance was astonishingly poor.

In Connecticut only one out of every five public school students met or exceeded the state's new academic standards in tests of reading, writing, and mathematics.[54] In 1993 California gave its new test, the California Learning Assessment System, to one million students in the fourth, eighth, and tenth grades; in each subject area, performance was ranked from one (lowest) to 6 (highest), and the kind of student performance that was expected at each level in each subject area was specifically defined. In mathematics only 7 percent of fourth graders, 11 percent of eighth graders, and 9 percent of tenth graders scored at the level of 4 or higher. In writing nearly half of fourth graders and eighth graders and 40 percent of tenth graders scored 4 or higher. In reading 30 percent of fourth graders, 38 percent of eighth graders, and 26 percent of tenth graders reached that level of achievement.[55] California's efforts to introduce performance assessments proved so controversial that some local school districts refused to administer the new state test, and it was subsequently canceled.

As part of a comprehensive reform program that included the introduction of explicit higher standards and new assessments, Kentucky began in 1992 to administer annual statewide tests, modeled on NAEP. Student scores were ranked on a four-level performance scale: novice, apprentice, proficient, and distinguished. In the first year, 1991–92, approximately 90–95 percent of students in the fourth, eighth, and twelfth grades scored in the bottom two levels in every subject tested. Only 10 percent of seniors ranked in the top two levels in reading and mathematics, and only 4 percent scored that high in science. By 1993–94, when the test was given a third time, the state reported dramatic improvements. In all three grades, the proportion in the bottom two levels declined to about 85 percent, and the percentages scoring in the top two levels increased. Among eighth graders, the top group increased from 8 percent to 18 percent in reading and from 13 percent to 19 percent in mathematics. Among twelfth grade students, the top two levels grew from 10 percent to 16 percent in reading, from 10 percent to 19 percent in mathematics, and from 4 percent to 7 percent in science. Tom Boysen, state commissioner of education, saw the results as evidence that the state's reforms were working. The assessments had given the citizens of Kentucky some bad news about student achievement, but they also showed that academic achievement would improve with sustained effort by teachers and students.[56]

The Public's View

What does the public think about the increasing attention to standards and assessments in American education? National pollsters found that the public has strong opinions about these matters and that they are more willing to consider a national curriculum and a national test than their representatives or the education interest groups in Washington. "If the public will governs," the Gallup Poll reported in 1991, "the following developments are inevitable in America: a national curriculum, national standards of achievement in five subjects and in thinking and writing skills; national tests to determine whether the national standards are being met; [and] report cards for individual schools, school districts, states, and the nation. . . . ." The Gallup pollsters found that:

- Sixty-eight percent favored "a standardized national curriculum."

- Seventy-seven percent favored "requiring the public schools in this community to use standardized national tests to measure the academic achievement of students"; of the 23 percent who were opposed or undecided, 57 percent said they would favor such a national test if it were optional for each district, rather than required.

- Eighty-four to 85 percent favored requiring the public schools in their community "to use standardized testing programs to measure students' achievement" in academic subject areas

(English, math, science, history, and geography), in problem-solving skills, and in writing skills.[57]

A poll conducted by the Louis Harris organization in 1991 documented strong public support for higher standards of achievement. It found that more than 80 percent of the public thought that the country "needs common national standards of performance that all schools should be expected to live up to" and nearly 90 percent thought that the United States needs "to reach higher standards of educational achievement" to be competitive in the world economy. Fully 95 percent of employers thought that such standards were needed. Interestingly, when asked whether schools already had clear standards, 37 percent of the public said yes; as did 44 percent of the recent graduates who took jobs upon leaving school, 31 percent of the recent graduates who went on to higher education, and 28 percent of parents, but only 20 percent of employers.[58]

To probe public opinion more deeply, the New Standards Project commissioned Public Agenda, an organization that studies public opinion, to talk to focus groups of parents, students, teachers, and members of the general public. In a report published in 1993, Public Agenda found "broad and spontaneous support for the notion that higher expectations will motivate improved performance. . . ." Those polled expressed a "bedrock belief that if you expect more from people, you will get more." But Public Agenda also found "deep concern about kids who can't achieve higher expectations" and fear about whether low-achieving students would fail; there was "a recurring assumption that . . . some students . . . could not achieve higher standards."[59]

The public was also skeptical of the claim by the New Standards Project that all children could reach high standards, a claim similar to the assertion by the Clinton administration that "*all* children in America will develop the knowledge, skills, and habits of mind we once expected of only our *top* students."[60] The opinion surveyors found that

Although people think most students can achieve more, they resist the generalization that *every single student* will be able to achieve the new standards. Their experience and intuition tell them otherwise. Exceptions automatically come to people's minds: children with disabilities, children whose first language is not English, etc. Many teachers feel that they are already struggling with overcoming differences of ability, aptitude and motivation among students. Parents referred to different patterns of achievement between their own children, as did students of their fellow classmates. Some of the general public sensed an inherent contradiction between the phrases 'all students' and 'high standards,' envisioning that either all students would not meet the standards or that the standards would not be that high after all.[61]

When the questioners compared American educational standards with those in other countries, people "recoiled." When comparison was made with Japan and Germany, almost every focus group "spontaneously brought up the image of Japanese students committing suicide after failing a test." When the comparison was made to Sweden and France, "the same recoil effect was triggered," as well as "the same stories about Japanese suicides." The respondents seemed convinced that other nations' school systems "succeed by excessive pressure and rigidity." (The oft-repeated assertion that Japanese students have a high suicide rate because of academic pressure is ironic, because the suicide rate of American adolescents is much higher than that of Japanese adolescents.)[62]

This survey was conducted to help the New Standards Project, but the results are instructive about the pitfalls likely to entangle efforts to raise standards or to change the status quo when the debate moves from Washington and state capitols to local communities.

First, the public likes the idea of raising expectations; it fits with their commonsense understanding of human nature and the way things work. But at the same time the public fears that higher standards will be accompanied by unacceptable levels of pressure on all students and by failure for some.

Second, the skepticism about utopian promises is enormous. People suspect that the promise that all children can succeed is either untrue, wholly unrealistic, or implies low standards for all.

Third, people are angry and defensive about claims that other nations do a better job of educating their children; they do not want to hear it. If some other country's students are doing better than American students are, it must be because they are putting too much pressure on their children (a claim that frequently appears in professional educational journals). As Harold Stevenson's work shows, Americans prefer to have children who are "well-rounded" rather than children who are good in school.

Fourth, the public likes the idea of portfolio assessments and other kinds of performance assessment, as well as open-ended test questions. People can see the advantage of nontraditional assessments—projects, activities, and other such demonstrations of student work. But they continue also to expect objective grades that compare student performance to others of their age. Thus, efforts to eliminate traditional grading are likely to encounter public resistance.

Fifth, people are worried about who will set the standards. Teachers are concerned that they will be set by "academics and educational administrators who have not been in a 'real' classroom for years." Members of the general public fear that national standards would entail "yet another federal bureaucracy based in Washington, D.C., inefficient and disconnected from local communities." People do not trust the federal government to set standards for their schools. Respondents also doubt the ability of the public school system to follow through on any real educational reform, and they are unwilling to pay higher taxes for systems that they see as "wasteful and top-heavy with administrators."[63]

Sixth, people express "powerful resistance" to the idea of grouping together students of different ability levels. Students and parents fear that low-ability students would be "subjected to ridicule" while high-ability students would be "held back." Although many educational policymakers and researchers embrace heterogeneous grouping, "it ran strongly counter to the intuition and experience of most people" and is "an extremely controversial and unpopular idea to many people, engendering opposition and intense disagreement."[64]

A Public Agenda survey in mid-1994 found that education experts and policymakers were dangerously out of touch with public opinion. By wide margins the public's major education concerns were safety, order, and mastering the basics. The public supports higher standards by huge margins: 88 percent thought that students should not be allowed to graduate from high school unless they had demonstrated the ability to write and speak English well, and 82 percent endorsed "very clear guidelines on what students should learn and teachers should teach in every major subject." But what really bothered respondents were issues that education leaders tended to ignore or belittle: discipline problems, metal detectors in schools, the failure of schools to enforce standards of appropriate behavior, and the schools' neglect of the basics (not only reading, writing, and arithmetic, but also grammar, spelling, and computation).

This poll carried a powerful message. When leading educators advocate high standards, they often link them to new teaching methods, new forms of assessment, and other classroom innovations. But when the public endorses high standards, it means a return to traditional education, with emphasis on the basics, an end to social promotion, removal of disruptive students from the classroom, firm disciplinary policies, and clear standards for promotion and graduation. People who were polled expressed skepticism, even outright opposition, toward innovative practices. NCTM leaders, for example, want children to use calculators instead of learning rote computation; but 86 percent of those polled think that children should first learn to do arithmetic "by hand," including memorizing multiplication tables, and only 10 percent agreed that young children should use calculators from the start. Leaders in English believe that children should be encouraged to write without having their errors corrected, but 60 percent of the respondents objected to teaching composition without also teaching spelling. Most people want schools that are cheerful, disciplined, and purposeful, where learning is interesting and enjoyable, where children are expected to meet clear demands for school work and good behavior, and where students learn such values as honesty, tolerance, and equality.[65]

These public attitudes—a mixture of hope and skepticism, of openness to change but not too much change—portend resistance to many current reform initiatives, unless reformers can make a better case for their proposals. What is more, the poll clearly reveals a deep fissure between the public's definition of high standards and the experts' definition. In the abstract everyone gladly pays homage to the idea of higher standards, but when state and local officials present a specific program that flies in the face of what the public thinks is needed, trouble lies ahead. And when that program is couched in jargon and laden with unrealistic promises, the public is likely to be unresponsive and suspicious. The public clearly supports national standards and national testing, but the way these initiatives are introduced and translated at the state and local level has the potential to generate intense controversy.

Political Obstacles to Standard Setting

This much is clear about the politics of standards: Getting legislation to establish national voluntary standards through Congress is difficult but ultimately easier than the process of actually developing meaningful standards. The diversity of political agendas that has fragmented the education system may also fragment the effort to establish standards. The multiplicity of often conflicting goals, purposes, and intentions that have become commonplace in American education will make it difficult, if not impossible, to establish high standards. The politics of education guarantees a veto to a broad assortment of interest groups, creates entitlements for others, and permits exceptions for still others. These are the very conditions that created the current educational system, in which schools expect little effort from students while offering them inflated grades and self-esteem. It is unlikely that standard-setting activities can be insulated from the interest group politics that promotes uniformity of practice and tolerance of mediocrity.

In each subject area mentioned in the national goals, and in some that are not mentioned, efforts are under way to forge national content standards. Each activity involves dozens of organizations and many hundreds of knowledgeable people, including teachers, scholars, administrators, laypeople, Washington-based lobbyists, and others. Each such group is working through a consensus process; their draft standards will be circulated widely for review and comment. NESIC, the agency created by Goals 2000, will certify voluntary national standards, as well as standards submitted by states.

The potential dangers and pitfalls in this process are numerous. In other nations, national standards are created by a highly professional ministry of education. Americans will learn in the next few years whether an elaborate negotiation among divergent groups can produce high national standards. If the negotiators are sufficiently representative of the field and the public, it might reproduce the current system, with its well-known aversion to real standards and accountability. The negotiation process itself might result in watered-down standards, to win the support of the broadest number of participants.

California succeeded in producing high standards because the state's educational leadership continually pushed and prodded participants in the consensus, insisting that the goal was not simply to reach agreement but to reach agreement on high standards. This process did not compromise every difference by acceding to every demand; a critical element of its success was a leadership willing to say no to inappropriate demands and pressures. The same determination will be necessary to prevent the dilution of national standards into minimum standards. The effort to create national standards will fail if the standards are so low that they challenge no one, so vague that no one takes issue with them or so vast in their coverage that they are beyond the comprehension of students and teachers alike. The fields of English and history face the challenges of multiculturalism. In the case of English, some partisans will be reluctant to agree that any particular language (say, English) deserves special status in the nation's classrooms. In the case of history, pressures to include coverage of everyone's ancestors and homelands, as well as multiple perspectives on every event, threaten to ignite divisive culture wars and turn the project into an encyclopedia instead of content standards that identify key concepts and essential knowledge and skills.

NESIC is supposed to review the draft standards to determine whether they are empirically sound; to measure them against the standards of successful school systems, both here and abroad; and to ensure that the proposed standards are clearly the best guides to high performance, rather than the most that could be expected from a process of negotiations. Empirical standards, such as those produced by athletes and scientists, are discovered, not negotiated. Given the political nature of NESIC's membership, will it be a body more attuned to negotiation and compromise than to empirical standard-setting? Will NESIC itself have the capacity to insist on standards that are high but attainable with sustained effort by students?

The difficulties at the state and local level will be no less challenging. Every state (and the District of Columbia) must shape new content standards and assessments, as well as opportunity-to-learn standards. Every state must develop and implement complex reform plans that affect every aspect of education and social services for children. Ahead lie countless battles over ideology, money, and control. Some state departments of education, never comfortable with focusing on academic content, will push neo-OBE concepts. Some educationists will insist that the new national standards—because they are grounded in the academic disciplines—are too hard, too narrow, and too confining, and they will seek ways to emasculate (or "coordinate" or "integrate") whatever is adopted at the national level. Some parent and community groups will object to any educational initiative that comes from Washington as a violation of local control. Some states will get it right, others will not. Goals 2000 could provoke a blizzard of activity and controversy, with no real results, or it could prove to be the most important education legislation in the United States since the passage of the Elementary and Secondary Education Act in 1965. Whether change or inertia prevails probably will not be known for fifteen to twenty years.

Federal funding will keep alive the discussion about standards as well as state-level activities. Hundreds of millions of dollars will be appropriated to encourage states to engage in their own standard-setting programs and to create state tests. Inside the nation's capital, Goals 2000 is seen as a mighty achievement, a forceful step in a new direction. Outside Washington, educators and ordinary citizens are confused. They are confused by the legislation because it is complicated and not easily understood. Even those in the field of education do not understand who will do what and how national standards will work. People are confused by declarations that all children can learn when they know that many students—especially in urban schools—are achieving at levels far below what is needed to enter college or take on a skilled job. It is not obvious how national standards, once adopted, will improve the achievement or motivation of students who are not now learning to read, write, or compute.

The sharp distinction between the rhetorical aims of Goals 2000 and the harsh realities of urban education may well induce cynicism. And yet poor and minority students suffer more from low standards than any other group in American education. It is they who are likeliest to endure years of workbooks, skill sheets, and meaningless drills. And it is they who are least likely to encounter good literature, challenging real-life problems in mathematics and science, and hands-on projects in history and English. The standards, if ever fully realized, can support inspired teaching. And they should be able to communicate clearly to students the message that success in school is within their reach and depends on their own efforts.

Is the goal—higher levels of academic achievement for all students—worth the effort? Absolutely. Although not every student will reach the highest levels of performance, all students can learn much more than they do now and improve their academic performance.

Irving Louis Horowitz of Rutgers University has described the shaping of standards as "a way of doing things by identifying or creating or constructing models of performance to which presumably rational persons can aspire." Two points in his description bear remembering. First, identifying models of performance must be a process of continuous improvement; second, the models of performance that serve as standards must be better than common practice; they must be models to which "presumably rational people can aspire." "Deep risks" must be taken in the process of setting and revising standards, Horowitz observes, but "there are catastrophes in the failure to run such risks."[66]

6

Conclusions and Recommendations

 THE DEBATE IN WASHINGTON, in the state capitols, and at the local level reflects a lack of consensus among Americans about what they expect from education and what they are willing to do to meet or raise their expectations. Higher standards are a good idea, Americans tell pollsters, but it is not clear that anyone is willing to concede anything to get them. Yes, higher standards are needed, but who can be trusted to set them? Yes, higher standards are needed, but no one should be examined or held accountable until everyone has access to equal resources, teachers, and facilities. Yes, higher standards are needed, but not if it means that students will feel pressured or that they will not have enough time for athletics or after-school jobs or a full social life.

Ultimately, the improvement of American education depends not on a technocratic solution, not on getting the right laws written, not even on reorganizing the schools' bureaucratic structures. The missing ingredient continues to be widespread agreement on the value of a challenging and rigorous education for everyone. One obstacle is sub-

177

tle elitism, a deeply ingrained belief that only the very smartest young-sters need or should get an excellent education; for most students, the elitist argues, punching the time clock at school is good enough. For most students, just getting by with minimal effort in school is good enough. Anything more would not be "appropriate" to their needs. And what needs are those? Well, their need to be entertained; their need to hang out with their friends; their need not to have their minds stretched too much or their imaginations opened too wide.

Do we really want higher standards? Do we want schools where students work hard and take their education seriously? Do we want a society in which everyone is well educated and knowledgeable about history, literature, science, mathematics, and the arts? Or do we want schools where academic studies are no more important, perhaps less important, than athletics and social activities?

Policymakers and educational experts paint an idealistic vision of schools where students cheerfully apply the principles of physics and geometry to the solution of real-life problems. But their vision com-petes with the anti-intellectualism that dominates both the American adolescent and popular cultures. It is no secret that high-achieving students risk being called "nerds," "geeks," "brainiacs," and other epithets. Adolescents, perhaps imitating adults, respect good looks, money, and athletic talent. The popular culture admires those quali-ties and rewards them.

If the world really is changing to one driven by brainpower rather than brawnpower, then that message must be conveyed to parents, children, and teachers alike. It must be conveyed to schools of edu-cation, state departments of education, employers, and universities. It must be recognized, too, by the mass media. If we are serious about building a society in which everyone is well educated, then we have to realize that our efforts must extend far beyond the walls of the school.

Children need to know that working hard in school is important and that they must devote themselves to their education. The adults in their lives—their family and teachers—must continually rein-force the value of learning, of investing in one's mind and skills. But this lesson cannot be taught unless adults believe it. Harold Stevenson's international studies have documented that American parents express high levels of satisfaction with average, even me-diocre, educational performance by their children. Many school administrators think that it is their duty to assure parents that their schools are doing an outstanding job, so that public confidence in the schools will remain high. Until some objective measures of school performance are devised, parents will continue to be uninformed about how their children are doing and whether they are getting a first-rate education.

A Louis Harris poll conducted in 1991 demonstrated just how wide the perception gap is. Large majorities of students and their parents believe that students are well prepared for work and higher education. Employers and college educators do not agree. Sixty-three percent of college educators say that the "high school education of their recently admitted students leaves them well short of being properly prepared" and that today's students are "worse prepared" than those of ten years ago. Although students arrive on campus eager to learn, the poll said, "almost entirely missing . . . are the disciplines necessary to achieve [their] goals: dedication to learning, discipline in work habits, and learning how to solve complex problems. And, underneath it all, of course, is the lack of functional literacy and basic skills in reading, writing, math, understanding written and verbal instructions, and doing arithmetic functions." Similarly, by large majorities, employers admire the positive attitudes of their new hires out of high school, but they are convinced that they are "by and large borderline in terms of functional literacy, their capacity to express themselves, and their basic functional skills. Most of all, they have little in the way of capacity for high concentration or creative and skillful application of their minds to work challenges." Yet in every area where employers and educators see a deficit in students' preparation, students believe that they are well prepared.[1]

How will students and their parents learn what employers and higher education expect of them? How can they reach for higher standards if they are satisfied with mediocre performance? How can they improve if they do not know that they need to improve? Clearly, employers and institutions of higher education must do a better job of communicating their expectations to the nation's schools. Some sort of testing or assessment that produces accurate and reliable information is needed so that students and their parents get an honest accounting of their readiness for the real world.

Will national standards improve student achievement? By themselves, probably not. If adults who are important in the lives of children do not set a good example and do not encourage children to excel in school, then national standards will be of little consequence.

Will systemic reform improve achievement? If systemic reform is understood to mean standards-based reform, then it suggests a reasonable scenario for dynamic and purposeful interaction on behalf of educational improvement. The first step in educational reform is to decide what children should learn. That provides a basis for changing teacher education, because teachers should learn what they are supposed to teach and how to teach it. It also provides a basis for teacher certification, because teachers should be certified only when they can demonstrate that they know what they are supposed to teach their students. Knowing what children should learn also provides a foundation for tests, because tests should assess what children have learned and whether they can apply what they have learned. Textbooks and technology should be prepared to help students meet high standards. Today, teachers teach what is in the textbooks and what is tested; that is backward.

Does the slogan "all children can learn" mean that the curriculum will be dumbed down, that bright kids will be held back until the slowest student catches up? No. It means that all children have the capacity to learn and that no child should be treated as a dummy and thrown on the ash heap. It means that, given enough time, all children can reach higher levels of learning than children currently achieve. It means that if more is expected of children, they will stretch to meet those expectations. It does *not* mean that all children should be taught at the same pace; some children learn faster than others, and they should move forward more quickly so they do not get bored. Every nation in the world has a spread of student achievement, with some students at the bottom and others at the top. The goal must be to raise achievement for all students, while narrowing the range from top to bottom. This does not mean dragging down the students at the top but expecting more of all students, especially those who are in the bottom half.

Does Goals 2000 offer the means to get from here to there? That is an impossible question to answer because Goals 2000 involves so many actors and so many contingencies. Most federal education programs consist of a relatively simple transaction: in return for federal funds, a state, district, or school must meet eligibility requirements and do certain things to accomplish the goal of the legislation. Sometimes the goal is to distribute federal dollars to schools where it is needed, a goal that can be easily tracked and measured.

But implementing Goals 2000 is far more complicated; it relies on many different moving parts. Many different panels must make sound decisions. The standard-setting groups must develop clearly stated standards that are concise and challenging, limited only to what is most important in each field. The National Education Standards and Improvement Council and the National Education Goals Panel must insist on high national standards and rigorous state standards. The states and territories must develop reform plans that set high standards and develop excellent student assessments. The national commission creating model opportunity-to-learn standards must propose practical steps that will encourage school improvement without suppressing innovation or busting state and local budgets. Everyone on every panel must be thoroughly nonpartisan and constantly wary of the dangers of overregulation. No one can know whether all of these things will happen, whether they will be done well, or what the unintended consequences will be. There will surely be lawsuits galore, for the legislation will predictably unleash new demands for equalization or fiscal "adequacy" (a concept that goes beyond equal resources).

What bears watching in Goals 2000 is the precedent it establishes for federal legislation that influences the kinds of textbooks, teaching materials, teacher training methods, and research findings that must be used in every school receiving federal funds. For many years, the federal government exercised great restraint by respecting state and local control of education. In the future, because of Goals 2000 and its tight linkage to the Elementary and Secondary Education Act (which allocates billions of dollars to the nation's schools and which, beginning in 1995, requires states to submit their standards and assessments to the federal government for approval), federal regulation may extend much more directly into what is taught, how it is taught, the conditions in which it is taught, and how it is tested. Restraint is still needed, however. Schools work best when they are managed by the people who are closest to them, not by Congress and interest groups in Washington, D.C., and not by state legislators and bureaucratic overseers.

The implementation of Goals 2000 will be the work of many years. In the meanwhile, here are some issues on which everyone can work.

First, whether Congress is controlled by Democrats or Republicans, it should pledge not to meddle in the educational affairs of the nation's schools. Congress should not write guidelines for tests, textbooks, sex education, teachers' preparation, discipline, or other matters that in a federal system properly belong to states, districts, and schools. Congress should remember that the intent of the national goals process is to create academic standards that are national, not federal. Congress should deregulate federal education programs and allow increased flexibility in the use of federal education funds. The overriding goal of education reform must be to improve student achievement, not to prod schools into a common mold by imposing regulations and mandates.

Second, Congress can substantially improve Goals 2000 by adopting four important changes:

Change the composition of the National Education Standards and Improvement Council (NESIC), whose presidentially appointed membership is dominated by education interest groups and may not necessarily be bipartisan. Replace it with a new council composed of educators, lay persons, and public officials and appointed by the bipartisan National Education Goals Panel. This was the original proposal of the National Council on Education Standards and Testing, which sought to depoliticize this crucial body and to shield it from partisan and interest-group pressure. The Clinton administration's original legislation contained a similar proposal.

Specify that any voluntary national standards and assessments must be approved by a two-thirds majority of NESIC (or its successor organization). The original Clinton bill included this provision; Congress changed it to a simple majority. A supermajority is necessary to prevent the adoption of content standards and assessments that are highly controversial and that lack broad popular support.

Eliminate the detailed requirements of the "state improvement plan," which compels states to appoint huge planning committees and mandates their composition and duties. States should be encouraged by new federal funding to establish academic standards and assessments, but the process of standard setting should be designed by states and localities, not by Congress.

Remove congressional restrictions on student testing. Congress is not competent to write technical specifications for educational testing; states and localities should make their own decisions about student testing.

Third, the national content standards should remain voluntary and should be regularly revised. They should serve as a vision of what is possible. They should be clearly understood as goals for academic achievement (unfortunately, the word "outcomes" has lost its value in this discussion). They should not be used to dictate instructional methods or to discredit unorthodox (or orthodox) educational programs. E. D. Hirsch Jr.'s "core knowledge" curriculum, for example, draws the wrath of the "language arts" professionals, but it appears to be extremely effective and is well liked by the educators who use it. National standards should not be used as a tool for pedagogical imperialism to silence innovators and dissidents. It matters not whether children learn to read using phonics, whole language, or some other method; it matters only that they learn to read well. If some visionary teacher finds a better way to teach mathematics or history or science, the national standards should not get in the way.

Fourth, multiple kinds of assessments will be needed to ensure that tests are used for the right purpose and to provide the information that is needed. *Congress must continue to support the National Assessment of Educational Progress*, which tests national and state samples on a regular basis. NAEP acts as a barometer of student achievement; it has proven its worth over a quarter of a century. Without a strong and independent NAEP (made so by its bipartisan governing board), little would be known about the performance of our schools and students. NAEP may not now be administered to any jurisdiction smaller than a state. Yet many school districts want to use NAEP tests on a sampling basis to find out how their students compare with others of their age and others in their state. Congress should permit such testing.

The customary method of testing in the classroom should be performance assessment, not multiple-choice tests. Students should be expected to demonstrate that they can apply what they have learned. Students should know that they will be expected to write essays, perform scientific experiments, engage in debates about historical issues, and exhibit in a variety of ways what they have learned.

Selection examinations, such as the SAT, should test not only reasoning ability and mathematical skill, but also school subjects such as science, history, geography, English, and civics, so that students know that what they learn in school will count on their college admission examination.

Something is missing from the menu offered thus far, and that is, *an examination for individual students that provides comparative performance data*. Some schools and districts will continue to use standardized, multiple-choice tests. But something more is needed. Because Goals 2000 does not lay the groundwork for a national examination system, private testing organizations have an opportunity to create an examination based on the new national content standards. A new examination should produce accurate information about student performance compared with others of the same age and grade, here and abroad. If such a test were widely recognized for its quality, students could submit their results with their college and employment applications.

Fifth, states and districts should create report cards for individual schools and districts. These report cards should provide relevant information for parents, students, and the public. They should include information about overall student performance, dropout and completion rates, staff qualifications, resources, facilities, program offerings, and course-taking patterns. Such report cards should be available not only because parents and others have the right to such information, but because the information helps to establish performance benchmarks and to determine where resources and improvements are needed. Utilizing school report cards, parents and students will be prepared to choose a school that is best for the student.

Sixth, a reliable system of standards and assessments will make it possible for districts and states to monitor school quality and to target assistance where it is needed. States and local school districts should focus on improving student performance and minimize regulations and mandates. Schools must be free to meet high standards in different ways. Clear measures of "value added" (that is, improved performance) must be developed, and assessments should measure progress toward meeting the standards. States and school districts must also take seriously their obligation to ensure that schools have adequate resources and that funding patterns among schools are fair. School-based budgeting will be necessary to make visible the equitable allocation and efficient utilization of resources. Schools with concentrations of disadvantaged or handicapped children will require extra resources. Debates over opportunity-to-learn standards should not be allowed to serve as excuses to defer or avoid setting content standards, performance standards, and assessments.

Seventh, parents must let their children know that nothing is more important than getting a good education and that they must apply themselves earnestly to their school work. Parents should read to their children when they are very young, set strict limits on television watching, monitor their homework, and visit regularly with their teachers. Parents can set a good example by reading and showing that they too want to keep learning. They should talk to their children about current events and take them to libraries, museums, concerts, and historical sites. Parents are their children's first teachers, and if they ignore their responsibilities, the schools are at an enormous disadvantage.

Eighth, every school and school district should reexamine its standards for promotion and graduation to determine whether students are learning the skills and knowledge that they will need for college, citizenship, personal development, and work. Educators should call on parents, local employers, colleges, and civic leaders to help establish academic standards for students and the schools. Schools and school districts should also adopt standards for student conduct.

Ninth, colleges and universities should be aware of the way that their entry standards affect the graduation requirements of the high schools. They should work closely with high schools to eliminate the necessity for remedial courses in college. Even when colleges intend to accept most applicants, they should make clear in advance what kind of educational preparation is needed for success in their institution.

Tenth, employers should insist on high school transcripts when they are hiring, and the schools should develop transcripts that are "employer friendly." These transcripts should provide clear information about grades, courses taken, attendance, behavior, effort, and extracurricular activities. Students need to know that their work in school will count in the world of work. Transcripts should include a teacher's recommendation.

Eleventh, in helping students prepare for the adult world, schools should teach standards of comportment as well as academic standards. New York City recently hired a firm to help people leave the welfare rolls. Payment to the firm is performance-based, paid only if the client is able to hold a job for at least four months. Before sending clients out for a job, the firm gives them training, teaching them, among other things, how to speak properly, how to dress for the world of work, and how to be punctual (if clients are late for a training class by as much as five minutes, they are dropped from the program). The city is paying the training agency to teach welfare clients what teachers used to teach as a matter of course. It is not outcomes-based education that is needed, but common sense, common decency, and a willingness to teach and learn the fundamental skills needed to succeed in the workplace.

Twelfth, the grownups in this society—parents, educators, civic leaders, neighbors, and everyone else—must resolve to take action against the violence, disorder, and crime that threaten too many children. Schools must be orderly, purposeful, cheerful places where children are safe and where learning can take place. Factory-style schools should be replaced with small schools where teachers and children know each other. Stronger bonds among teachers, parents, and students will facilitate not only a sense of community, but also higher standards of learning.

Finally, a system of standards and assessments, no matter how reliable, will not solve all the problems of American education. It will not substitute for the protection of a loving family, it will not guard children against the violence of the streets, it will not alleviate poverty, and it will not turn off the television at night. But a system of standards and assessments might help to focus the priorities of the educational system on teaching and learning, which is no small matter in a world where what you are and what you can aspire to depends increasingly on what you know. As a society our goal must be to see that knowledge is broadly democratized, that *all* children in America have equal educational opportunity, that the work of teachers is valued and respected, that the brainpower of this nation is treated as its most precious resource, and that we do not waste the educational potential of even one of our citizens.

Appendix

The National Education Goals

1. *School Readiness. By the year 2000, all children in America will start school ready to learn.*
   The objectives for this goal are that

   - All children will have access to high-quality and developmentally appropriate preschool programs that help prepare children for school;

   - Every parent in the United States will be a child's first teacher and devote time each day to helping such parent's preschool child learn, and parents will have access to the training and support parents need; and

As adopted by Congress in March 1994, as part of the Goals 2000: Educate America Act.

- Children will receive the nutrition, physical activity experiences, and health care needed to arrive at school with healthy minds and bodies, and to maintain the mental alertness necessary to be prepared to learn, and the number of low-birthweight babies will be significantly reduced through enhanced prenatal health systems.

2. *School Completion. By the year 2000, the high school graduation rate will increase to at least 90 percent.*
   The objectives for this goal are that

   - The Nation must dramatically reduce its school dropout rate, and 75 percent of the students who do drop out will successfully complete a high school degree or its equivalent; and

   - The gap in high school graduation rates between American students from minority backgrounds and their non-minority counterparts will be eliminated.

3. *Student Achievement and Citizenship. By the year 2000, all students will leave grades 4, 8, and 12 having demonstrated competency over challenging subject matter including English, mathematics, science, foreign languages, civics and government, economics, arts, history, and geography, and every school in America will ensure that all students learn to use their minds well, so they may be prepared for responsible citizenship, further learning, and productive employment in our Nation's modern economy.*
   The objectives for this goal are that

   - The academic performance of all students at the elementary and secondary level will increase significantly in every quartile, and the distribution of minority students in each quartile will more closely reflect the student population as a whole;

   - The percentage of all students who demonstrate the ability to reason, solve problems, apply knowledge, and write and communicate effectively will increase substantially;

- All students will be involved in activities that promote and demonstrate good citizenship, good health, community service, and personal responsibility;

- All students will have access to physical education and health education to ensure they are healthy and fit;

- The percentage of all students who are competent in more than one language will substantially increase; and

- All students will be knowledgeable about the diverse cultural heritage of this Nation and about the world community.

4. *Teacher Education and Professional Development. By the year 2000, the Nation's teaching force will have access to programs for the continued improvement of their professional skills and the opportunity to acquire the knowledge and skills needed to instruct and prepare all American students for the next century.*
The objectives for this goal are that

- All teachers will have access to preservice teacher education and continuing professional development activities that will provide such teachers with the knowledge and skills needed to teach to an increasingly diverse student population with a variety of educational, social, and health needs;

- All teachers will have continuing opportunities to acquire additional knowledge and skills needed to teach challenging subject matter and to use emerging new methods, forms of assessment, and technologies;

- States and school districts will create integrated strategies to attract, recruit, prepare, retrain, and support the continued professional development of teachers, administrators, and other educators, so that there is a highly talented work force of professional educators to teach challenging subject matter; and

- Partnerships will be established, whenever possible, among local educational agencies, institutions of higher education, parents, and local labor, business, and professional associations to provide and support programs for the professional development of educators.

5. *Mathematics and Science. By the year 2000, United States students will be first in the world in mathematics and science achievement.* The objectives for this goal are that

- Mathematics and science education, including the metric system of measurement, will be strengthened throughout the system, especially in the early grades;

- The number of teachers with a substantive background in mathematics and science, including the metric system of measurement, will increase by 50 percent; and

- The number of United States undergraduates and graduate students, especially women and minorities, who complete degrees in mathematics, science, and engineering will increase significantly.

6. *Adult Literacy and Lifelong Learning. By the year 2000, every adult American will be literate and will possess the knowledge and skills necessary to compete in a global economy and exercise the rights and responsibilities of citizenship.*
The objectives for this goal are that

- Every major American business will be involved in strengthening the connection between education and work;

- All workers will have the opportunity to acquire the knowledge and skills, from basic to highly technical, needed to adapt to emerging new technologies, work methods, and markets through public and private educational, vocational, technical, workplace, or other programs;

- The number of quality programs, including those at libraries, that are designed to serve more effectively the needs of the growing number of part-time and midcareer students will increase substantially;

- The proportion of the qualified students, especially minorities, who enter college, who complete at least two years, and who complete their degree programs will increase substantially.

- The proportion of college graduates who demonstrate an advanced ability to think critically, communicate effectively, and solve problems will increase substantially; and

- Schools, in implementing comprehensive parent involvement programs, will offer more adult literacy, parent training and life-long learning opportunities to improve the ties between home and school, and enhance parents' work and home lives.

7. *Safe, Disciplined, and Alcohol- and Drug-Free Schools. By the year 2000, every school in the United States will be free of drugs, violence, and the unauthorized presence of firearms and alcohol and will offer a disciplined environment conducive to learning.*
The objectives for this goal are that

- Every school will implement a firm and fair policy on use, possession, and distribution of drugs and alcohol;

- Parents, businesses, governmental and community organizations will work together to ensure the rights of students to study in a safe and secure environment that is free of drugs and crime, and that schools provide a healthy environment and are a safe haven for all children;

- Every local educational agency will develop and implement a policy to ensure that all schools are free of violence and the unauthorized presence of weapons;

- Every local educational agency will develop a sequential, comprehensive kindergarten through twelfth grade drug and alcohol prevention education program;

- Drug and alcohol curriculum should be taught as an integral part of sequential, comprehensive health education;

- Community-based teams should be organized to provide students and teachers with needed support; and

- Every school should work to eliminate sexual harassment.

8. *Parental Participation. By the year 2000, every school shall promote partnerships that will increase parental involvement and participation in promoting the social, emotional, and academic growth of children.*
The objectives of this goal are that

- Every State will develop policies to assist local schools and local educational agencies to establish programs for increasing partnerships that respond to the varying needs of parents and the home, including parents of children who are disadvantaged or bilingual, or parents of children with disabilities;

- Every school will actively engage parents and families in a partnership which supports the academic work of children at home and shared educational decisionmaking at schools; and

- Parents and families will help to ensure that schools are adequately supported and will hold schools and teachers to high standards of accountability.

Notes

Introduction

1. National Education Goals Panel, *National Education Goals Report: Building a Nation of Learners* (Government Printing Office, 1992), pp. 321–22.

2. Australia, Belgium, Canada, France, Ireland, Japan, the Netherlands, New Zealand, and Spain have a higher proportion of their population ages 2–29 enrolled in school than does the United States; Denmark, Finland, France, Germany, Ireland, Japan, Sweden, and Switzerland have higher rates of secondary school completion than does the United States. Organization for Economic Cooperation and Development, *Education at a Glance: OECD Indicators* (Paris: 1992), p. 97.

3. Frank Levy, with Richard Murnane and Lijian Chen, "Education and Skills for the U.S. Work Force," *Aspen Institute Quarterly*, vol. 6 (Winter 1994), pp. 42–61.

4. The tests administered to random samples by the federally funded National Assessment of Educational Progress (NAEP) are widely respected as a gauge of student achievement, but NAEP does not report the scores of individual students, nor does it report scores for jurisdictions smaller than states.

5. Committee for Economic Development, *Putting Learning First: Governing and Managing the Schools for High Achievement* (New York: 1994).

Chapter 1

1. *Merriam-Webster's Collegiate Dictionary,* 10th ed. (Springfield, Mass., 1993), p. 1145.

2. Albert L. Batik, *The Engineering Standard: A Most Useful Tool* (Ashland, Ohio: Bookmaster/El Rancho, 1992), pp. 2, 5, 6, 9.

3. U.S. Constitution, art. 1, sec. 8.

4. *Promises to Keep: Creating High Standards for American Students,* Report on the Review of Education Standards from the Goals 3 and 4 Technical Planning Group to the National Education Goals Panel, November 15, 1993, p. 9.

5. Ibid., p. 22.

6. National Center for Education Statistics, *NAEP 1992 Writing Report Card* (U.S. Department of Education, 1994), p. 22.

7. For a valuable discussion of the history of state responsibility for opportunity-to-learn standards, see Richard F. Elmore and Susan H. Fuhrman, "Opportunity to Learn and the State Role in Education," *The Debate on Opportunity-to-Learn Standards* (Washington: National Governors' Association, 1993), pp. 73–102.

8. Government of Japan, Ministry of Education, Science, and Culture, *Course of Study for Elementary Schools in Japan* (Tokyo: 1983), p. 65.

9. Ibid., p. 50.

10. John H. Bishop, "Impacts of School Organization and Signalling on Incentives to Learn in France, The Netherlands, England, Scotland, and the United States," Working Paper 93-21. Cornell University, Center for Advanced Human Resource Studies, November 9, 1993.

11. American Federation of Teachers and National Center for Improving Science Education/The NETWORK, Inc., *What College-Bound Students Abroad Are Expected to Know about Biology* (Washington: American Federation of Teachers, 1994), pp. 3, 30, 48.

12. The SAT (formerly the Scholastic Aptitude Test), administered by the Educational Testing Service and sponsored by the College Board, consists

of sections on verbal ability and mathematics; 42 percent of all high school graduates took this test in 1994. The ACT, administered by the American College Testing program, consists of tests of English, reading, science, and mathematics; about 35 percent of all high school graduates took it in 1994. College Board, *College Board Scores: 1994 Profile of SAT and Achievement Test Takers* (New York: 1994).

13. Stephen Arons, "The Threat to Freedom in Goals 2000," *Education Week*, April 6, 1994, p. 52.

14. Theodore R. Sizer, *Horace's School: Redesigning the American High School* (Houghton Mifflin, 1992), p. 111; see also Theodore R. Sizer and Bethany Rogers, "Designing Standards: Achieving the Delicate Balance," *Educational Leadership*, vol. 5 (February 1993), pp. 24–26.

15. For various criticisms of a national curriculum, see Elliott W. Eisner, "Invitational Conference on the Hidden Consequences of a National Curriculum," *Educational Researcher*, vol. 22 (October 1993), pp. 38–39.

16. Michael W. Apple, "The Dangers of a National Curriculum," *In These Times*, vol. 17 (November 15, 1993), pp. 26–27.

17. Jeannie Oakes, *Multiplying Inequalities: The Effects of Race, Social Class, and Tracking on Opportunities to Learn Mathematics and Science* (Santa Monica, Calif.: Rand, 1990), p. vii.

18. College Board, *EQUITY 2000 News*, vol. 3 (Spring 1994), pp. 1, 2, 8.

19. Larry Cuban, "A National Curriculum and Tests: Charting the Direct and Indirect Consequences," *Education Week*, July 14, 1993, pp. 25, 27.

20. Apple, "The Dangers of a National Curriculum," pp. 26-27; see also Cuban, "A National Curriculum and Tests," p. 27, note 22, who predicts that failure of standards and assessments to improve achievement will lead to "renting of public school children to private firms to produce academic achievement and the use of government vouchers for parents to send their children to any private school of their choice."

21. John Jacob Cannell, *Nationally Normed Elementary Achievement Testing in America's Public Schools: How All Fifty States Are Above the National Average* (Daniels, West Virginia: Friends for Education, 1987).

22. The author, as assistant secretary for the Office of Educational Research and Improvement (1991–93), had primary responsibility within the U.S. Department of Education for awarding grants for the development of voluntary national standards.

Chapter 2

1. Edwin Cornelius Broome, *A Historical and Critical Discussion of College Admission Requirements* (Macmillan 1903), p. 18.

2. Ibid., p. 30.

3. Ibid., p. 34.

4. Claude M. Fuess, *The College Board: Its First Fifty Years* (New York: College Entrance Examination Board, 1967), p. 6.

5. The National Educational Association was a forerunner to today's National Education Association. At that time, however, it was not a teachers' union; most of its members were school superintendents, not teachers.

6. David Angus and Jeffrey Mirel, "Rhetoric and Reality: The American High School Curriculum, 1945–1990," in Diane Ravitch and Maris A. Vinovskis, eds., *Learning from the Past: What History Teaches Us about School Reform* (Johns Hopkins Press, 1995).

7. The report of the Committee of Ten is reprinted in Theodore R. Sizer, *Secondary Schools at the Turn of the Century* (Yale University Press, 1964), pp. 209–71; or see National Educational Association, *Report of the Committee on Secondary School Studies Appointed at the Meeting of the National Educational Association, July 9, 1892; with the Reports of the Conferences Arranged by This Committee, and Held December 28–30, 1892*, Document 205 (U.S. Department of Interior, Bureau of Education, 1893).

8. Edward A. Krug, *The Shaping of the American High School, 1880–1920* (University of Wisconsin Press, 1964), p. 147.

9. Until mid-twentieth century, many selective colleges routinely used quotas to limit the number of Jewish and Catholic students, and these colleges would have been reluctant to embrace any scheme that would cause them to accept students strictly on the basis of test scores.

10. Commission on the Reorganization of Secondary Education, *Cardinal Principles of Secondary Education* (Department of the Interior, Bureau of Education 1918; reprint, Government Printing Office, 1928).

11. Fuess, *The College Board*, p. 104.

12. Ibid., p. 57.

13. Ibid., p. 113.

14. Clifford Adelman, "Devaluation, Diffusion, and the College Connection: A Study of High School Transcripts, 1964–1981," Paper prepared for the National Commission on Excellence in Education (U.S. Department of Education, 1983).

15. Paul Davis Chapman, "Schools as Sorters: Lewis M. Terman and the Intelligence Testing Movement, 1890–1930," Ph.D. diss., Stanford University, 1979, pp. 165–80.

16. Arthur Woodward, David L. Elliott, and Kathleen Carter Nagel, *Textbooks in School and Society* (New York: Garland Publishing Company, 1988), p. 7.

17. Daniel Marks, "Statewide Achievement Testing: A Brief History," *Educational Research Quarterly,* vol. 13 (3, 1989), pp. 40–41.

18. National Center for Education Statistics, *120 Years of American Education: A Statistical Portrait* (U.S. Department of Education, 1993), pp. 91, 55. NCES, *Digest of Education Statistics, 1992* (U.S. Department of Education, 1992), p. 107.

19. Diane Ravitch, *The Troubled Crusade: American Education, 1945–1980* (Basic Books, 1983), chap. 7.

20. Adelman, "Devaluation, Diffusion, and the College Connection," abstract, pp. 17, 22.

21. Annegret Harnischfeger and David E. Wiley, *Achievement Test Score Decline: Do We Need to Worry?* (Chicago: CEMREL, 1975), pp. 1, 2, 17, 107–112.

22. College Entrance Examination Board, *On Further Examination* (New York: 1977); see also William Turnbull, "Student Change, Program Change: Why the SAT Scores Kept Falling," College Board Report 85-2 (New York: 1985).

23. The President's Commission on Foreign Language and International Studies, *Strength through Wisdom: A Critique of U.S. Capability* (Washington: 1979), p. 6.

24. National Science Foundation and U.S. Department of Education, *Science & Engineering Education for the 1980's & Beyond* (Washington: 1980), pp. 3, 46–48.

25. Southern Regional Education Board, *The Need for Quality* (Atlanta: 1981), pp. 16–20.

26. National Commission on Excellence in Education, *A Nation at Risk: The Imperative for Educational Reform* (Washington: 1983), p. 5.

27. Ibid., p. 14.

28. Ibid., pp. 18–22.

29. *The Nation Responds: Recent Efforts to Improve Education* (U.S. Department of Education, 1984), pp. 12–19.

30. SREB, *Looking Back at a Decade of Educational Improvement* (Atlanta: 1993), pp. 4–5.

31. National Governors' Association, *Time for Results* (Washington: 1986), p. 3.

32. William J. Bennett, *James Madison High School: A Curriculum for American Students* (U.S. Department of Education, 1987).

33. Allan Bloom, *The Closing of the American Mind: How Higher Education Has Failed Democracy and Impoverished the Souls of Today's Students* (Simon & Schuster, 1987); E. D. Hirsch, Jr., *Cultural Literacy: What Every American Needs to Know* (Houghton Mifflin, 1987).

34. The National Assessment of Educational Progress is a federally funded testing program that was initiated in 1969–70; it regularly tests national samples of American students in different subject areas.

35. SREB, *Measuring Student Achievement: Comparable Test Results for Participating SREB States, the Region, and the Nation* (Atlanta: 1986), pp. iii, 2.

36. *The Nation's Report Card: Improving the Assessment of Student Achievement,* Report of the Study Group, Lamar Alexander, Chairman, H. Thomas James, Vice-Chairman, with a Review of the Report by a Committee of the National Academy of Education (Cambridge, Mass.: National Academy of Education, 1987), p. 11.

37. National Education Goals Panel, *National Education Goals Report: Building a Nation of Learners* (Government Printing Office, 1992), p. 321–22.

Chapter 3

1. A norm-referenced test is one in which students are compared with a national sample and ranked according to whether they are above, at, or below the average of the sample. It is not referenced to an absolute standard, but to an average of test-takers.

2. John Jacob Cannell, *Nationally Normed Elementary Achievement Testing in America's Public Schools: How All Fifty States Are above the National Average* (Daniels, W. Va.: Friends for Education, 1987); John Jacob Cannell, *How Public Educators Cheat on Standardized Achievement Tests* (Albuquerque, N.M.: Friends for Education, 1989), p. 7.

3. George F. Madaus, "The Influence of Testing on Teaching Math and Science in Grades 4–12," report of a study funded by the National Science Foundation and conducted by the Center for the Study of Testing, Evaluation, and Educational Policy, Boston College, October 1992, p. 2.

4. Gerald W. Bracey, "Why Can't They Be Like We Were?" *Phi Delta Kappan,* vol. 73 (October 1991), p. 106. See also Gerald W. Bracey, "The Second Bracey Report on the Condition of Public Education," *Phi Delta Kappan,* vol. 74 (October 1992), p. 107. Researchers from the Sandia National Laboratories held that student achievement is "at least as high as any previous generation" but added that "challenging subject matter for the 21st century may demand even higher performance levels." See C. C. Carson, R. M. Huelskamp, and T. D. Woodall, "Perspectives on Education in America," *The Journal of Educational Research,* vol. 86 (April 1992), p. 305. See also Iris C. Rotberg, "Myths in International Comparisons of Science and Math-

ematics Achievement," *The Bridge*, vol. 21 (Fall 1991), pp. 3–10; Iris C. Rotberg, "I Never Promised You First Place," *Phi Delta Kappan*, vol. 72 (December 1990), pp. 296–303; Richard M. Jaeger, "World Class Standards, Choice, and Privatization: Weak Measurement Serving Presumptive Policy," *Phi Delta Kappan*, vol. 74 (October 1992), pp. 118–128.

5. A useful critique of the revisionist position is offered by Lawrence C. Stedman, "The Condition of Education: Why School Reformers Are on the Right Track," *Phi Delta Kappan*, vol. 75 (November 1993), p. 216, who points out that the danger of the revisionist message is that it "will be misconstrued as a call to abandon school reform in general."

6. Bracey, "Why Can't They Be Like We Were," p. 111–12.

7. Arthur Bestor, *Educational Wastelands: The Retreat from Learning in Our Public Schools*, 2d ed. (University of Illinois Press, 1985), pp. 4–6.

8. Verbal scores went as high as 431 in 1985 and 1986 and dropped to 422 in 1991. Mathematics scores rose steadily but modestly (with a one-year drop in 1991) each year. See Fiske, "College Entry Test Scores Drop Sharply," *New York Times*, September 7, 1975, p. 1; National Center for Education Statistics, *The Condition of Education 1993* (U.S. Department of Education 1993), p. 243; and College Board, *College-Bound Seniors: 1994 Profile of SAT and Achievement Test Takers* (New York: 1994).

9. Before 1972 the Educational Testing Service counted the number of tests administered, not the number of students who took the test. Starting in 1972 each student was counted only once. The scores before 1972 are now considered estimates. Changing the method of counting test-takers did not appreciably affect the size or slope of the score decline.

10. For the numbers of high-scoring students, see the annual reports, College Board, *College-Bound Seniors* (New York). For an analysis of the decline of high-scoring students, see Charles Murray and R. J. Herrnstein, "What's Really Behind the SAT-score Decline?" *Public Interest*, vol. 106 (Winter 1992), p. 52. For discussion of the implications of the decreasing number of students with high verbal scores, see Daniel J. Singal, "The Other Crisis in American Education," *Atlantic Monthly*, vol. 268 (November 1991), pp. 59–73.

11. College Board, *College-Bound Seniors: 1993 Profile of SAT and Achievement Test Takers* (New York: 1993), p. iii; College Board, *College-Bound Seniors: 1994*, p. iii.

12. See, for example, Harold Howe II, "Let's Have Another Score Decline," *Phi Delta Kappan*, vol. 66 (May 1985), 599–602.

13. Daniel Koretz, *Trends in Educational Achievement* (Congressional Budget Office, 1986), p. 53.

14. Daniel Koretz, "What Happened to Test Scores, and Why?" *Educational Measurement: Issues and Practice* (Winter 1992), p. 7.

15. Daniel Koretz, *Educational Achievement: Explanations and Implications of Recent Trends* (CBO, 1987), pp. 32–33.

16. Murray and Herrnstein, "What's Really Behind the SAT-score Decline?" pp. 34, 37, 40, 49, 52.

17. Ibid., p. 43.

18. National Center for Education Statistics, *Digest of Education Statistics 1994* (U.S. Department of Education, 1992), p. 108.

19. The college-going rate reached a high of 63.2 percent for males in 1968, a likely response to the student deferment from the military draft during the Vietnam War. NCES, *Digest of Education Statistics 1994*, p. 188.

20. NCES, *Condition of Education 1993*, p. 243; College Board, *College-Bound Seniors: 1993*, p. ii.

21. NCES, *Digest of Education Statistics 1994*, p. 188; College Board, *College-Bound Seniors: 1994*, p. iii.

22. College Board, *College-Bound Seniors: 1994*.

23. "Note Book," *Chronicle of Higher Education*, February 2, 1994, p. A31.

24. Southern Regional Education Board, *Measuring Student Achievement: Comparable Test Results for Participating SREB States, the Region, and the Nation* (Atlanta: 1986), p. iii.

25. Ina V. S. Mullis and others, *NAEP 1992 Trends in Academic Progress* (U.S. Department of Education, 1994), p. 17.

26. Mullis and others, *NAEP 1992 Trends in Academic Progress*, p. 19.

27. ETS Policy Information Center, *ETS Policy Notes*, vol. 5 (Summer 1993), p. 5.

28. Mullis and others, *NAEP 1992 Trends in Academic Progress*, pp. 2–5

29. Ina V. S. Mullis and others, *Trends in Academic Progress* (U.S. Department of Education, 1991), pp. 4–5. The critical judgments that typified NAEP reporting for twenty years disappeared after 1990, as a result of a decision by the U.S. Department of Education to convert what had been a grant to the Educational Testing Service (which administers NAEP) into a contract. After 1990 NAEP reports were written to conform to the requirements of a statistical agency, with a minimum of judgmental terminology.

30. National Assessment of Educational Progress, *The Science Report Card: Elements of Risk and Recovery* (Princeton: Educational Testing Service, 1988), pp. 5–7, 45.

31. National Center for Education Statistics, *The 1990 Science Report Card* (U.S. Department of Education, 1992), pp. 36, 136, 142–43, 28, 24.

32. Mullis and others, *NAEP 1992 Trends in Academic Progress*, p. 57.

33. National Assessment of Educational Progress, *Changes in Mathematical Achievement, 1973–78* (Denver: Education Commission of the States, 1979), pp. 5, 14.

34. John A. Dossey and others, *The Mathematics Report Card: Are We Measuring Up?* (Princeton, N.J.: Educational Testing Service, 1988), pp. 36–43, 10, 16

35. Mullis and others, *NAEP 1992 Trends in Academic Progress*, p. 64.

36. John A. Dossey, Ina V.S. Mullis, and Chancey E. Jones, *Can Students Do Mathematical Problem Solving?* (National Center for Education Statistics, 1993), pp. 2, 193.

37. Ibid., pp. 2–3.

38. Ibid., pp. 19, 92, 93–95.

39. Ina V. S. Mullis and others, *NAEP 1992 Trends in Academic Progress,* pp. 136–39.

40. Ibid, pp. 171, 173, 178.

41. Diane Ravitch and Chester E. Finn, Jr., *What Do Our 17-Year-Olds Know? A Report on the First National Assessment of History and Literature* (Harper & Row, 1987), pp. 263–69. A mainstay of the "revisionist" (the-schools-are-better-than-ever) argument was that this assessment was "norm-referenced," which meant that it was composed of items that half the test-takers were expected to get wrong. But, in fact, the assessment was "criterion-referenced," which meant that it was designed with the expectation that most students would know most items. See Dale Whittington, "What Have 17-Year-Olds Known in the Past?" *American Educational Research Journal,* vol. 28 (Winter 1991), pp. 759–80; Bracey, "The Second Bracey Report on the Condition of Public Education," p. 107; and response, Diane Ravitch, "Letters," *American Educational Research Journal,* vol. 30 (Fall 1993), pp. 515–16. The "revisionist" claim is that, because American students in the past did not know much history, it is unreasonable to expect current students to know much history.

42. National Assessment of Educational Progress, *The U.S. History Report Card* (Princeton, N.J.: Educational Testing Service, 1990), p. 10.

43. The International Association for the Evaluation of Educational Achievement is a multinational consortium of national research centers and education scholars. The Educational Testing Service of Princeton, New Jersey, conducts the International Assessment of Educational Progress, together with the National Assessment of Educational Progress and the SAT.

44. Norman M. Bradburn and Dorothy M. Gilford, eds., *A Framework and Principles for International Comparative Studies in Education* (Washington: National Academy Press, 1990), p. 2.

45. Elliott A. Medrich and Jeanne E. Griffith, *International Mathematics and Science Assessments: What Have We Learned?* (U.S. Department of Education, 1992), p. vii.

46. National Commission on Excellence in Education, *A Nation at Risk: The Imperative for Educational Reform* (Washington: 1983), p. 8.

47. Country rankings are often misleading. The score differences among several nations are often insignificant, but it is difficult for casual readers to know that Country A got the highest score but that Countries B, C, D, and E were tied for second.

48. Torsten Husen, ed., *International Study of Achievement in Mathematics: A Comparison of Twelve Countries,* vol. 2 (John Wiley & Sons, Inc. 1967), pp. 21n, 22, 24, 25.

49. L. C. Comber and John P. Keeves, *Science Education in Nineteen Countries* (John Wiley & Sons, Inc., 1973); and Medrich and Griffith, *International Mathematics and Science Assessments,* pp. 79–81.

50. Curtis C. McKnight and others, *The Underachieving Curriculum: Assessing U.S. School Mathematics from an International Perspective* (Champaign, Ill.: Stipes Publishing Co., 1987), pp. 17, 26–27.

51. Willard J. Jacobson and Rodney L. Doran, *Science Achievement in the United States and Sixteen Countries: A Report to the Public* (New York: Teachers College, 1988), pp. 30, 37, 45.

52. Robert L. Linn and Stephen B. Dunbar, "The Nation's Report Card Goes Home: Good News and Bad about Trends in Achievement," *Phi Delta Kappan,* vol. 72 (October 1990), p. 131.

53. Archie E. Lapointe, Nancy A. Mead, and Gary W. Phillips, *A World of Differences: International Assessment of Educational Progress* (Princeton, N.J.: Educational Testing Service, 1989), p. 24.

54. Archie E. Lapointe, Nancy A. Mead, and Janice M. Askew, *Learning Mathematics* (Princeton, N.J.: Educational Testing Service, 1992), pp. 18, 84; Archie E. Lapointe, Janice M. Askew, and Nancy A. Mead, *Learning Science* (Princeton, N.J.: Educational Testing Service, 1992), pp. 18, 83.

55. Stephan Lazer, *Learning about the World* (Princeton, N.J.: Educational Testing Service, 1992), p. 15.

56. Warwick B. Elley, *How in the World Do Students Read?* (Hamburg: International Association for the Evaluation of Educational Achievement, 1992), p. 15.

57. Lazer, *Learning about the World,* pp. 74–75; Elley, *How in the World Do Students Read?* pp. 17, 70–72.

58. For a debate about the technical validity of the international assessments, see Rotberg, "I Never Promised You First Place," pp. 296–303; Norman Bradburn and others, "A Rejoinder to 'I Never Promised You First

Place,'" *Phi Delta Kappan,* vol. 72 (June 1991), pp. 774–77; Iris C. Rotberg, "How Did All Those Dumb Kids Make All Those Smart Bombs?" *Phi Delta Kappan,* vol. 72 (June 1991), pp. 778–81.

59. Medrich and Griffith, *International Mathematics and Science Assessments,* pp. 29, viii.

60. McKnight and others, *The Underachieving Curriculum,* pp. 106–111; Jacobson and Doran, *Science Achievement in the United States and Sixteen Countries,* p. 103.

61. Medrich and Griffith, *International Mathematics and Science Assessments,* p. 35.

62. McKnight and others, *The Underachieving Curriculum,* pp. vi–vii.

63. Ian Westbury, "Comparing American and Japanese Achievement: Is the United States Really a Low Achiever?" *Educational Researcher,* vol. 21 (June-July 1992), p. 22; David P. Baker, "Compared to Japan, the U.S. Is a Low Achiever . . . Really: New Evidence and Comment on Westbury," *Educational Researcher,* vol. 22 (April 1993), pp. 18–20; Ian Westbury, "American and Japanese Achievement . . . Again: A Response to Baker," *Educational Researcher,* vol. 22 (April 1993), pp. 21–25; David P. Baker, "A Rejoinder," *Educational Researcher,* vol. 22 (April 1993), pp. 25–26.

64. McKnight and others, *The Underachieving Curriculum,* pp. xii–xiii.

65. A front-page story in the *New York Times* (December 9, 1993), was headlined "International Report Card Shows U.S. Schools Work" and cited a report by the Organization for Economic Cooperation and Development. The *Times* article said the OECD report "indicated that American students lag only slightly behind their counterparts around the world in math and science. . . ." Actually, the OECD offered no judgment about how American schools were doing; its description of educational outcomes was based on two international tests cited above: the international reading assessment, in which 14-year-old Americans performed well; and the Second International Assessment of Mathematics and Science, in which American 13-year-olds performed poorly in both subjects. The *Times* reached its positive conclusions because the OECD report did not include the scores of non-OECD nations (including high-scoring nations such as Korea, Taiwan, Hungary, the Soviet Union, and Slovenia). That omission moved U.S. students from thirteenth out of fifteen in science to eighth out of ten, and from fourteenth out of fifteen in mathematics to ninth out of ten. See Center for Educational Research and Innovation, *Education at a Glance* (Paris: OECD, 1993, pp. 153, 161, 167; Lapointe, Mead, and Askew, *Learning Mathematics*; and Lapointe, Askew, and Mead, *Learning Science.*

66. William H. Schmidt, "High School Course-Taking: A Study of Variation," *Journal of Curriculum Studies,* vol. 15 (April-June, 1983), pp. 167,

182; William H. Schmidt, "High School Course-Taking: Its Relationship to Achievement," *Journal of Curriculum Studies,* vol. 15 (July-September, 1983), pp. 311, 332.

67. Sol H. Pelavin and Michael Kane, *Changing the Odds: Factors Increasing Access to College* (New York: College Board, 1990), pp. 76, 79.

68. David Angus and Jeffrey Mirel, "Rhetoric and Reality: The American High School Curriculum, 1945–1990," in Diane Ravitch and Maris Vinovskis, eds., *Learning from the Past: What History Teaches Us about School Reform* (Johns Hopkins Press, 1995).

69. Clifford Adelman, "Devaluation, Diffusion and the College Connection: A Study of High School Transcripts, 1964–1981" (U.S. Department of Education, 1982), p. 1.

70. William B. Fetters, George H. Brown, and Jeffrey A. Owings, *High School Seniors: A Comparative Study of the Classes of 1972 and 1980* (U. S. Department of Education, 1984), p. 9.

71. Ibid., pp. 5, 6, 19.

72. Ibid., pp. 20–21, 24.

73. Jeannie Oakes, *Multiplying Inequalities: The Effects of Race, Social Class, and Tracking on Opportunities to Learn Mathematics and Science* (Santa Monica, Calif.: Rand, 1990), p. xi. See also Jeannie Oakes, *Keeping Track: How Schools Structure Inequality* (Yale University Press, 1985).

74. Oakes, *Multiplying Inequalities,* p. 102.

75. National Center for Education Statistics, *The Condition of Education 1994* (U.S. Department of Education, 1994), pp. 3–4.

76. Ibid., pp. 78–79, 248.

77. Ibid, pp. 74–75, 240–41; NCES, *Digest of Education Statistics 1994,* p. 135. Slight variations in the percentages occur between the two sources.

78. NCES, *The Condition of Education 1994,* p. 241.

79. Ibid., pp. 40.

80. National Center for Education Statistics, "Understanding the Performance of U.S. Students on International Assessments," *Education Policy Issues: Statistical Perspectives* (February 1994), p. 2.

81. NCES, *Digest of Education Statistics 1994,* p. 132.

Chapter 4

1. Mortimer J. Adler, a philosopher, wrote *The Paideia Proposal: An Educational Syllabus* (Macmillan, 1984) and encouraged the creation of Pai-

deia schools devoted to intellectual development and Socratic teaching; William Bennett was U.S. secretary of education during the mid-1980s; Ernest L. Boyer, president of the Carnegie Foundation for the Advancement of Teaching and a former U.S. commissioner of education, wrote several books about American education, including *High School: A Report on Secondary Education in America* (Harper & Row, 1983); Albert Shanker, president of the American Federation of Teachers, used his weekly column in the *New York Times* as a platform to advocate education reform; and Theodore R. Sizer wrote *Horace's Compromise: The Dilemma of the American High School* (Houghton Mifflin, 1984) and *Horace's School: Redesigning the American High School* (Houghton Mifflin 1992); he also founded the Coalition of Essential Schools, a network of more than two hundred schools.

Ronald R. Edmonds wrote numerous articles about effective schools, including "Making Public Schools Effective," *Social Policy,* vol. 12 (September-October 1981), pp. 56–60. Marva Collins created a private school for inner-city children in Chicago, Jaime Escalante was the subject of a movie called *Stand and Deliver* about his experiences teaching mathematics in a tough inner-city school in California, and Deborah Meier founded a model public school (Central Park East) in New York City and won a MacArthur Fellowship.

2. Lauren B. Resnick and Leopold E. Klopfer, "Toward the Thinking Curriculum: An Overview," in Lauren B. Resnick and Leopold E. Klopfer, eds., *Toward the Thinking Curriculum: Current Cognitive Research* (Reston, Va.: Association for Supervision and Curriculum Development, 1989), pp. 2–3.

3. Robert Glaser, "The Future of Testing: A Research Agenda for Cognitive Psychology and Psychometrics," *American Psychologist,* vol. 36 (September 1981), p. 924.

4. Ibid.

5. See John T. Bruer, *Schools for Thought: A Science of Learning in the Classroom* (MIT Press, 1993) for an excellent survey of cognitive science.

6. Robert Glaser, "The Integration of Instruction and Testing," in E. Freeman, ed., *The Redesign of Testing in the Twenty First Century: Proceedings of the 1985 ETS Invitational Conference* (Princeton, N.J.: Educational Testing Service, 1986), p. 56.

7. Lauren B. Resnick and Daniel P. Resnick, "Assessing the Thinking Curriculum: New Tools for Educational Reform," in B. R. Gifford and M. C. O'Connor, eds., *Changing Assessments: Alternative Views of Aptitude, Achievement, and Instruction* (Boston: Kluwer Academic Publishers, 1992), p. 38.

8. Daniel P. Resnick and Lauren B. Resnick, "Improving Educational Standards in American Schools," *Phi Delta Kappan,* vol. 65 (November 1983), p. 180.

9. Daniel P. Resnick and Lauren B. Resnick, "Standards, Curriculum, and Performance: A Historical and Comparative Perspective," *Educational Researcher,* vol. 14 (April 1985), p. 17.

10. Lauren B. Resnick, "Performance Assessment and Educational Quality," paper presented at the annual meeting of the American Educational Research Association, April 1992, p. 9.

11. Ibid., pp. 4–5.

12. New Standards Project, "Checker Tournament," in *New Standards Project: Mathematics: Elementary School Pilot Assessment* (Washington: National Center on Education and the Economy, 1993), p. 4.

13. Most of their studies examined students and schools in these three cities. Later they included students from Chicago and Beijing. Minneapolis was chosen specifically because its residents "tend to come from native-born, English-speaking, economically sound families. . . .If problems were found in Minneapolis, we assumed they would be compounded in other American cities," the authors wrote. Harold W. Stevenson, Shin-Ying Lee, and James W. Stigler, "Mathematics Achievement of Chinese, Japanese, and American Children," *Science,* vol. 231 (February 14, 1986), p. 694.

14. For a full discussion of the cross-national studies, see Harold W. Stevenson and James W. Stigler, *The Learning Gap: Why Our Schools Are Failing and What We Can Learn from Japanese and Chinese Education* (Summit Books, 1992).

15. Stevenson, Lee, and Stigler, "Mathematics Achievement," p. 694.

16. Harold W. Stevenson, Chuansheng Chen, and Shin-Ying Lee, "Mathematics Achievement of Chinese, Japanese, and American Children: Ten Years Later," *Science,* vol. 259 (January 1, 1993), pp. 54–55.

17. Ibid., p. 55. Because Harold W. Stevenson is the lead author with various colleagues in several different studies describing the same research project, the studies are identified in the text by his name; the reader should refer to the footnote for the full list of authors.

18. Stevenson, Lee, and Stigler, "Mathematics Achievement," pp. 695–96.

19. Harold W. Stevenson, "Learning from Asian Schools," *Scientific American,* vol. 267 (December 1992), pp. 75–76.

20. Stevenson, Lee, and Stigler, "Mathematics Achievement," p. 697.

21. Stevenson, Chen, and Lee, "Mathematics Achievement . . . Ten Years Later," pp. 55–57.

22. Stevenson, Lee, and Stigler, "Mathematics Achievement," p. 697.

23. Stevenson, Chen, and Lee, "Mathematics Achievement . . . Ten Years Later," p. 57.

24. Ibid.

25. Stevenson, Lee, and Stigler, "Mathematics Achievement," p. 695.

26. Stevenson, Chen, and Lee, "Mathematics Achievement . . . Ten Years Later," p. 55.

27. Ibid., p. 57.

28. This finding was corroborated by a survey conducted by Louis Harris & Associates, which found that students and their parents thought that the students were well prepared by their schooling but that employers had "serious doubts about the functional literacy of the vast majority of the labor pool from which they must find new employees." Louis Harris & Associates, "An Assessment of American Education: The View of Employers, Those Running Higher Education, the Public, Former Students, and Their Parents" (New York: Committee for Economic Development, 1991), p. 6.

29. Peter F. Drucker, *Post-Capitalist Society* (Harper Business, 1993), pp. 73–74.

30. Lester Thurow, *Head to Head: The Coming Economic Battle among Japan, Europe, and America* (William Morrow, 1992), pp. 39–52.

31. Martin Neil Baily, Gary Burtless, and Robert E. Litan, *Growth with Equity: Economic Policymaking for the Next Century* (Brookings, 1993), pp. 122–23.

32. Commission on the Skills of the American Workforce, *America's Choice: High Skills or Low Wages!* (Rochester: National Center on Education and the Economy, 1990), pp. 3–5.

33. See, for example, Commission on Workforce Quality and Labor Market Efficiency, *Investing in People: A Strategy to Address America's Workforce Crisis* (U.S. Department of Labor, 1989); Education Subcouncil of the Competitiveness Policy Council "Building a Standards-Based School System," in *A Competitiveness Strategy for America* (Washington, March 1993), pp. 11–37.

34. John H. Bishop, "Why High School Students Learn So Little and What Can Be Done About It," working paper 88-01, Center for Advanced Human Resource Studies, Cornell University, p. 4.

35. Theodore R. Sizer, *Horace's Compromise,* p. 54.

36. John H. Bishop, "Why the Apathy in American High Schools?" *Educational Researcher,* vol. 18 (January/February 1989), pp. 7–8, 9, 10.

37. Albert Shanker, "National Standards and Exams," *New York Times,* March 1, 1992, p. E7.

38. Robert J. Samuelson, "Hollow School Reform," *Washington Post,* April 28, 1993, p. 19.

39. Arthur G. Powell, Eleanor Farrar, and David K. Cohen, *The Shopping Mall High School: Winners and Losers in the Educational Marketplace* (Houghton Mifflin, 1985), p. 66–67.

40. Michael W. Sedlak and others, *Selling Students Short: Classroom Bargaining and Academic Reform in the American High School* (New York: Teachers College Press: 1986), pp. 5–7, 180.

41. James E. Rosenbaum, "Empowering Schools and Teachers: A New Link to Jobs for the Non-College-Bound," a paper prepared for the U.S. Department of Labor, Commission on Workforce Quality and Labor Market Efficiency, April 1989, pp. 3, 5, 9, 10; see also James E. Rosenbaum, "What If Good Jobs Depended on Good Grades?" *American Educator* (Winter 1989), pp. 10–15, 40–42; and James E. Rosenbaum and Takehiko Kariya, "From High School to Work: Market and Institutional Mechanisms in Japan," *American Journal of Sociology,* vol. 94 (May 1989), 1334–65.

42. Rosenbaum, "Empowering Schools and Teachers," pp. 5, 6, 7.

43. *Wisconsin Performance Assessment Development Project: Annual Report for Fiscal Year 1992–93* (Madison: Wisconsin Center for Education Research, 1993), pp. 152–53.

44. Maryland State Department of Education, "Maryland State Department of Education: 1993 MSPAP Outcome Score Report," *Maryland School Performance Program Report, 1993: State and School Systems* (Baltimore 1993).

45. See, for example, "Model Competency-Based Social Studies Program," draft report prepared by the Ohio Department of Education, Division of Curriculum, Instruction, and Professional Development, 1993, where chronology is minimized and the term "history" is replaced by the term "cultural heritage."

46. Diane Ravitch and Chester E. Finn, Jr., *What Do Our 17-Year-Olds Know? A Report on the First National Assessment of History and Literature* (Harper & Row, 1987), pp. 1–3.

47. California State Department of Education, *History-Social Science Framework* (1987).

48. Bradley Commission on History in Schools, *Building a History Curriculum: Guidelines for Teaching History in Schools* (Washington: 1988), p. 7.

49. National Council for Geographic Education and the Association of American Geographers, *Guidelines for Geographic Education* (Washington: 1984).

50. "Geographic Knowledge Deemed Vital, But Many Lack Basic Skills," *The Gallup Report,* Report 277 (October 1988), p. 35.

51. The star-crossed effort to set English standards is indicative of the ideological turmoil in the field. In November 1992, after the presidential election, the Bush administration awarded funds to create English standards to a consortium of three organizations: the National Council of Teachers of English, the International Reading Association, and the Center for the Study of Reading at the University of Illinois. In March 1994 the Clinton administration canceled the contract, citing a lack of progress. When the Department of Education placed a notice in the *Federal Register* about its plans to rebid the award, several members of the organizations that participated in the original project wrote to express their fear that the department would seek standards based on "traditional English" and to warn that they would not cooperate with any other standard-setting project. Kenneth Goodman, a past president of the International Reading Association, expressed the hope that the department would receive "no credible responses" and concluded that "I believe your office has already decided to award this contract to far-right ideologues and enemies of children and teachers." See Karen Diegmueller, "Flap Over English Standards Sparks Strong Words," *Education Week,* Sept. 7, 1994, p. 9; and Kenneth S. Goldman, "Standards, NOT!" *Education Week,* September 7, 1994, p. 39.

52. For a useful review of the history of new math, see Bruce R. Vogeli, "The Rise and Fall of the 'New Math,'" Inaugural lecture, Teachers College, Columbia University, 1976.

53. Diane Massell, "Setting Standards in Mathematics and Social Studies," *Education and Urban Society,* vol. 26 (February 1994), p. 121.

54. Conference Board of the Mathematical Sciences, National Advisory Committee on Mathematical Education, *Overview and Analysis of School Mathematics, Grades K-12* (Reston, Va.: National Council of Teachers of Mathematics, 1975), p. 138.

55. National Council of Teachers of Mathematics, *An Agenda for Action: Recommendations for School Mathematics of the 1980s* (Reston, Va.: 1980), p. 1.

56. Thomas A. Romberg, *School Mathematics: Options for the 1990s* (U.S. Department of Education, 1984), pp. 9–10.

57. National Council of Teachers of Mathematics, *Curriculum and Evaluation Standards for School Mathematics* (Reston, Va.: 1989).

58. Thomas A. Romberg, "The NCTM Standards as a Model for Discipline-Based School Reform," in Charles M. Firestone and Catherine H. Clark, rapporteurs, *Telecommunications as a Tool for Educational Reform: Implementing the NCTM Mathematics Standards* (Queenstown, Md.: Aspen Institute, 1992), pp. 20–21.

59. Thomas A. Romberg, "Changes in School Mathematics: Curricular Changes, Instruction Changes, and Indicators of Changes," paper prepared for Center for Policy Research in Education, Rutgers University, 1988, pp. 16–17.

60. As discussed in Anne Turnbaugh Lockwood, "Mathematics for the Information Age," *Focus in Change* (Winter 1991), p. 3.

61. Thomas A. Romberg,"Changes in School Mathematics," pp. 7–9.

62. Zalman Usiskin, "What Changes Should Be Made for the Second Edition of the NCTM *Standards?*" *UCSMP Newsletter,* no. 12 (Winter 1993), p. 10.

63. Bill Honig, *Last Chance for Our Children* (Reading, Mass.: Addison-Wesley, 1985), pp. 43–44.

64. Ibid., pp. 54–55.

65. Francie Alexander, "What I Saw at the California Education Revolution," in Chester E. Finn, Jr., and Herbert Walberg, eds., *Radical Education Reform* (Berkeley: McCutchan, 1994).

66. "Adoption" means that the state board of education chooses specific textbooks for use in public classrooms, after review and discussion; textbooks that win state approval are widely used and purchased with state funds. Textbooks that do not win adoption are at an enormous disadvantage. See Alexander, "What I Saw."

67. Bill Honig, "How Can Horace Best Be Helped," *Phi Delta Kappan,* vol. 75 (June 1994), pp. 790–96.

68. Honig was forced to resign early in 1993 after he was convicted on a charge of conflict of interest because the state education department awarded funds to schools that worked with a parent-involvement project managed by his wife. No state funds went to his wife, and some observers saw the prosecution as politically motivated, the culmination of efforts by politicians to eliminate him as a potential candidate for governor and by right-wing critics to punish him for his stands on controversial issues such as evolution and abortion.

Chapter 5

1. The controversy over opportunity-to-learn standards became clear shortly after the passage of Goals 2000 in March 1994, when the Office of Civil Rights in the U.S. Department of Education threatened to sue Ohio because some students had failed a high school graduation test. According to the civil rights office, the students had not had "opportunity to learn," which made the test invalid; according to the state, the students' failure

occurred not because of an unequal opportunity to learn, but because of their poor school attendance.

2. President George Bush, "Remarks by the President at the Presentation of the National Education Strategy," *America 2000: An Education Strategy: Sourcebook* (Government Printing Office, April 18, 1991), p. 5.

3. National Council on Education Standards and Testing, *Raising Standards for American Education* (Washington: 1992), pp. 1, 15, 3, 4, 15, 4, 5, 7. The statement about "high-stakes" testing was inserted at the insistence of Albert Shanker, with strong support from other NCEST members, who agreed with economist John Bishop about the importance of establishing incentives for students to take school seriously and making what is learned in school consequential.

4. Jonathan Kozol, *Savage Inequalities: Children in America's Schools* (Crown Publishers, 1991).

5. NCEST, *Raising Standards for American Education*, p. E-5.

6. Ibid., p. 13.

7. "Response to National Testing Proposals," n.d. See "Prominent Educators Oppose National Tests," *New York Times*, January 29, 1992, B9; and *Education Week*, vol. 11 (January 29, 1992), p. 30. Neither newspaper reprinted the statement in full.

8. For the latter reason, the House Education and Labor Committee later proved to be almost as much of a stumbling block for President Clinton as it had been for President Bush.

9. Letter from Secretary Lamar Alexander to House Minority Leader Robert H. Michel, September 30, 1992, p. 1.

10. Julie A. Miller, "Reform Measure Dies—Except as Campaign Issue?" *Education Week*, vol. 11 (October 7, 1992), p. 32.

11. Office of Educational Research and Improvement, "World Class Standards for American Education" (U.S. Department of Education, October 1992), p. 3. This pamphlet was distributed to every school in the country.

12. Bill Clinton, "The Clinton Plan for Excellence in Education," *Phi Delta Kappan*, vol. 74 (October 1992), p. 134.

13. Bill Clinton and Al Gore, *Putting People First: How We Can All Change America* (Times Books, 1992), pp. 18, 85–86.

14. HR 1804, Sec. 213 (a) (B) (i); (b).

15. HR 1804, Sec. 213 (c).

16. Julie A. Miller, "Administration Readies Reform, Assessment Bill," *Education Week*, vol. 12 (March 24, 1993), p. 1.

17. Andrew C. Porter, "School Delivery Standards," *Educational Researcher*, vol. 22 (June-July 1993), p. 25.

18. "Riley Defends Federal Intrusion in Schools," *Greenville, S.C., News,* July 18, 1993, p. 10. See also "Chucking Educational Standards," *The Washington Times,* June 3, 1993, p. G2; "Schools Subverted," *Augusta (Ga.) Chronicle,* July 14, 1993, p. 10.

19. Jill Zuckman, "School Improvement Bill Snagged by Standards," *Congressional Quarterly Weekly Report,* May 22, 1993, p. 1297.

20. Letter from Governors Roy Romer and Carroll A. Campbell, Jr., chairman and vice-chairman of the National Governors Association, to U.S. Secretary of Education Richard Riley, May 6, 1993.

21. Letter from Governor Carroll A. Campbell, Jr., to U.S. Secretary of Education Richard Riley, May 6, 1993.

22. Letter from U.S. Secretary of Education Richard Riley to Governor Carroll A. Campbell, Jr., May 24, 1993.

23. "Washington Focus: Administration Bills Move Ahead," *Department of Education Reports,* June 21, 1993, p. 3. The letter from President Clinton to Representative William Ford was written on June 3, 1993.

24. Letter from Governors Roy Romer and Carroll A. Campbell, Jr., to Senator Edward Kennedy, July 20, 1993. Nonetheless, Congress added two new national goals. One called for increased parental involvement in the schools; the other for increased professional development opportunities for teachers. Because each goal becomes a spur for new federal programs, interest groups lobbied furiously to get new goals added to support their activities.

25. Letter from Governor Carroll A. Campbell, Jr., to President Clinton, March 1, 1994.

26. Letter from President Clinton to Governor Carroll A. Campbell, Jr., March 3, 1994.

27. PL 103-227, Goals 2000: Educate America Act, sec. 306(d); sec. 213(c).

28. Ibid., sec. 212(b)(3).

29. Marshall S. Smith, Jennifer O'Day, and David K. Cohen, "National Curriculum, American Style," *American Educator* (Winter 1990), p. 42. Smith also signed the report criticizing the NCEST report.

30. "Let Us Resolve to Continue the Journey of Renewal," text of President Clinton's State of the Union Address, *Washington Post,* January 26, 1994, p. A12.

31. Albert Shanker, "Let's Suppose," *New York Times,* June 20, 1993, p. E7.

32. PL 103-227, Goals 2000, sec. 1029(a)(b); Title II, sec. 213(f)(C).

33. PL 103-33, General Education Provisions Act, sec. 432.

34. "Text of Final Summit Statement Issued by President, Governors," *Education Week,* vol. 8 (October 5, 1989), p. 6. The rhetoric of the summit

statement echoed *Time for Results,* the report issued by the National Governors' Association in 1986, in which Lamar Alexander wrote that the governors were "ready for some old-fashioned horse-trading. We'll regulate less, if schools and school districts will produce better results." (p. 3).

35. NCEST, *Raising Standards for American Education,* p. 3.

36. Ellen M. Pechman and Katrina G. Laguarda, "Status of New State Curriculum Frameworks, Standards, Assessments, and Monitoring Systems," a report prepared by Policy Studies Associates for the U.S. Department of Education, Washington, February 1993, p. 1.

37. The National Science Foundation's "state systemic initiative" made large, multiyear awards ($10 million) that supported a variety of reforms (including both curriculum and assessment), while the relatively small (less than $1 million) awards from the U.S. Department of Education supported only curriculum improvement by state officials.

38. Pechman and Laguarda, "Status of New State Curriculum Frameworks," pp. 3–5.

39. National Governors' Association, "State Strategies for Restructuring the Education System" (Washington: 1993).

40. State Board of Education, Commonwealth of Pennsylvania, *Draft Student Learning Outcomes,* July 30, 1991.

41. From the Harrisburg, Pa. *Patriot-News,* as quoted in "Outcome-Based Ed: Rally Delares War on PA Proposals," *Daily Report Card* (American Political Network Inc., November 18, 1992). See also Lonnie Harp, "Rebel Mom," *Teacher,* October 1993, pp. 24–29; James A. Barnes, "Parent Power," *National Journal,* vol. 24 (June 12, 1993), pp. 1399–1401.

42. Judith McQuaide and Ann-Maureen Pliska, "The Challenge to Pennsylvania's Education Reform," *Educational Leadership,* vol. 51 (December 1993/January 1994), p. 18.

43. See "What's Wrong with Outcome-Based Education?" *The Phyllis Schlafly Report,* vol. 26 (May 1993); see also Robert L. Simonds, "A Plea for the Children," *Educational Leadership,* vol. 51 (December 1993/January 1994), pp. 12–15.

44. Pennsylvania Business Roundtable, "Student Learning Outcomes as drafted by the Pennsylvania Business Roundtable" (Harrisburg, Pa.: November 1991), p. 3.

45. Chapter 5 of the State Board of Education Curriculum, printed in the *Pennsylvania Bulletin,* vol 23 (July 24, 1993), p. 3553.

46. National Center for History in the Schools, *National Standards for United States History: Exploring the American Experience* (Los Angeles, 1994), p. 72.

47. Jean Johnson and John Immerwahr, *First Things First: What Americans Expect from the Public School* (New York: Public Agenda, 1994), p. 20.

48. Lynn Olson, "Who's Afraid of O.B.E.?" *Education Week,* vol. 12 (December 15, 1993), p. 26.

49. Albert Shanker, "Outrageous Outcomes," *New York Times,* September 12, 1993, p. E7.

50. George Judson, "Bid to Revise Education Is Fought in Connecticut," *New York Times,* January 9, 1994, p. A21. See also Kenneth Von Kohorn, "Educational 'Restructuring' Hits Connecticut," *The Weston Forum,* October 20, 1993.

51. Lynn Olson, "Who's Afraid of O.B.E.?" *Education Week,* vol. 12 (December 15, 1993), 25–26, 27.

52. State of Michigan, 87th Legislature, Regular Session of 1993, House Bill No. 5121, Sec. 1278 (1).

53. "Statement on Voluntary National Education Content Standards," in *Promises to Keep: Creating High standards for American Students,* Report on the Review of Education Standards from Goals 3 and 4 Technical Planning Group to the National Education Goals Panel, November 15, 1993.

54. "Most Students Score Poorly on New State Test," *New York Times,* January 15, 1994, p. A24.

55. California Department of Education, "Statewide Student Assessment Results Released," press release, March 9, 1994.

56. Kentucky Department of Education, "KIRIS Tests Show Substantial and Dramatic Growth," press release, Frankfort, Kentucky, September 29, 1994; Lynn Olson, " 'Dramatic' Rise in Ky. Test Scores Linked to Reforms," *Education Week,* vol. 13 (October 5, 1994), p. 13.

57. Stanley M. Elam, Lowell C. Rose, and Alec M. Gallup, "The 23rd Annual Gallup Poll of the Public's Attitude Toward the Public Schools," *Phi Delta Kappan,* vol. 73 (September 1991), p. 46.

58. Louis Harris & Associates, Inc., "An Assessment of American Education: The View of Employers, Those Running Higher Education, The Public, Former Students, and Their Parents," prepared for the Committee for Economic Development, the Business Roundtable, the National Education Goals Panel, and the National Council on Education Standards and Testing, New York, September 1991, pp. 14–17.

59. Public Agenda Foundation, *Effective Public Engagement* (Washington: New Standards Project, 1993), pp. 2, 3.

60. U.S. Department of Education, "Improving America's Schools Act of 1993: The Reauthorization of the Elementary and Secondary Education Act," September 13, 1993, Introduction, p. 1.

61. Public Agenda Foundation, *Effective Public Engagement,* p. 4.

62. Ibid., p. 7. For youths aged 15–19, the suicide rate is 4.4 per 100,000 in Japan and 11.3 per 100,000 in the United States. David S. Crystal and others, "Psychological Maladjustment and Academic Achievement: A Cross-Cultural Study of Japanese, Chinese, and American High School Students," *Child Development,* vol. 65 (June 1994), pp. 738–53; U.S. Department of Education, *Youth Indicators 1991* (1991), p. 116. The suicide rate for youths 20–24 was 11.0 in Japan and 15.0 in the United States. In the United States, white males had the highest suicide rate in both age ranges, 19.6 among the 15–19 group, and 27.0 among the 20–24 group.

63. Public Agenda Foundation, *Effective Public Engagement,* p. 8, 16–17. Also, telephone interview with Steve Farkas, Public Agenda Foundation, February 8, 1994.

64. Public Agenda Foundation, *Effective Public Engagement,* p. 20.

65. Johnson and Immerwahr, *First Things First,* pp. 13, 15, 17, 18, 21, 24–25.

66. Irving Louis Horowitz, "Democratic Forms: The Place of Scientific Standards in Advanced Societies," in Steven M. Spivak and Keith A. Winsell, eds., *A Sourcebook on Standards Information: Education, Access, and Development* (Boston: G. K. Hall, 1991), p. 12.

Chapter 6

1. Louis Harris & Associates, "An Assessment of American Education: The View of Employers, Those Running Higher Education, the Public, Former Students, and Their Parents," prepared for the Committee for Economic Development, the Business Roundtable, the National Education Goals Panel, and the National Council on Education Standards and Testing, New York, September 1991, pp. 7–14.

Index